Educating the Imagination

Essays and Ideas
for Teachers and Writers

Volume 1

Edited by Christopher Edgar & Ron Padgett

Teachers & Writers Collaborative

New York

Educating the Imagination, Volume 1

Teachers & Writers Collaborative
5 Union Square West
New York, N.Y. 10003–3306

Library of Congress Cataloging-in-Publication Data

Educating the imagination / edited by Christopher Edgar & Ron Padgett.
  —1st ed.
    p. cm.
    Contents: v. 1. Writing poetry. Writing fiction. Inventing language. Bilingual & Cross-cultural. Evaluation. Reading. First & last. A look back.— v. 2. Letting go. Writing poetry. Writing plays. Writing across the curriculum. Parody & humor. Reading. On language. My high school English teacher. Exemplary models.
    ISBN 0-915924-42-0 (v. 1 : acid-free). — ISBN 0-915924-43-9 (v. 2 : acid-free)
1. English language—Rhetoric—Study and teaching.   I. Edgar,
Christopher, 1961– .   II. Padgett, Ron.
PE1404.E29 1994
808'.042—dc20   94-1182
                            CIP

Printed by Philmark Lithographics, New York, N.Y.
Design: Christopher Edgar

Acknowledgments

Teachers & Writers Collaborative is supported in part by grants from the New York State Council on the Arts and the National Endowment for the Arts.

T&W programs and publications are also made possible by funding from The Bingham Trust, American Stock Exchange, The Bydale Foundation, The Witter Bynner Foundation for Poetry, Chemical Bank, Consolidated Edison, Aaron Diamond Foundation, New York Community Trust, New York Times Company Foundation, Henry Nias Foundation, Helena Rubinstein Foundation, The Scherman Foundation, and the Lila Wallace-Reader's Digest Fund.

Gratitude is also due to the following publishers and writers who permitted T&W to quote from their work:

"Period Styles: An Abbreviated History of Punctuation" © Ellen Lupton. "Semicolon; for Philip Whalen" from *Meat Air* by Ron Loewinsohn reprinted by permission of the author. "Beautiful" and "l(a" reprinted from *Complete Poems, 1904–1962*, by E. E. Cummings, edited by George J. Firmage, by permission of Liveright Publishing Corporation. Copyright © 1958, 1986, 1991 by the Trustees for the E. E. Cummings Trust. "Nadie" ("Nobody") by Nicanor Parra from *Poems and Anti-Poems*. Copyright © 1967 by Nicanor Parra. "Sorpresa" and "Cancíon de Jinete" by Federico García Lorca from *Blackburn/Lorca*, translated by Paul Blackburn and published by Momo's Press, copyright © 1979. "64" and "69" by Sappho, translated by Mary Barnard in *Sappho: A New Translation*. Copyright © 1958 by The Regents of the University of California; © renewed 1984 by Mary Barnard. "Pleiades" and "I don't know" by Sappho, translated by Guy Davenport in *Archilochos, Sappho, Alkman: Three Lyric Poets of the Late Greek Bronze Age*. Copyright © 1980 by The Regents of the University of California. "Pleiades" by Sappho, translated by Kenneth Rexroth in *Poems from the Greek Anthology*. Copyright © 1962 by Kenneth Rexroth. "Shall I" and "Alone" by Sappho, translated by Willis Barnstone in *Sappho and the Greek Lyric Poets*. Copyright © 1962, 1967, 1968 by Willis Barnstone and reprinted by permission of Schocken Books, a division of Random House, Inc. "Phrase" by Robert Fitzgerald from *Spring Shade: Poems 1931–1970*. Copyright © 1953, 1971 by Robert Fitzgerald and reprinted by permission of New Directions Publishing Corp. Two poems from *Ghost Tantras* by Michael McClure reprinted by permission of the author. "A Poem about a Wolf Maybe Two Wolves" translated by Jerome Rothenberg, in *Shaking the Pumpkin*. Reprinted by permission of Jerome Rothenberg. "Primrose"

Table of Contents

xi   Foreword ❖ Joe Brainard

xii   Preface ❖ Christopher Edgar and Ron Padgett

1   Robert Coles, Maria Irene Fornes, Lewis Hyde, and Julie Patton ❖ Educating the Imagination

WRITING POETRY

25   Bill Zavatsky ❖ Class Walk with Notebooks after Storm

31   Larry Fagin ❖ Fantasy Helmets

44   William Bryant Logan ❖ Sound, Rhythm, Music

51   William Bryant Logan ❖ Verbs and Whitman

54   Phillip DePoy ❖ Saying What Can't Be Said

61   Jane Augustine ❖ The World of Color

64   Mary Swander ❖ About a Wolf Maybe Two Wolves

75   Jeffrey Schwartz ❖ Renga: Teaching a Collaborative Poem

81   Grady Hillman ❖ Writer's Block: Poetry-in-the-Schools in Prison

WRITING FICTION

89   Alan Ziegler ❖ Writing about People

101   Meredith Sue Willis ❖ Writing Dialogue

116   Walter Dean Myers ❖ Maria

123   Meredith Sue Willis ❖ Deep Revision

INVENTING LANGUAGE

141   Peter Sears ❖ Learning Language by Invention

150   Priscilla Alfandre ❖ Inventing Primitive Languages

164   Ellen Lupton ❖ Period Styles: An Abbreviated History of Punctuation

BILINGUAL & CROSS-CULTURAL

169   John Oliver Simon ❖ Poetry across Frontiers

182   Dale Davis ❖ Sing in Me, Muse: Ancient Greek in the Elementary School Classroom

195   Shelley Messing ❖ Teaching Poetry en Dos Languages

209   Bill Bernhardt ❖ Individual Writing in a Collective Country

214   Kenneth Koch ❖ I'll Carry You Off to Sing with the Train, Maria

EVALUATION

224 Jack Collom ❖ What I See in Children's Writing
238 Peter Sears ❖ What Do You Say about a Terrible Poem?

READING

244 Ron Padgett ❖ Creative Reading
260 Lorna Smedman ❖ Collage

"FIRST & LAST"

261 Stephen Vincent ❖ The First Time I Heard the Word *Voluptuous*
262 Peter Schjeldahl ❖ The First Poem I Ever Wrote
263 Suzanne Zavrian ❖ The First Poem I Ever Wrote
264 Larry Zirlin ❖ My First Metaphor
265 Madeline Tiger ❖ The First Poem
266 Francelia Butler ❖ Meeting Louis Untermeyer

A LOOK BACK

267 Jeff Morley ❖ Wishes, Lies, and Dreams Revisited

281 Notes on Contributors

Foreword

by Joe Brainard

Preface to Volume 1

by Christopher Edgar and Ron Padgett

The two volumes of *Educating the Imagination* are comprised of articles
from the past seventeen years of *Teachers & Writers,* the bi-monthly
magazine of Teachers & Writers Collaborative. Most of the articles
are by teaching writers or creative teachers. Our initial idea was simply to pick those pieces that might qualify as "greatest hits," but having
done so, we found that together they were more than that. They reso-
nated among one another, exemplifying the myriad approaches to
teaching imaginative writing that might be termed (very loosely) the
Teachers & Writers approach. Shortly after the birth of Teachers &
Writers Collaborative, the poets, fiction writers, playwrights, and other
artists working in its program realized that there is no one way to teach
writing; that different people teach different ways; that different students learn differently; and that to reduce the teaching of writing to a
codified method was to falsify (ossify) the entire process.

Of course this is not to say that there aren't many wonderful and
useful techniques for teaching writing. In fact, many of the essays here
are practical—for immediate adaptation and use in classrooms at all levels—but at the same time there is always a "theoretical" side that comes
through, not to mention a "human" side. One thing the authors have
in common is a great faith in and respect for their students as writers and
as thinkers. Perhaps the ultimate beauty of this book is that it reminds us
that it's hard *not* to get inspired by students' imaginations; in a number
of ways, the students are the real stars of these two volumes.

The first volume begins with a lively discussion between Robert
Coles, Maria Irene Fornes, Lewis Hyde, and Julie Patton of the themes
that are at the core of this book.

The poetry section begins with Bill Zavatsky's poem "Class Walk
with Notebooks after Storm," with its close attention to the immediate.
This is followed by Larry Fagin's detailed account of writing two collaborative poems with his students ("Fantasy Helmets"). William Bryant
Logan's "Sound, Rhythm, Music" explores the uses of chant and sound
poetry, and his second essay discusses the ways strong verbs can help
students write vivid poems. Phillip DePoy's "Saying What Can't Be
Said" shows how posing unanswerable questions can liberate the imagination and result in good poems. Jane Augustine demonstrates how
color can infuse a poem, as in William Carlos Williams's "Primrose."
Mary Swander finds connections between Native American poems and
concrete poetry in her "About a Wolf Maybe Two Wolves." Jeffrey

Schwartz's piece on renga, the traditional Japanese form, returns to the theme of collaboration, and Grady Hillman gives us an insider's view of his poetry residency at a correctional facility.

The next section, on teaching fiction writing, includes pieces by Alan Ziegler (on creating characters) and Meredith Sue Willis (on dialogue). Walter Dean Myers's "Maria" is a chapter from his reader-interactive young adult novel, *Sweet Illusions*. The section concludes with Willis's discussion of learning revision by revising existing literature, in her "Deep Revision."

The theme then moves to language, in the broad sense: our own and other languages, and the nature of language. Peter Sears's students learn about English via codes, dialects, and "difficult" language such as Chaucer's Middle English and Joyce's supermodern English. Priscilla Alfandre has her students learn about prehistoric people(s) by having them invent a language for a stone-age tribe. Ellen Lupton takes us on a typographical trip through the history of punctuation. Essays by John Oliver Simon and Shelley Messing focus on teaching poetry to Spanish-speaking students (in Mexico City; Oakland, California; and New York City). Dale Davis teaches her students in Greece, New York, about Ancient Greek literature (and translation) in a residency that includes a visit from noted Homer translator Robert Fitzgerald. Bill Bernhardt discusses writing and individuality in China, and Kenneth Koch describes his experiences as a poet teaching writing in China, France, Italy, and Haiti.

In the section on evaluation, Jack Collom grapples with elusive but important qualities of children's poetry, and forms for teaching it, in "What I See in Children's Writing." Peter Sears gives advice on how to wean high-school age poets from the high-blown winds of over-philosophizing and the aversion to revision typical of late adolescence.

Ron Padgett then presents new ways to read, and shows how experimental modernist writing has changed us as readers. Lorna Smedman's piece redefines "getting into a text."

For several years, *Teachers & Writers* asked its readers to send in accounts of "first times" and "last times." We include here a selection of the sweet and bittersweet results.

This first volume concludes with a meditative piece by Jeff Morley, one of Kenneth Koch's *Wishes, Lies, and Dreams* students in the late 1960s, who takes a clear-eyed look back at Koch, himself, his classmates, and poetry writing, asking questions about the imagination that are at the very heart of this book.

Robert Coles, Maria Irene Fornes, Lewis Hyde,
and Julie Patton

Educating the Imagination

To celebrate the twenty-fifth anniversary of Teachers & Writers Collaborative,
four distinguished panelists—Lewis Hyde, Julie Patton, Robert Coles, and
Maria Irene Fornes—came together to discuss the elusive subject "Educating
the Imagination." The discussion was moderated by Wesley Brown.—Editor

Lewis Hyde: I'm going to tell a bit of an ancient Hindu story and
comment on it. The question that lies behind this short narrative has
to do with the ethical function of imagination—whether or not the
imagination is moral, amoral, or immoral. I'm not going to answer this
question, but to try to complicate it.

In ancient times the world was dominated by an evil tyrant,
Kamsa, so much so that the Earth herself went to heaven pleading for
intercession from the gods. The gods agreed to help and they created
Krishna to try to clear things up. He was taken from his birth mother
and given to a foster mother so as to protect him from evil forces. He
was raised by this foster mother, Yasoda, who is a cowherd woman, as
they call her. So he's raised in this barnyard setting, and there are many
amusing stories about discovering the god in the barnyard.

But the one that interests me has to do with Krishna as a thief. It's
morning and Krishna's asleep and Yasoda keeps trying to get him to
wake up: she's got all this breakfast ready and he won't wake up. Finally she gives up and goes away. Immediately he wakes up and, in the
little plays that they put on in India, you see him sneaking around the
stage looking for the butter. He is the butter thief. He finally finds the
big urn in which his mother keeps the butter—it's the Hindu equivalent of cookies—and he breaks it open and eats the butter. Yasoda then
comes home and discovers him—he's the dark god—with the white
butter smeared on his black face. She confronts him and asks, "Krishna,
did you steal the butter?" and he says, "I didn't steal the butter, Ma."

That's the canonical reply. And then he has a whole series of charming replies for wriggling out of the impending doom, and the pertinent one here is: "How could I steal the butter? Doesn't everything in the house belong to us?" His mother typically smiles at that point and lets him off.

There are similar stories all over the world—in Greece, there's the story of Hermes's birth. On the day of his birth he steals Apollo's cattle, and then he's confronted by the gods about this and he tells these fabulous lies to try to escape. In the Raven cycle in the Pacific Northwest, it's the child thief who steals daylight. And so forth and so on. I would argue that these stories are partly about the imagination and that the telling of these stories is one way in which the imagination is educated. I want to try to make three or four quick points about what I see in these tales.

The first thing is that these are stories about children, and so, in a way, they are stories about the first theft, and also, then, about the first lie, and they are creation stories about the creation of theft and the creation of lying. Because these characters are creative themselves, the stories seem to imply that both thieving and lying are part of creativity at one level. In terms of personal psychology, if you want to have a lively dinner table conversation, ask people to tell the story of their first theft, or think back on your own, and also then the first lies that had to follow, and also then how the elders handled this event.

Which brings me to the second point about these stories: the shamelessness of the lying. In the Homeric hymn to Hermes, when Hermes has stolen the cattle and comes home to his mother, and they have a boy-mom argument at dawn at the door, she tries to shame him. She says, "You who wear the cloak of shamelessness." Hermes can't be shamed, nor can Krishna, and so in a way these stories are fantasies about that first instance of thieving and lying, but relieved of all the possible shame or guilt that might come with them. John Stratton Hawley, who's written a wonderful book about Krishna the butter thief, actually went to India and asked mothers how they felt about their children lying and thieving, and it turned out that the mothers would be upset if their children up to a certain age didn't have a little bit of Krishna in them, didn't have a little bit of devilishness, that in fact the child who never lied or thieved would be the child who was somehow in trouble and in need of help. Up to a certain age, of course—there is a kind of cutoff point.

The third point comes from Umberto Eco, who is not just a novelist, but also has written books on semiotics. In his *Theory of Semiotics* he talks about what makes something a sign, and says that a sign is anything that can be taken as significantly substituting for something else. Then he says, "Thus, semiotics is, in principle, the discipline studying everything which can be used in order to lie. If something cannot be used to tell a lie, conversely it cannot be used to tell the truth, it cannot in fact be used to tell at all." I find this a fascinating idea. In these trickster stories the theft is a sort of a substitution of objects or a moving of objects from one context to another, and lying is the verbal equivalent. In fact the first lie is a moment in which a child is discovering the plasticity and the figurative nature of language—until you can tell a lie, you're in this delusion that language has a sort of one-to-one relationship to its objects. Thus lying is the beginning of fiction, it's the beginning of fabulation. With it then too come the philosophical questions about what is true and what isn't. Thus begins the battle between imagination and the kind of fundamentalism that insists that all the stories are literally true, a battle that continues in this nation.

At any rate, the final point I'd like to make here is that Krishna's lie is one that tells a greater truth. When Krishna says, "I didn't steal the butter," that's a lie. However, he then widens the context. When he says, "Doesn't everything in the house belong to us?" it changes the situation of the question, and at that point, if you take his reformulation as apt, he changes what seems to be a lie into something that is in fact a truth. Such lies call into question the standards of truth of the community. Remember that Krishna has come to earth because an evil tyrant is ruling. Perhaps the local ethical standards are not in tune with the sacred. There comes a time when you have a president whose policies are out of line with people's true needs and then you suddenly get darker people stealing and the question of whether this is true theft or not. That's part of what's in this Krishna story: tricksters (or characters) who lie and cheat in order to try to change the terms of local morality. In this line there is a long tradition of artists who have spoken of their work in exactly this way. You may know Picasso's remark: "We all know that art is not truth; art is a lie that makes us realize the truth, at least the truth that is given us to understand." Or Oscar Wilde's: "The telling of beautiful untruths is the proper aim of art." This is from his wonderful essay, "The Decay of Lying." And the final one I'll offer is from Czeslaw Milosz, who writes of "the right of the poet to invent—that is, to lie." Milosz also warns against what he calls "an attachment to ethics at the expense of the sacred," that is to say, an attachment to a sort of local moral structure that has in some way begun to exclude what we think of as the sacred, which is how I'm reading these stories about prophetic tricksters.

In terms of educating the imagination, or situations in which these things actually arise, my feeling would be that some sort of delicacy and restraint is in order so as not to shame the young, or even to shame professional artists, when they imagine worlds different than our own. Such education is difficult, especially in a country whose first president could not tell a lie.

★　　★　　★

Julie Patton: In thinking about the topic of educating the imagination, at first I thought, "Oh, you know, that's simple." I thought about all of the different things that I've done with kids over the years regarding imaginative play, and then I realized that *imagination* is a word that I've always taken for granted, and I began to ask myself, "What exactly is the imagination?" I finally settled on imagination as a process of transformation and the multiplication of meanings. But first of all I want to say that for me, as an artist and visual writer, the imagination is not detached from my artistic practice: imagination exists in the doing. Defining what this activity consists of and how it is applied means confronting a web of issues, topics, concerns, and considerations that I will touch on today.

The word *imagination* is one we usually associate with artists and children, with their minds and their relationship to reality. The closest word to imagination for me is *dreaming*. Both are parts of the process of transformation and involve the multiplication of meanings. In our society we tend to marginalize the imagination as an inverse function (or flip side) of reality precisely because of its transformative power—that is, its power to produce alternative versions of reality. Having said that, I am faced with the demands of my own imagination, begging a question usually reserved for lovers; that is, "Why do you need me?" My response is, "Because our vision of the world is not enough. Faced with the many problems that reality can produce, I see two ways to respond to them; one is to repress them, the other is to find new ways to resolve them, using the imagination."

Another thing that occurred to me is that *imagination* is a loaded word that suggests other, equally significant words, including the word *image*. We need to make a distinction between the two. *Image* comes from the Latin verb *imaginor,* to picture. In the West, we tend to compartmentalize our senses. I believe, as musicologist Joachim-Ernst Berendt says, that we are constantly intensifying the domination of seeing and the seeable, and we primarily relate images to what can be seen. That's because a description of forms is easier than a description of movement or process. Berendt believes that eye thinking is "polarized thinking," and points out an abundance of words that illustrate this fact: we see, scrutinize, look, contemplate, reflect, see through, observe, eye something, inspect, discriminate, examine, discern, note, mark, regard—all of which get us into right-and-wrong responses. So when the teacher comes into the room with her marking pencil, what is she crossing out or erasing? The forms that tumble into a jumble as the child struggles with mastering script, or the ideas themselves as represented by the images?

This is problematic for two reasons: one is that, as Gaston Bachelard says, while the imagination lays down images, it exists beyond them. The imagination is more than images, and more than the production of images. I care about the whole journey. The poem is a description of the stay. I try to remember that something is going on in the mind or spirit of a child whether it's manifested on paper or not. I can be content with interpreting the energy that happens around the making of a poem. I can see scribble as impulse, long stretches of silence as meaningful, the movement of a hand as dance, script as drawing, the rolling of an eye, the bounce and the bop as expression. Sometimes this is all that may happen for weeks, and then slowly the hand moves, grabs the pencil, and then begins to make the gestures that will give body to formerly immobile characters.

But it's a mistake to think of images as being only positive. In fact, as Bachelard says, "stable and completed images clip the wings of the imagination" instead of encouraging us to dream and to reflect. Such images compel us to consume them and to be dominated by them. My biggest struggle in the classroom involves trying to pry the imagination from confining images. Such images include Ninja Turtles, Freddy Krueger, the educational system, and even styles imagined by young people on the streets of Harlem and repackaged and sold back to them as something new, fresh, and necessary enough to kill for. Meanwhile, the young people themselves will be reprocessed as images, frightening ones, such as "gorillas in the mist" heading for Simi Valley, or "children at risk." The message to such young people is not to trust themselves, the power and validity of their own imaginations, and so fire speaks for those who cannot speak or those whom we do not hear.

Increasingly, my role in the classroom reminds me of a tale from Amos Tutuola's "Feather Woman of the Jungle," in which he talks about two kids journeying into a forest, where they encounter the ostrich woman. She tells them not to look into a certain pit, because if they uncover it, they will see two ostrich eggs that will turn them into images. There are lots of people who had wandered into the forest and become images. Every night she comes to the images and beats them. That's what I do in the classroom. I try to drive the images out of my students, so that the children can return to their own vital visions.

Bachelard describes imagination not as "the faculty of forming images of reality, but rather the faculty of forming images that go beyond reality, that sing reality." As someone else said, "To read a poem is to hear it with our eyes, to hear it is to see it with our ears." The richest events occur in us long before we perceive them. When we open our eyes to the visible we have long committed ourselves to the invisible. I muse over this idea, perhaps thinking that the imagination begins in the dark sea of the womb, as we bend our ear towards our mother's heartbeat, where sound filters in as the only available light source. In the dark, the attentive ear tries to see. Creation myths describe the creation of the world as beginning with a sound. And often this sound accompanies the idea of an intermingling of light and sound. Turning off the lights and closing the blinds encourages us to look inward, to let go of the world, to nurture imagination as insight. Poets don't see the muse, they hear her. Rilke talks of hearing the wind and being inspired to create his *Duino Elegies*. The fact is, we perceive through the fabric of our entire being, feeling our way through the world, which reverberates in us. So, much of my work involves saying, "Away with boundaries, let distance appear and the depths speak," and the depths *do* speak. The walls we define as real are precisely the same ones that the imagination can and should tear down. Imagination is a yes to all the resounding *no*'s and *cannot*'s fencing children in. It is flight, not escape. And transcending the immediate world, we enter the space of elsewhere. Dimming the classroom lights and lowering my voice, I transport students with the rudder and oar of my tongue, with the song of poets resonating from all over the world. Sometimes one word can send children dreaming: *void, vast, night, space, river*, even *gravity*. These words are elastic enough to create impressions of immensity that reflect the children's own imaginative capacities.

I see this work as empowering, bound up with survival. Bell Hooks, in her book *Yearning: Race, Gender, and Cultural Politics*, describes her grandmother's ability to make a space livable, and in a lot of ways this is what I'm talking about—how to transform the classroom to allow space for imagination:

Baba was certain that the way we live was shaped by objects, the way we looked at them, the way they were placed around us. She was certain that we were shaped by space. Her house is a place where I am learning to look at things, where I am learning to belong in space. In rooms full of objects, crowded with things, I am learning how to recognize myself. 'Look,' she tells me, 'what the light does to color.' Do you believe that space can give life or take it away, or that space has power?

Baba taught her how to look at the world and to see beauty, but *seeing* in this instance is meant metaphorically as insight or awareness or understanding. The question is: what is the role of language in this context, and how can paper, or a slightly altered classroom, mirror this expansion of space that will hopefully enable children to relax into their own rhythms, set their own paces, and, with a stroke of the pen, name themselves masters of the world?

This year I struggled to resolve the nagging question of what is the real value of writing for children. How natural is it? How does working with language in non-oral ways orient them to the world? What impact will it have on their eyes? And is this really what they would choose to do with their hands and bodies were they not in school? I interviewed a lot of students about their attitude toward writing outside of school. I wanted to know what spaces they take to, what compels them to write on their own time, what gets them in the mood, what tools they use, what kind of light or what time of day or night they prefer. The answers were interesting and startling, but one of the things I noticed was how and where movement ushered in—or followed—a gathering-in of body and mind and the act of writing. Some students said, "Writing is playing, constructing, working, hammering. Writing is where a pen and a pencil can move to letters. Dancing is similar to writing because you have to think before doing the next step. When I see action, it encourages me to write. I feel another world in myself. It is like people working with my brain. It feels like wheels circulating in my head. I like to write in the living room with soft, slow music, drinking lemonade, writing with a black pen." Another student said, "I feel like a cartoon and nothing can stop me but cartoon acid." For these students, words come out of movement. In a similar sense, Foucault says, "To read and to journey are one and the same thing." Reading, I noted, was one of the most common activities that stimulated children to pick up the pencil and write. Reading appears to be an immobile activity, but actually it has a tempo of reflective thought, in which words recover their movement, running, skipping, jumping, falling. This mobility and its counterpoint require space. Sixth grader Ron Taylor's comment that "you need writing to go through the world" mirrors the aboriginal concept of language as migration, in which the melodic contour of song describes the nature of the land over which it passes. For an aboriginal these song lines are as legible in the dirt as a poem is on paper. The hands are ex-feet, remembering and relishing and requiring movement. The earth has become paper, paper the earth we dig, scratch, and etch our lives into. The pencil is a digging stick, nicking the skin of a former tree whose memory of horizons comes back to spin blue lines that extend as far as the imagination will go.

★   ★   ★

Robert Coles: In recent years I've been teaching a fourth grade class in what is called, I guess, a difficult neighborhood, and a lot of the children are unruly, provocative, or angry, and don't pay attention. I got into this because one of my students, an art history major, was interested in what their reactions would be to some of his slides. He showed them Picasso's *Les Saltimbanques* and they wondered what was the matter with these people: they seemed very unhappy, and some of them seemed malnourished. And as he collected some of these responses, I went with him to the classrooms and ended up teaching English in a fourth grade class at the Martin Luther King School in Cambridge, Massachusetts.

The children told me that they were not interested in writing and they weren't interested in reading. Trained in psychoanalysis to ask questions like "What's your favorite subject?" or "What do you like to do here?" in order to elicit responses, I got responses like "Recess is my favorite subject and eating is a close second or sometimes first, and the best subject of all is when the day is over." They asked me what I was doing there and why I wanted to do this, and I told them that I wanted to be there and to find out more about them, but that didn't register too well. Then I told them a truth of sorts—which at the time I thought was a lie—namely that I wanted to get away from where I was, that I was sick of where I was, and I was glad to be there instead. Some of them bought this, others wanted to know where I was before I came there. And then I started hearing stories of their experiences in the same city—Cambridge—where I've taught for a long time. What it means to go through that well-known place that calls itself and is called a Yard. What those buildings mean. Who those people are who have been seen by these children in that area and going in and out of some of those buildings.

I told them that I wasn't going to try and teach them how to write—I didn't know how anyone ever did that anyway—but I was going to continue the tradition of showing them some pictures, and I started in with a collection of slides of the work of Edward Hopper. I use those slides in a college freshman seminar, which I've called American Light, in which we read Raymond Carver's short stories and poems, and then we look at Hopper's pictures. My students are eighteen-year-old men and women, ten to twelve of them, who want to do this for a term. With the fourth graders, though, I certainly wasn't going to start in with Carver's stories. Instead I brought in those slides, and started out with the best known of them, namely *Nighthawks*. As soon as I showed *Nighthawks*, the class quieted down. It was the quietest class I'd had with them. I'd been struggling for several weeks with their noisiness: kids getting up and walking around, ignoring the schedule I was trying to keep, and ignoring me while I tried to read to them. Now they quieted down, and they asked me where the scene in this picture was. I said, "Where do you think?" And then a girl told me that her mother worked the night shift in Dunkin' Donuts. And she started telling the class about the people who come into Dunkin' Donuts in the middle of the night, the good people and the bad people. And this picture got us going on nightlife in restaurants and elsewhere, and I noticed that the children waited out their turn, and were even raising their hands for me to recognize them, something that had not been taking place before, although I had tried to tell them, "Please, there has to be *some* routine and order and structure in this class." Now they politely raised their hands, and one after the other they told stories about eating at night, and restaurants, and places that are open at night, and streets where you can go and always get something at night, and places where you can't, and on and on.

Then I showed them some other slides of Hopper, some of his restaurant automat scenes, some of his street scenes, some of his office scenes, some of his home scenes, some of his sailing scenes, and his on-the-road scenes. He was one of the first people in America to go on the road, so to speak. He and his wife got into a car in the twenties and drove across the country, and out of this came some of his Mobil gas pictures and roadside stand pictures, visual evocations that he'd connected to that trip out west. And these children were enormously interested—and continue to be interested—in the relationships between the men and the women in the homes and offices. Unerringly they pick up that strange mixture of intimacy and huge distance that Hopper was such a genius at rendering. In abstract terms, what I began to hear from them was a rather lively narrative response to visual images. I brought in other slides, from Picasso, from Renoir, from Pissarro, and some fell over like duds, and got nothing going, but others did get a lot going.

A favorite one of mine, which goes back to my mother's taking me to the Boston Museum of Fine Arts, is Renoir's *Le Bal à Bougival*, which hung for many years in one place in the museum and now has been moved. I told the children that I remembered my mother's bringing me to look at that picture and telling me about it, and they were interested in that, they were interested in the Boston Museum of Fine Arts. I found out that none of them had been there. They wanted to know where it was, and so of course I had the idea that we could all go there. And I took them there, and the guards followed us around, which immediately turned these children on enormously. They wanted to know who the guards were. When I said, "I don't know, but we could go and ask them," one kid went up and said, "Who are you?" to the guard, and the guard said, "I work here," and fortunately he was a nice man, although a worried man, and a nice conversation got going, and the children began to connect with him in such a way that I noticed they were behaving a little better, almost in order to please him. That lasted while we were in his turf, but when we went into some other turf, there was trouble: the guard screamed at a couple of the kids and told them to get their hands off the wall, or off the frame, to which one kid said, "What's it to you?" and we were off and running. Pretty soon I saw we had to get out of there. But we'd had a good time, we'd had a good time in the van, and we'd had a good time with one of the guards.

I was fascinated by the way the kids looked at this part of Boston—the buildings and the people—and I felt myself learning something about a viewpoint, a viewpoint that has its own kind of muckraking populism to it, a lack of interest in the stuffy and the pompous. The students don't use words like *stuffy* and *pompous*, but perhaps I shouldn't use some of the words that I've heard from them about some of these institutions. But the more I heard, the more I thought I would tell them that hearing them was to a certain extent a little music to my ears. It got me away from the university and the psychoanalytic institute. It's nice to get away from all that talk and it's also nice to get a viewpoint that reminds one of one's own imprisonment in a world of pretentious language, self-importance, and constraint—constraint through phrases like "character disorder" and "acting out." As I tried to make connections with these children, I kept hearing the voices that I'd been trained to hear—and those voices are hard to get out of one's head—like "acting out," a lot of which goes on in that fourth grade classroom. My wife and I once spent a whole weekend at the Waldorf Astoria where the American Psychoanalytic Association had a two-day symposium on acting out. When we left, my wife said to me, "I have a question for you." I said, "What is the question?" She said, "I want to know the difference between acting out and living."

The children were acting out and they were also—I began to realize after weeks and weeks—willing to settle down, scratch their heads, and notice some of the sadness and loneliness in those Hopper pictures, but also notice the light, the shadows, and the mixture of the sinister and the apparently intimate, and even connect it to their own lives and to the world that they inhabited. I don't want to forgo mentioning that this worked with some and didn't with others, and some were vastly bored. I love the way they kept on pushing at me, in what I initially felt to be a rude and insolent way, as to my own reasons for doing all this, and in fact when I told my wife about this she said, "You're calling them rude and insolent for doing to you what you do all the time with patients."

So it has been an interesting experience that I can't let go of, and it's a pleasure to have children look at these pictures without using words like *chiaroscuro* and all that other stuff. I wanted to take them to the Fogg Museum, but then I thought I would be undone by the wish I would have that they would go on a wholesale rampage, and I thought I had better just—how do they say in the English school of psychoanalysis?—keep on splitting.

★　　★　　★

Maria Irene Fornes: I'm writing a play in which one of the characters talks about the violence and despair in the world today. Speaking right after the L.A. riots have taken place, she says that the problem is that people look too much to themselves and are less able to look outside themselves—that they are self-centered and selfish and that they don't think of others. She says, "By 'to think of others' I don't mean to be kind to others, but to be curious. To observe other people and be interested in what other people do. What other people are like. Whether with kindness or unkindness." She says that when we look too much into ourselves we lose our balance, but that when we look outside ourselves we feel in a state of bliss. I think my character is very smart, and I think that when she says that looking outside ourselves is creative, she is right. She says it is like when you are learning to ride a bicycle: if you look right down in front of you, you lose your balance and you fall, but that to look out in front and to have a perspective is what brings you to balance. Looking out in front of you not only means that you are conscious of and generous to the world, but also is actually for your own good and your own sense of center.

I have been aware of this fact, and of how important it is for the creative process of the writer, ever since I started teaching playwriting a long time ago. Actually I don't really teach playwriting. My responsibility as a teacher is not to teach people how to compose, not to teach people to create a structure, not to teach people how to decide on an interesting subject and then bring it out and implement it, nor to think of a pertinent idea that would be relevant to everyone today and would perhaps even contribute to the improvement of the world, but rather to show them that they must go inside themselves. Now, this sounds contradictory, because the character in my play is saying not to go inside yourself. But you have to go inside yourself in order to be able to look out—that is the creative process. You have to become centered so that you can look outside yourself, but since you have to look outside yourself in your imagination rather than in reality, therefore you have to first be able to center yourself inwardly to then be able to look out and to imagine. In a sense you have to disappear, otherwise you'll have a very hard time. You have to stop thinking about questions such as what should I write, how should I write, what should be the first word that I write, because it often happens that you start writing and you look at the first sentence and then say, "This could not possibly be the first sentence of a great work of art." You throw it out and you start again, and of course this same thought comes back. Sometimes I hear people quote the first sentence of a novel as if that line was so good that it was a reason for the greatness of the rest of the work, when in fact it is the other way around.

I would like to talk now about the importance of creativity for the ordinary person, not for the artist but for the ordinary person. It seems that when a new concept evolves, it circulates at lightning speed. Often it's just a phrase, naming a particular kind of problem. Then people start bouncing it around and accusing other people of having that problem. There are so many such phrases that it's hard to think of one, but let's take for example the word *dysfunctional*. This word is used these days like a weapon, so that you're afraid to say anything, because somebody's going to say, "Well, you grew up in a dysfunctional family." You talk about a friend who has a problem and people say, "Well, that's a dysfunctional person."

I remember that when I first came to live in New York, in 1945, Freud and psychoanalytic terms were becoming fashionable. These things really are like fashions. Finally these terms went out of fashion, but new ones came into fashion. Such systems—and they *are* systems—accumulate. It's not as though one system replaces the other and there's always a sort of natural human being and then there is this little space reserved for those systems. Those systems stay, they are like dormant germs that live there and they keep adding up and they keep occupying the human space inside us. And I don't know where we are now, how far down we have gotten, but I do feel there are times when I meet people who are almost completely made up of layers of different systems and there's maybe just a little bit of the human being left around the ankles. Every time I go to California I hear a new phrase. I say, "What does that mean?" I remember one word, and it's not the most recent, that took me a while to understand was "You have an *attitude*." And you even have to say *AT-TI-TUDE*, because it has a little more punch to it. And I remember that I said, "Uh, yes, I . . ." and then I realized that it was an accusation! They didn't seem to realize that you could have a *friendly* attitude, or all sorts of attitudes. Not all these concepts and phrases get East, but about half of them do become part of our language.

What does this have to do with the importance of creativity in the ordinary person? I feel that creativity is probably about the only thing—creativity, and maybe love—that really can break through those systems. Because being in love is such a powerful thing that it destroys all these structures. But I wonder whether in the end we will perish, because real emotions and real connections are going to become so feeble that in the end we'll die, we'll just die. Maybe we'll become like space people or automatons. Maybe we will survive, but not our humanity, as science fiction sort of creatures. I do think it's possible, because I think we are already at least halfway there.

*   *   *

Wesley Brown: Thank you all very much. I'm going to pose four questions related to things that have intrigued me about what each of the panelists has spoken about. Any of you can respond to the questions in any order that you choose. I guess, in Lewis Hyde's sense, you could steal the question that belongs to someone else and then trade lies about whose response it is.

I was struck by what Lewis Hyde was saying about thieving and lying as a function of imagination and one of the questions that came to mind was: Are there any other examples of enlightened forms of thievery that you might feel are crucial to the education or to the educating of the imaginations of children? Julie Patton was speaking about imagination as a process of transformation, and how images are often regarded as an expression of imagination, when in fact they often stunt the possibilities for children to create their own visions. And I was interested in what responses she might have, as a teacher and a poet, to the power that images have to take the lives of children away from themselves. When Robert Coles was talking about *Nighthawks* and how the Hopper images were a catalyst for what he called the "lively narrative responses" from children that he was working with, I was wondering if he might be able to speak more about what might be some of the qualities of these lively responses and how they might have been useful to him in his work with children over the years. And finally, I was very taken with Irene Fornes's speaking about how our lives are so categorized. And I was reading an interview with you, Irene, in which you spoke about the ways in which you attempt to deal with the difficulties that some beginning playwrights have in trying, as you say, to take an inward journey, one that is not freighted with the categories of living that we all have to contend with. Those are the four questions.

Maria Irene Fornes: You could ask one at a time.

Wesley Brown: Well, the reason for just asking them all at once is so that they could be switched and transformed, so there could be thievery and lying.

Maria Irene Fornes: Well, I was last, so I'll go first. I think that people in their own work, including myself, are either extremely stupid or stubborn. For example, there is a person who wants to go out, and all they have to do is open the door. What they do is stand in front of the wall and press against it and say, "I want to get out." They are right there like that, and they will not think for a moment, "Let me see whether this is the best spot, the best point of exit or entry," just like the most stupid animal. If you see an animal that's trying to do something and they do it that way you say, "This is"—hens are supposed to be very stupid—you say, "This animal is more stupid than a hen, this is the most stupid animal." I find that all I have to do when I am teaching is distract people enough, like give them something fast so they don't have time to turn it into what's familiar to them. So they are not quite sure why I'm asking them to do what I'm asking them to do. So they go to their most talented place rather than the habitual one. There's a kind of obstinacy in the way people think. They "know" how it should be done: it *must* be done like that. So it never occurs to them to just move, remove themselves, just do something different. I suffer from the same problem. And since I don't have a teacher, I don't have someone who pushes me. . . .

Robert Coles: You have an attitude.

Maria Irene Fornes: There are times when I have been stuck with that obstinacy, which is something that can give you many sleepless nights and anxiety. I mean it's serious, it's not like, "Oooh, well, I haven't been able to write for two weeks." Sometimes it's a desperate situation and I don't realize that what I have to do is to do one of my own exercises. Instead I keep doing what my students do, which is to push at the same place.

Lewis Hyde: One thing to say about this thieving and lying mythology is that in fact it's about marginalized or powerless characters. These are stories about children, whose only access to power is through cunning. The issues about shame are in the same realm. I'm interested in the problem of creating a space in which you do not feel ashamed of yourself or ashamed of what comes up in your own imagination, and I think that when that happens you no longer have to lie or steal. There's a kind of open playfulness involved. I was moved by Bob Coles's story of working with these kids, because part of the story is about finally coming to a space in which the children feel free to be themselves—particularly the story about the child whose mother works nights in the Dunkin' Donuts. You know, children feel ashamed of their own lives and therefore are unable to relax and play the way you would if you knew that the people around you trusted you and cared for you. And when that happens, you're freed also of this lying and stealing business. The thing I keep coming back to in terms of educating the imagination is that everybody is born with an imagination, and that it's only a matter of trying not to damage it and of trying to provide situations in which it can grow. And that begins with just being attentive to the child who's in front of you, which takes time and energy and silence and money.

Julie Patton: I agree with Mr. Hyde and with Irene Fornes. The categorization that you talk about is what I meant in reference to children appropriating images. Well, it's actually not that they appropriate concepts, it's just that the concepts are dumped on them. I try to keep the children moving past them, but more and more I see that it's a very difficult job. For example, in the last three years images of violence seem to dominate a lot of the discussions I've had with children. It's not that images are wrong in themselves—of course as a poet I use them—it's just the images that they get from TV and from the media, images of themselves, and I see that process as repressive. It's as if the children who are most susceptible to this are the children who lack a belief or conviction in themselves, so I try to engage with them in such a way that they begin to celebrate who they are, and often it comes out of the writing, the writing itself is a process for producing a type of magic that will help them find interest in their own minds. But more and more I do see it as a very difficult battle, this year in particular, because of all the violence in the media. I remember asking a group of sixth graders about people knocking you over your head for a coat. I had been talking about which clothes were no-no's for me when I was a child—windowpane stockings or platform shoes or Afro wigs—and we were discussing their struggle with trying to be cute or beautiful or attractive and how the parent may say yes or no, and that led to a discussion that was very strange because it made me realize how much fear these children live with: though they may want certain types of clothing, be it a leather coat or a certain brand of tennis shoes, those pieces of clothing are dangerous because you can be killed for wearing them. And that was odd, because we got into a discussion about the right and wrong of that, and a lot of them felt that it was valid for someone to strike someone or do whatever they felt necessary to survive. That's what it amounted to. And then we talked about images from religion. I asked how many of them go to church on Sunday. About half of the class did, and then in the course of this discussion I realized that they didn't see the contradictions between the forms of behavior that they were told to practice in church and the violence they found acceptable. Right and wrong and all these edges are very blurred.

Robert Coles: That brings up a serious educational issue: the role in the culture of the forms of constraint that are exerted upon children.

In many classrooms, the flag is gone, the Bible is certainly gone, and texts are deconstructed, but the school psychologists live on forever, and I suspect that no Supreme Court is going to get rid of them for us. The role, however, of self-consciousness, not to mention a kind of moralistic self-consciousness in the name of science directed at people by those who have the power to do so, is a major question and needs plenty of discussion still. You would have thought this would have gone away by now. These fads do come and go but they keep regenerating new and essentially the same—to use the word—"attitude."

As far as working with children—I've been working with children through their drawings and paintings all my working life. It started out when I was in pediatrics at the Children's Hospital. We had a polio epidemic and a lot of the kids were very upset by what had suddenly happened to them, and as I would sit and talk with them, sometimes there was nothing more to say, and I remembered what I used to see William Carlos Williams do when he'd go on house calls. He carried in his black bag some little Hershey Kisses—which live on forever—and he carried some crayons and some paper, and sometimes he'd get the parents out of the way, he'd sit on the floor, and he and the children would draw pictures together. I will never forget some of the drawings those kids did when they got out of the iron lungs, the ones who had bulbar polio, like getting out of prison. When I started working with children under the rubric of child psychiatry, I used to ask them to draw and paint, sometimes just to settle them down. They didn't want to talk very much, and some of them were very rambunctious, and they'd start tearing up my office with all my toys and stuff, and I'd either want to take them for a walk, to get them out of my office, or I'd try to sit down with them, and we'd both draw. Sometimes they drew a hell of a lot better than I did, and they would see that, and that was a first step. Some of them thought that I secretly could draw better, that I was drawing down, so to speak. But I can tell you from the bottom of my heart that I really think that drawing and painting is a much-neglected instrument of communication between all of us, and especially between teachers and children in our schools, and it could be the subject of a long discussion about what it is, especially in American education, that has pushed so-called "art education" out of the schools, or derogated it as a transient kind of behavior permissible at a certain age but something one must outgrow in the name of more serious matters, like—"God forbids," Flannery O'Connor would say—spelling. I've collected thousands of drawings and paintings and sometimes tried to make sense of them. I'll never forget a scene in a *favela* [Brazilian shantytown], I was with two of my sons and a translator, and I was stumbling around with my effort to begin something and one of my sons nudged me and said, "Daddy, why don't we just sit down with some of those crayons and paper and ask the translator to tell them what we should all draw?" And then he decided not to be at the mercy of the translator, and he pointed up, and there was that statue of Jesus that dominates Rio, and he didn't say a word, he pointed and he made do with the paper and the crayons, and pretty soon we were all sitting out there in this field doing these Jesus drawings. And then we got some stories about what Jesus thinks of Copacabana and Ipanema versus the *favelas*, and I wish that some of our well-known American ministers and cardinals and others who go in and out of the White House could have heard some of those comments. Some nuns ran a kitchen at the base of that *favela*. In the *favelas* in Rio, the real estate values go up as the land goes down, in contrast to the way most of us are taught to think. In Rio, you go up high in the hills and real estate means nothing there, and there are these beautiful what we would call "views."

One of the "girls" who drew some pictures for me was thirteen years old. She drew a picture of Jesus as a whore, a slut on the Copacabana streets. And later the nun told me a story about her, how she'd go and do tricks for fat cats. But she told me something else, that she came back and she split the cruzeiros: half of what she made went to the nuns for the soup kitchen—even with the serious character disorder that this girl had, and even with her acting out. And I thought to myself, it would be interesting to see how many Harvard professors and training analysts at the Psychoanalytic Institute tithed themselves fifty percent for the soup kitchens in Boston. So what one is left with always, as you who write stories and struggle with human complexity know, what one is left with is all the ironies and the contradictions and the inconsistencies and the paradoxes that ought to haunt us and ought not to drive us, as you well said, ought not to drive us to these dreary simplifications directed sometimes in such a mean-spirited way at others and therefore as a means of elevating ourselves as so smart, so wholly smart.

Wesley Brown: Let's open the discussion to the audience. Are there any questions on anything? Yes, Tillie?

Tillie Olsen: My question for the panel is about the working of the imagination. In Robert Coles's haunting instance of the Brazilian girl who split half and half, was she not exercising what might be called

Blake's "divine imagination?" She was *being* those others, as well as herself. Of course her grounding was her own experience of gnawing poverty and homelessness. But—in the same vein—I'd like to say something contrary to Lewis Hyde's statement that the first evidence of the imagination in little children is their lies. Even with babies in arms (except for the damaged ones) there's the first rudimentary expression of the innate human capacity for what later—unless impeded—develops into what we call empathy, identification. Cry, and there are tears on that baby's cheeks; laugh—and how can they know what the laughing's about?—and they're crowing with laughter too. Later, the second, the third year they're into pretend, dress-up, acting out situations and relationships around them—and more. The walk, the gestures, the tone of voice, yes the very characterizing phrase that the person whom they're pretending to be would use in that situation. It's not blind imitation—it's observation, trying to understand, embellishing—the unfolding human child way of *imagining* being another, in other situations. So we need to remember that the imagination is not only make-believe, fantasy, but is "divine" capacity—more necessary than ever today—to understand, feel what others are feeling, even thinking, to *be* those others. My question for the panel is: what more can or has been done to shelter, educate, or bring back this aspect of the imagination?

Wesley Brown: Would anyone on the panel like to respond to that?

Maria Irene Fornes: Well, I don't know whether this answers your question, but in talking about the importance of drawing, part of my method of teaching has to do with drawing. I usually teach playwrights, who are not children, but in a sense what I have to do is bring them to the state of being childlike in order to get them to stop conceptualizing, and one very specific way and very effective way that people can stop conceptualizing is through visualizing. I have them visualize different things, whatever—it's not something specific. I give them a general subject and their visualization is very personal. Then, before the writing starts, I have them draw what they have visualized, and I make sure that they don't think that this has to be an artistic drawing. I tell them it is just a way of writing something down to anchor themselves. The drawings are important no matter how they look, what is important is that their imagination does not exclude what is material, that the imagination is not conceptual and verbal. One of the main problems in writing is that the writing very soon becomes repetitive and exhausted. If the imagination doesn't conceive matter (the life, the physical life of the persons that they're writing about, or the place, the physical life of the place, the air, the tone of the light), if all of that is not in the imagination the writing is disembodied and quickly asphyxiates itself. The drawing helps with that in a very easy manner.

Man in audience: Mr. Hyde made some rather interesting allusions to fundamentalism as a battle we are fighting in this country. I just wondered what was behind that.

Lewis Hyde: Well, I'm thinking of the people who want to take everything literally, as opposed to those who understand that there are several layers of meaning in any utterance. Take the fight over Serrano's *Piss Christ*, just as a small example. I once worked in a hospital, and one of the remarkable things about working in a hospital is that you work close to people's bodies, you work with blood and piss, and there's a kind of an enlivening contact with what is usually hidden. When I saw Serrano's photos I thought that in a funny way what he's trying to do is to ponder the mystery of the body in Christianity, where Christ's body—you know, his actual body—is nailed up on the cross, and he actually bleeds. Some people take this image and turn it into a shibboleth that doesn't have any liveliness in it anymore. Part of what I thought Serrano was trying to do was to rethink the image of Christ and to say, "Okay, this is about a body suffering." Of course I'm doing a kind of a complicated personal take on this image, as opposed to the way it's attacked by fundamentalists in this country, who think it's simply an insult to a tradition. To my mind, what's actually going on is that there are people in this country who are not interested in the imagination, because the imagination does put you in contact with other people, because the imagination is how we create the future, and if we're going to get out of our political logjams or any other kind of logjams we have to have a free imagination. But that kind of fight between the literal reading of a sacred text versus an imaginative reading is an old one. Blake says that the suppression of mental war leads to corporeal war. If you don't allow there to be imaginative fights and intellectual fights, then you're going to have to have physical fights, and if you don't have a debate over what it means to go into the Persian Gulf, then you're going to have to *go* into the Persian Gulf. Or if you don't have an actual political process that can deal with the inner cities, then you're going to have to have riots. I see this as all connected, and that's what I was thinking of when I mentioned fundamentalism.

Julie Patton: I would like to respond to Tillie Olsen's question. What Tillie mentioned about kids imitating or wanting to be other people made something else click in my mind. Children do a lot of mimicking and what I think they mimic is what they guess is what the teacher wants to hear. I don't see them as lacking imagination. I think that there's still a lot of make-believe and play, but I think that their response to me in the school and what they think they're giving me is what they think I want to hear. That goes back to this whole idea of society's treating the imagination as the opposite of reality. When children really try to go off on their own imaginations, a lot of educators respond by saying "But that's not *true*." The educators immediately want to bring the children back to "reality," but what I try to do is to keep them moving, to make the world bigger and bigger and bigger. That may mean going for a walk in their minds down 125th Street and gathering in all the different languages, customs, and rhythms, or looking at the lines radiating in a broken glass and seeing beauty in that. It may mean going within and going to outer space—all of those things.

I brought up the ear because I know that in my own writing I tend to hear things first—that's generally my stimulus. And I was struck by something I was reading recently that said that we can see only three dimensions, but we don't know how many we can hear. Anyway, having kids close their eyes and go within is a way of helping them get in touch with their feelings and be honest with themselves and push aside the frozen images that they're given all the time.

Woman in audience: For fifteen years I wrote for various educational publishing houses. I wrote for English students who were second-language learners and who were in crisis situations in the South Bronx, in places with Hispanic students all over the country, and year after year my editors would come to me and say, "We're tired of your endings. Your endings always end with hope, with an open door, and we want you to change them." I didn't change my endings, because if I did, those children would never have a feeling of themselves—and I'm talking about adult children, adult children who needed to perceive, who needed to identify, like one girl in Pelham who worked in a grocery store yet wanted to be a tennis player like Althea Gibson. These people *had* to have something to hold on to, *had* to know that the door was open, or that it would open. I think we do not have enough talented role models for children in crisis in this country, and we will not have that unless the voices are heard.

Julie Patton: That reminds me of something else. This voyage of the imagination that I try to induce in the classroom has an end, and this is something that's important to the work that I do, and that is this idea of creating a memory and thinking about how a memory is bound up with the imagination and vice versa. And I see all of this gathering primarily because when I work in the classroom I bring in my own childhood. I remember what it was like encountering museums and feeling that you couldn't enter certain worlds, that there were all these *no*'s, and children not claiming space. It's my hope that when they are adults they'll look back and see what Gaston Bachelard calls "the motionless childhood," this center that stays still within us, that we can begin to make use of as adults.

Man in audience: I was struck by Ms. Fornes's and Mr. Coles's comments on concepts and labels. At the end of her presentation, Ms. Fornes spoke about love as a way of cutting through all of this to some personal authenticity. Is there some pure love that you're speculating about?

Maria Irene Fornes: No, I was thinking more of mad love, when you're madly in love. When you are just sweetly in love you may very, very easily fall into all kinds of concepts, but when you are madly in love then you become totally irrational, and you do things that can be very embarrassing and very awful—*that* is what I'm talking about.

Wesley Brown: One final question.

Stephen O'Connor: I was just thinking how the remarks I've heard here have brought up problems I have as a writer and teacher working with kids who are often very fearful, very desperate. It seems there are two aspects of using the imagination. You talked a lot about the relationship between imagination and truth, but in art the imagination does another thing, which seems to be the same thing but isn't really, which is to create beauty. And I find that my desperate, frightened students are not very interested in the beauty aspect. They really are interested in using imagination, using stories as a way of investigating the world, as a way of lying to discover the truth, using imagination to get in somebody else's mind. But I have to wonder: What about beauty? What about that good feeling we have when we read stories— I just reread *Dubliners*, and I found myself feeling really good. They're very depressing stories, but I was feeling good because they were so beautifully written, so beautifully constructed. And what about the role of aesthetics and the imagination creating aesthetics in education?

Lewis Hyde: You might look at that essay of Oscar Wilde's that I mentioned, "The Decay of Lying." When he talks about lying he says, "The function of art is to tell *beautiful* untruths." The second thing that comes to mind is that one sort of works in stages. It's often the case that the first stuttering version of one's story is not beautiful, and that you sit with it and work with it, trying to perfect it on its own terms. I think that it's a question of where you are in this process. For many people, often all you're involved with in the time you're in the school is trying to get something started, and beauty is a later concern.

Robert Coles: And there are the moments of beauty, even in the midst of the chaos. Since Tillie Olsen is here I'll say that one of the things I've done is to read "I Stand Here Ironing" to the children, just as I get my college students to read all four of the stories in *Tell Me a Riddle*, and it is astonishing how the children respond not only to the substance, but also to what she's done, to the mystery of these stories. And remember, just talking about the visual—that our dreams are visual—can serve as a reminder of our aesthetic capacity in the middle of the night to make pictures and to respond to them.

Man in audience: I need to know if I understand your question. Were you talking about beginning a process whose only goal is beauty?

Stephen O'Connor: No, I guess what I meant was a question of emphasis. For instance, take something like Gertrude Stein's *Tender Buttons*. I mean, where's the "truth" in *Tender Buttons*? There's humor and beauty in *Tender Buttons* and in other works that seem to be less referential to the world and more just about themselves. My students have trouble with that. So it makes me think, How much do I value beauty? How much do I value aesthetics? How serious and important a goal is it? It's not only a philosophical question, but it relates to teaching too.

Maria Irene Fornes: I feel that beauty, whether it is for the observer or for the creator, is a question of true contact with the thing we're talking about, whether it is the beauty of a shirt, a fabric, a pair of sneakers, a dog or a cat, anything that you truly open yourself to and become familiar with. If you see, say, this glass only once, you don't know whether it is a beautiful glass or not. But if you become interested in it and you begin to observe, you will, as a natural function of the human being, end up being able to tell which is the beautiful one and which is the poor one. But the moment you start thinking, "Oh, this is *supposed* to be the good one, and this is *supposed* to be the bad one," you are not progressing at all. I would say don't mention the word *beauty*. The children will learn what is beautiful if you teach them how to come close to it.

Bill Zavatsky

Class Walk with Notebooks after Storm

These puddles floating
down this street
must lead somewhere."

Or so I think
but don't tell
the whole third grade

trailing behind me
stopped to lean on cars
or telephone poles

scrawling their seeing
on spiral pads
or blowy paper sheets.

I want them to stalk
their own lives, to see
that all of matter matters

and so—outdoors! Arms
flying into sleeves
down the rickety stairs

into the rain-wet streets
all eyes and ears
with ballpoint pens alert

to make sense of this town
that's made them much
of what they are.

A wandering pooch
plots afternoon smells.
I too lead my students

by the nose, exhibiting
everything: the basketball
ogled by a fishtank fish

in Don's Hobby Store window;
the candy store's weathered wood
—"like the gravestones"

notes one melancholy
boy I can't help patting
on the head

he reminds me so
of my gloomy self
at that age, when

"Smile!" my parents chirped
"Smile!" and I would answer
"What is there to smile about?"

"Write that down!" I urge
us both as we pass the diner
popping with pinball bells,

ajump with light. "What
crazy kind of food could they
be cooking there?" I blurt,

biting my tongue and begging
of the Muses
their forgiveness.

Then unto the barber
—"He's always standing there,"
a girl at the window mutters

jotting down his white suit,
eternally folded arms,
the monumental bald head

which ushers us toward
the adjacent darkness
deepening the Funeral Home

its dripping canopy
like a coffin maw
waiting to clamp shut.

Each glowing clapboard
a stroke of chalk
on the blackboard of eternity

so perfectly drawn
the whole shebang might
lift into heaven tonight!

A turn onto Main Street,
we go feasting
on flashes of imagery:

a stately 1928 engine
fenders drawn by eagles
pulling strands of firehouse gold

glides past us. I think
of the gold five
Williams watched clanging

through his darkened city
and his friend Charlie
Demuth painted, gleaming

on a firetruck door
"Among the rain
and lights," he wrote

—like us, skirting
the sunlit puddles, the
fallen sky framed

in odd nooks and crannies
all over town.
"Look down and see

the sky, the clouds.
Look at the mirrors
at your feet!" I shout,

thinking how nice
to snuggle in a hole
the world has made for you,

your job finally through
as part of the sky;
at last allowed to stare

at the home you came from
all the time
intent on going back,

Yes, everything's looking up
A fireman's rubber boot
smack in a wavery cloud

as he motions that engine
(hunks of red and gold)
back to its berth, pausing

to smile and let pass
two nyloned women scissoring
long legs over

a slippery patch
of pavement, gliding angelically
while we scribble.

Some big bruiser splashing
his cuff, ticked off,
wipes and smirks.

That dog, still following
us with long pink tongue,
pauses to lap up bits

of cloud, his eyes
mirroring the chills
along the water's spine.

And water itself, crushed
by clumsy shoes,
regains composure,

collecting itself in
the mantra of reflection
for a haiku:

Puddles in the street—
at last the dog gets a chance
to see its own face

We halt for mirrors, too:
a sundry shop of images
browsed by the glare

of my own horse face
haloed by the faces
of the kids

shows me dawning
to the idea that
this little town

with its one main street
and local shops
is itself a collection

of knickknacks
balanced carefully
on a shelf

in the mind of the boy
who lived where
I grew up!

That is, me—
walking around
a new town

letting my eye
embrace the real
like a hungry rose

that gulps a drop
of wetness, like
the roses that

exploded every spring
as my grandmother coaxed
with her clippers and her hose.

All of this pleasure
I squeeze from a morning's rain
in residence around us.

Let me tell my students
these puddles are fallen stars
they must write down

whose light will guide them
to where they live on earth,
scattered up and down

the streets we walk
all day, heaven grounded
temporarily, the sky

one constellation shy

Larry Fagin

Fantasy Helmets

Recently I worked with a small, pullout group of talented third, fourth, and fifth graders at P.S. 31 in the Bronx, selected by their teachers. We met nine times. Two terrific poems came out of four meetings toward the middle and end of the series: "The Beautiful Poem" took one and a half sessions, "Life on Earth" two.

All the children were bright, but one, Steven Figueroa, was particularly loquacious and imaginative. He had adult, sophisticated frames of reference, and he came up with a lot of urbane phrases and comments, not all of which we used.

The kids dictated the lines to me, but I orchestrated and edited the poems somewhat. Sometimes we disagreed about the direction of the poem, and sometimes I'd give in and let them have their way, partly because I was curious as to how far they would take a particular tack. The poems were written spontaneously and quickly, and a lot was thrown out, by me or by the students, on the spot or later. For instance, both poems have "catalogue" sections that were originally much longer than they are in the final versions. Here is the first poem:

The Beautiful Poem

The beautiful dresses that ladies wear in the spring
With patterns of stripes and daisies
The beautiful songs that come from the heart
In church soft music blessing Jesus
5 Beautiful toot from toy trumpet
Music of beautiful party people
Lovely sparkling punch
Beautiful conversations in quiet tones of adorable friends and family
Hot music of fast dancing
10 Beautiful white rain pouring down on beautiful blue iron roofs
Glorious birds soaring in the trees with pieces of fruit and beautiful
     worms
Flowers wake up, get out of bed
Yellow tulips, roses red
Gorgeous rainbows looping over the clouds

15 Cute toys—bright transformers click and squeak
Hearts are so lovely I can't resist them
Happy are mothers after you've kissed them
Everybody stick together
Going up in the elevator
20 Into the beautiful mountain of gold
Stay in line
Beautiful shoeshine, shoes reflect your image
Small things are beautiful—hamsters, hamburgers
Tinier still—jewelry and coins, butterflies, ladybugs, dominoes, string,
  clover and candy, erasers and baseballs
25 Snowflakes vanishing in a twinkle
Beautiful lipstick applied on lips
Blush and shadow
Powder and perfume
Make women look like Egyptian princesses
30 Make men flip like hot Mexican jumping beans
Pretty sky
Pretty plane
Swans and flamingoes walking on water
Long sticky legs stirring and paddling
35 Dolls, angelfish, woodpeckers, tweetybirds
The beauty of Barbie and her gigantic wardrobe
She flies by in her Porsche with her lovely Ken
Heartbreaking beauty of the death of innocent kittens
Newborn beauty of sunny chicks
40 Beauty of Paris—its bridges and pools
The glory of the Eiffel Tower shaped like a black A
Delicate accents of French and Italian like bubbles and flutes
Beautiful sleep
Pleasant dreams
45 Of marriage and kids and love and respect
Beautiful basketball dunked through the hoop
Beautiful school team, beautiful group
Beautiful teacher who cares for us all
Beautiful textbooks, beautiful fall
50 The bell rings
School is out
I run to the candy store
Glamorous licorice, Hersheys, and gum
Extravagant Skittles, cherry and plum
55 Delicious Starburst and 3 Musketeers
Nestle's Crunch and Baby Ruth
Beautiful eyeballs
Beauty of tooth

Under my pillow
60 The beautiful fairy leaves $10
My beautiful rich grandfather
Who gave me an antique
It's one of a kind
Uniquely designed
65 An ancient green porcelain Chinese flowerpot
Its color is lime
It's cold to the fingers
Beautiful time . . . running out for this poem
Beautiful poem
70 Beautiful afternoon—misty sky
What'll we do now
The beautiful composition
The beautiful end

    —Rebecca Rosada, Ruben Bermudez, Arnulfo Batista, Michele LaSalle,
Zulma Alicea, Steven Figueroa, Marcus Guyton, Melissa Caldero, and
José Maldonado

In the workshop in which "The Beautiful Poem" began, I didn't
have any idea that we would be writing about beauty, or about any
particular subject. I said to the kids, "Somebody, just begin. Poems
can start anywhere."

One kid said, "We should say something beautiful."

"Okay. What's beautiful? What's the most beautiful thing in the
world?"

"A dress."

"What dress?"

"The beautiful dresses that ladies wear in the spring" (line 1).

I wrote that down and asked, "What else is beautiful?"

No answers.

"Okay, let's stick with the dresses. What do they look like?"

"The ones with patterns, you know, with stripes and daisies."

"Okay. Now what else is beautiful?"

The kids were timid about getting started. One offered, "Music."

"What kind?"

"Songs."

"What kind of songs?"

"Beautiful songs."

"Where do they come from?"

"From the heart."

I wrote down line 3 ("The beautiful songs that come from the
heart") and asked for another kind of beautiful music, because by now

I could see that the poem was organizing itself around the idea of beauty.

When "lovely" got into it (line 7), I asked, "What are some other words that mean *beautiful?*" We made a list, which we used later in the poem: gorgeous, lovely, extravagant, elegant, and so on. The first suggestion for line 10 began, "Beautiful rain falling down. . . ." I pointed out that rain *always* falls, so it's boring to say. "What's a different verb?" (These children have good vocabularies, and even if they hadn't I would have used the word "verb" anyway; I call them verbs because that's how the kids learn what verbs are. I don't present a textbook definition of what a verb is.) "Falling" became "pouring." I also asked for an adjective to describe the rain. Among the suggestions "white" seemed the most inspired.

As we went along, a couple of kids began to catch on to the fact that I wanted stronger verbs and more descriptive adjectives: "Glorious birds soaring. . . ." But this takes a lot of work. If teachers would emphasize a more vivid vocabulary and use it every day in their lessons, the students would start picking it up on their own, and we'd see a dramatic improvement in their writing.

The "beautiful worms" (line 11) must have led to the ground and the flower bed (line 12). One student, Arnulfo Batista, a third grader, came up with the next line (13), which introduced rhyme and a rhetorical inversion new to the students' writing. I thought that rhyme might then invade the poem, but it didn't, although it did pop up nicely from time to time, as in lines 16–17. Steven Figueroa suggested, "Mothers are happy after you've kissed them" (line 17). I took a hint from Arnulfo's line (13) and supplied the inversion "Happy are mothers. . . ."

I'm not sure how we got the idea of line 19, "Going up in the elevator." I think it happened this way: it started with the gold (line 20), a mountain of gold, a beautiful mountain of gold, and when I asked how we'd get to the top, someone said, "By going up in the elevator!" So we worked backwards from line 20 to get line 19, which at this point has the effect of a sudden acceleration. I think I moved line 18 up to its present position—originally it was just before "Stay in line" (line 20), which one of the kids kept repeating to me. Only later did I realize that he was referring to my handwriting, which was wandering all over the sheet. "Stay in line" suggested "Everybody stick together," hall monitor talk, or maybe the advice of a nature guide in an adventure story.

Rhyme came back in lines 21–22, with "line" and "shoeshine," and the nicely polished shoes yielded the idea of something reflected in them. (The idea of a small, reflected image recurs in the poem we wrote a few sessions later, "Life on Earth.") The tininess of the image suggested other small things (lines 23–25).

Somehow this led to things that women use to beautify themselves, and to the sky and birds. The kids saw now that any common thing, like a Barbie doll, could be seen as beautiful, as long as you described it well.

The poem turned out to be a catalogue poem about beauty, with brief digressions and narrative moments, all among beautiful things. The result is fast, free, and full of gorgeous surprises.

★   ★   ★

Working with pullout groups is different from working with full classes. Pullout groups are special, and the kids in them are well aware of it. (I worked with the same students in their regular classes as well.) The pullout group size—in this case about eight kids—affects what you can and can't do. For instance, with a small group you can move very quickly in collaborative poems, and the poems reflect this agility. You can also focus on drawing out each individual student, especially the shyer ones. The kids become more involved because each one has immediate and direct access to how the poem is taking shape. They don't have to raise their hands and, too often, compete with their thirty classmates for attention.

With a group like this I become quite excited myself. As editor/orchestrator I am right in the thick of it with them. We write the poem together. I'm not the impassive scribe who accepts everything, good and bad. Teacher participation intensifies the whole process, and it puts a premium on performance, because no one can hide in such a small group. Of course, not everyone performs well under these circumstances, and some kids are less spontaneous than others. The tactful editor/orchestrator will see to it that everyone benefits from the experience.

Had I worked with these particular students longer, I would have broken the group up into, say, pairs, and had them work on such poems on their own, without my direction or interference. Gradually I would have eased the kids into writing alone silently at their desks back in their regular classrooms. You can't expect them to internalize immediately everything they've experienced in a couple of quick workshop sessions. If I'd had more time I'd have typed up the poems and given the kids written copies for us to revise.

★   ★   ★

The first draft of "Life on Earth," also dictated to me, was visually a mess, written all over the paper and other scraps. Because of the briefness of my residency, I didn't type it all up neatly and give it back to them for revision. As with "The Beautiful Poem," we did it all pretty much on the spot. At several points in the writing, someone objected by saying, "But that doesn't make sense." So we talked about what did or didn't make sense, and what that meant, "to make sense." I welcomed criticism as we wrote, but I didn't let the talk degenerate into a gab-session that would turn the kids away from their energy for writing. After maybe a minute I'd get everyone back to the poem.

Like "The Beautiful Poem," this poem started naturally. One of the kids asked, "What are we going to write about today?" I said, "I don't know." One of the other kids said, "Let's write about everything!" And I said, "Good idea, why not. What is 'everything'?"

Then I got inspired by this question. I talked about trying to think of everything, from the greatest to the smallest, from the most distant to the nearest. The things that were closest were the things in the room, so that's where we started: some chemical bottles turned upside down for a science demonstration and some *papier-mâché* puppet and theater displays. That accounts for the first few lines of "Life on Earth." After line 5, I asked, "What are other good and bad characters?" and one kid asked, "Do you mean fictional or real?" "Anything—characters from history or legends or stories." This would send the kids off on a burst of energy that would roll for a while, then things would calm down and we'd have another quick little discussion, which would send them off again.

Life on Earth

Upsidedown chemical bottles
Projects for fairy tales
Shoemaker and elves
The rabbit's bride
5 Good and bad characters
Princess Pandora
Hitler with a big army
Slave owners
Jesse James
10 Inhumane pet owners
Poisoners of Tylenol
Godzilla
Wonderful heroines like Harriet Tubman, Martha Washington,
    Blondie, Firestar

Madonna
15 Courageous heroes such as King Tut, Iceman, Spiderman, Bobby
   Kennedy
All great actors and freedom fighters
Tibet where Mr. Tut lived who ruled the Egyptians with his jewelry
   and power
Lyons, France, where some people go to school and eat french fries
Ethiopia—skinny children suffer
20 Please help them
Give canned food, flour, equipment, sheets, doctors, money
Help these poor souls, pray for them
Hawaii, where the luau is happening—big table of people eating like
   pigs on Love Boat
Beautiful hula hula dreams
25 Coconuts bounce off your head
Smooth sand, bare feet
Hot volcano
Look out! It's erupting!
Lava pours out, flowing down the mountain
30 People run and scream
Their skin is burning
Hard to breathe
Let's get out of here!
Tokyo
35 People with pop-out eyeballs make vases, plates, dolls, transformers,
   jewelry boxes, watches, electric appliances, long silk robes
Haiti—poor people wearing rags and scraps—not enough to cover
   their backs—no roofs over their heads—pacing and praying in
   little shacks—dying from hunger every day—all because of one
   greedy man—Baby Doc who is fat and rich and splurges on fancy
   food and clothes—all for him
But now the people have kicked him out
And he goes to Red Lobster under heavy guard
Too clumsy to even wash dishes
40 Canberra, New South Wales, Australia—koalas chewing eucalyptus
   leaves—nobody bothers them
I love these cute bears
We should import them
Zambia—hot—doubletime summertime all the time—men in biki-
   nis—bongos and congas—papaya jungle—piranhas mutilate
   toes—ancient moondancing around bonfires—white stripes on
   your forehead—poison arrows zip through the leaves—old tombs
   with booby traps—gold and ivory under a pyramid—you walk
   down a secret passage with a torch—the wind blows it out—it's
   pitch black—all of a sudden a slimy finger touches your ankle

Fun with slimy fingers
45 Each player gets one finger
Soap & water
Blob of jelly
Instructions: . . . (unreadable)
Life on earth
50 Adam & Eve step into the mud
Earth developed from small to big
Stars exploded and cooled down
The Big Guy shaped them like Play-Doh
He blew life into animals
55 Light into night
Put down the animals and organic bushes
Made jelly brains pumping in your skull
Meat, water, blood, skin, bones, clay, liver, vessels, kidneys, tissues,
    cells, germs, antibodies, static, tubes, wires
Jesus taught respect, love, care, patience, kindness, intelligence
60 Ideas
Moses came down the mountain and smashed the great tombstones
Ten Commandments
1. Thou shalt not kill
2. Thou shalt not steal
3. Thou shalt not take God's name in vain
4. Respect your parents
5. Thou shalt not invade another's privacy
6. Never tell a lie
7. Commit no sins
8. Don't make fun of handicapped people or mental sickness
9. Don't rub your help in anybody's face
10. Try not to spread colds
Who follows these rules?
Dr. King, Mrs. Emma Merced, and Carmen Fernandez
75 That's all
Everybody else needs to work on this
The Pope of St. Peter's prays to St. Patrick to guide Arnulfo Batista in
    spiritual behavior and math
Years ago dinosaurs fought for fun
Now some people don't even care about their families
80 In Chicago, who cares?
Who cares about life anyway?
We are all going to die
BUT
While we're alive
85 We'll keep writing poems like these
About how things are and could be

In life on earth
Poems that are truthful and beautiful
Poems that come straight from the spirit
$1.75 per poem
Special offer
Mail today
Last chance
Life goes on

It so happened that there was a globe on our table, the perfect focal point—or prop—for a poem about life on earth. That's how various countries got into the poem, beginning with Tibet (line 17). Anytime we wanted to go somewhere else, we'd just spin the globe. It's a little like Guillaume Apollinaire's poem "Zone," whose narrator has a bird's-eye view of the whole world.

At the end of the long line about Zambia (line 43) a "slimy finger" entered the poem. That was a reference to a soap bubble kit one of the kids had, but I can't remember how it got into the poem here. I decided to go with it (and later to keep it, unlike some other tangents we dropped, such as one on William "The Refrigerator" Perry, because the kids got hung up on him too much and it got boring). The soap bubble kit tangent led to a point where the energy subsided, so I looked at the globe and, instead of spinning it again, asked "How did all this begin? How did life begin?" The kids contributed various creation theories, with Biblical references (lines 50–62).

A funny thing happened here. One kid said, "Moses came down the mountain and smashed the tombstones," and another kid said, "It wasn't tombstones, it was. . . . What was it, Mr. Fagin?"

"You mean the tablets?"

"Tablets, that's aspirin. He didn't smash *aspirins*."

I was tempted here to write down "Moses came down the mountain and smashed the great aspirin," but I didn't want to manipulate *that* much, so I stuck with "tombstones" because that sounded good to me and the tablets *do* look like tombstones.

Then (line 62) I asked them to name the Ten Commandments. When we got to the end, one girl asked, "Who is able to follow these rules?"

Another answered, "Dr. Martin Luther King."

"Who else?" I asked.

And they named their next-door neighbors, Mrs. Emma Merced and Carmen Fernandez, as exemplary people.

"Anybody else?"

Silence.

Steven Figueroa commented, "Everybody else needs to work on this" (line 76).

There's a lurch in line 78, back to the dinosaurs. I didn't know how it came up but I put it in, just for fun—like the dinosaurs fighting.

The poem now gets into social criticism (lines 79–82). The children are aware of the various kinds of poor behavior unearthed by the media, in shows such as *60 Minutes*.

At this point the poem starts to end; in fact I said to them, "Okay, let's wind this up." And so we did. The last line was "Life goes on" (line 94). The whole session took forty-five minutes.

★ ★ ★

When I got home and read what we had, I was pleased. But I also had the feeling that the poem could go on. So at the next session I walked right in and said, "Guys, let's revive this poem! Let's give it new life."

The kids shouted, "Hurray!" They really *liked* the poem. And so we continued:

```
 95 We go on
    You go on
    This poem goes on
    A beautiful girl
    9 years old
100 Red sweater
    Red ribbon
    Reflected in her glasses: my tiny face
    I look like a frog with blue skin
    The United States of Orangutan
105 Each orangutan has a license to eat bananas
    The young orangutans slide in the peels on snow days
    Down the mountain
    Into the valley
    Over the bridge
110 Through the village
    The villagers come out and say
    "Get those orangutans out of here!"
    The baby orangutans go to jail for stealing bananas and disturbing the
       peace
    This does not take place in Mexico
115 Where there's a landslide
    Land is sliding into the ocean
    Out on the ocean the captain of Love Boat screams,
    "Get that land out of here!"
    The land goes to jail for disturbing the peace
```

120 Love Boat passengers go back to their kissing
When they kiss
Nothing happens
They are boring
Disturbed
125 Lipless
Loveless, brainless, alcoholic, no personalities
Stowaways on welfare
Meanwhile the land and the baby orangutans plan their escape
But Bruce Lee is hot on their tail
130 Their tail is on fire
"Fire!" screams Bruce Lee
He drops the land back into the ocean and the Love Boat sinks to
the bottom
And meets the Titanic
Where there's a party going on
135 Skeletons in fur coats doing the body hustle
Everybody drinking salt water
Eating taffy
All the taffy comes together to make Gumby
Who can't swim
140 So he drowns
But Bruce Lee come to save him in a water taxi
Which is not in the dictionary
Other words are there
Like water tank, waterbaby, waterbed, waterballoon, tapwater,
sweetwater, slopwater, club soda
145 The orangutans open their dictionaries
When they find the word *banana* they eat it
In Wyoming scientists discover a cure for being boring
It's a fantasy helmet
Put it on and you become exciting
150 Like every time you want to eat you drive a motorcycle through a
restaurant, grab a meal, and do a wheelie over the head of the head
waiter
By the way, how long does the earth have to go?
As long as the Russians and Americans feel like it
Why can't they get along?
Because they are retarded
155 These government bums need special help
Psychiatrists
Something . . .
And now, Arnulfo, it's time for your nap.

—*Rebecca Rosado, Steven Figueroa, Melissa Caldero, Arnulfo Batista,
Ruben Bermudez, and Michele LaSalle*

"We go on" (line 95) means "human life continues," but in the context of the workshop meant simply that we were continuing the poem. At that point I had the kids go back to what was right in front of us, in this case a "beautiful girl" (line 98).

One of the boys noticed his reflection in the girl's glasses. I asked him what he looked like there. He said, "I look like a frog—"

"—with blue skin," added another.

Then, as I recall, we noticed the American flag in the room. So we did a parody of the Pledge of Allegiance, beginning, "I pledge allegiance to the flag of the United States of Orangutan" (line 104). Later I cut it, leaving only "The United States of Orangutan."

Throughout this whole process there was a tremendous amount of talking going on, some soft, some loud. At one point it got out of hand, with one kid shouting at the top of his lungs. I had to calm him down: I couldn't hear the other kids. But that happens. It's crazy to expect kids to become excited and energized and just sit quietly.

In the orangutan section (lines 104–146), things move easily from line to line: orangutan leads to banana, which leads to sliding, which leads to snow, which leads to "Down the mountain," which leads to other prepositional phrases, which lead to villagers, and so on. The globe comes back briefly with "Mexico" (line 114), but generally the poem moves quite naturally to water and the Love Boat (line 117), from one association to another. This associative movement has become a standard (though still nameless) technique of modern poetry.

Throughout the workshop, I urged the kids to include action verbs. Such verbs tend to induce narrative, but I don't do it for that reason. I do it because verbs are the weakest part of children's writing, the part most in need of improvement.

The technique of one thing leading to another takes a new turn in lines 129–130: "But Bruce Lee is hot on their tail / Their tail is on fire." Here the correct and usual expression ("hot on their *trail*") has been mislearned, and then taken literally, with interesting results: "hot" and "tail" lead to "Their tail is on fire."

For lines 132–135 I asked, "What happened to the land?" It gets dropped back into the ocean. "What happened to the Love Boat?" It sinks and meets the Titanic. "What happens then?" There's a party going on. "But the people on the Titanic are all dead." Yes, they're skeletons and they're dancing. "What are they wearing?" Fur coats (the kids knew the Titanic victims were people with money). "What kind of dance?" The body hustle.

You see the question-and-answer method here. Every once in a while there'd be such clusters, especially at those points where I felt the poem to be foundering a bit, for lack of energy.

When the "water taxi" (line 141) appeared, I asked what that was. The dictionary got included because we had a dictionary on the table. That led to thinking of other words with "water" in them, and clustering them the way they might be in a dictionary. The globe, which comes back in with "Wyoming" (line 147), served the same purpose as my questions: to pick up the energy.

Steven Figueroa's "fantasy helmet" (line 148) was one of my favorite phrases in the poem. The helmet inspired a long list of things you can do with it, but the list turned out to be surprisingly predictable, so I cut that part out.

The last line of the poem was written in response to the bell ringing. The poem could have gone on, but this seemed like a good place to stop. It runs about seven pages typed. Had it been twenty-five pages it might have collapsed under its own weight. On the other hand, had it gone on for 100 pages it might have been a masterpiece.

★   ★   ★

How much of this is of use to the classroom teacher? A lot, provided that the teacher is fairly spontaneous. Unfortunately, some teachers are firmly convinced that everything has to be based on lesson plans backed by what is called solid academic research. This rigor leads to a rigidity that causes these teachers to recognize only one kind of system. They are unable to see other systems, such as those working naturally in human spontaneity.

For instance, in "Life on Earth" we used the globe as an organizing device. It just happened to be there in the room. We could have used something else, accidentally or deliberately. In "The Beautiful Poem" it could have happened that the organizing device was the word *ugly*, instead of *beautiful*. In both poems we used the catalogue (or list) as an organizing system. In "The Beautiful Poem" rhyme popped up, another organizing system. Both poems use these various systems in a kind of mix-and-match variety. That such systems are not prescribed keeps them—and us—fresh for imaginative use.

William Bryant Logan

Sound, Rhythm, Music

I like to use models when I'm trying to let my elementary school students see the terrific textures that are possible in language. Using models is important not only because it adds energy to students' writing, but also because when they write more energetic lines, they find them easier to remember and to read out loud with gusto.

Two models have been particularly useful, both involving magic and incantation. The first is by the Cuban poet Nicolas Guillen (followed by my translation):

Sensemayá

Mayombé - bombe - mayombé!
Mayombé - bombe - mayombé!
Mayombé - bombe - mayombé!

La culebra tiene los ojos de vidrio;
la culebra viene y se enreda en un palo;

con sus ojos de vidrio, en un palo
con sus ojos de vidrio.
La culebra camina sin patas;
la culebra se esconde en la yerba;
caminando se esconde en la yerba;
caminando sin patas.

Mayombé - bombe - mayombé!
Mayombé - bombe - mayombé!
Mayombé - bombe - mayombé!

Tu le das con el hacha, y se muere:
dále ya!
No le des con el pie, que te muerde,
no le des con el pie, que seva!

Sensemayá, la culebra,
sensemayá.
Sensemayá, con sus ojos,
sensemayá.
Sensemayá, con su lengua,

sensemayá.
Sensemayá, con su boca,
sensemayá . . .

La culebra muerta no puede comer;
la culebra muerta no puede silbar;
no puede caminar;
no puede correr.
La culebra muerta no puede mirar;
la culebra muerta no puede beber;
no puede respirar,
no puede morder!

Mayombé - bombe - mayombé!
Sensemayá, la culebra . . .
Mayombé - bombe - mayombé!
Sensemayá, no se mueve . . .
Mayombé - bombe - mayombé!
Sensemayá la culebra . . .
Mayombé - bombe - mayombé!
Sensemayá, se murio!

★   ★   ★

Sensemayá (Song to Kill a Snake)

Mayombé - bombe - mayombé!
Mayombé - bombe - mayombé!
Mayombé - bombe - mayombé!

The snake has eyes of glass;
the snake comes and wraps around a stick;
with its eyes of glass, on a stick,
with its eyes of glass.
The snake walks without feet;
the snake hides in the grass;
walking, it hides in the grass,
walking without feet.

Mayombé - bombe - mayombé!
Mayombé - bombe - mayombé!
Mayombé - bombe - mayombé!

You hit it with an ax and it dies:
Hit it now!
Don't hit it with your foot, or it'll bite you,
don't hit it with your foot, or it'll run!

Sensemayá, the snake, the snake,
sensemayá.
Sensemayá, with its eyes,
sensemayá.
Sensemayá, with its tongue,
sensemayá.
Sensemayá, with its mouth,
sensemayá . . .

The dead snake can't eat;
the dead snake can't hiss;
it cannot walk,
it cannot run.
The dead snake can't see;
the dead snake can't drink;
it cannot breathe,
it cannot bite!

Mayombé - bombe - mayombé!
Sensemayá, the snake, the snake . . .
Mayombé - bombe - mayombé!
Sensemayá doesn't move . . .
Mayombé - bombe - mayombé!
Sensemayá, the snake, the snake . . .
Mayombé - bombe - mayombé!
Sensemayá is dead!

I then talk about poems as magic and ask the students to imagine writing a poem that would compel an animal to act in a certain way. The students and I think of examples of the repetition of words, phrases, and names that exercise a power over the hearer. Finally, I suggest that the students include a refrain of pure sound—musical, guttural, whatever—as a sort of *coup de grâce* to make the spell effective.

With this idea, I've gotten songs to Elevate an Elephant, to Sauté a Sloth, to Tame a Horse, to Put a Hippo to Sleep, to Make a Fish Swim to the Center of the Sea. Using the repetition of names and syntax and a refrain of pure sounds, the poems are always energetic. But there was one unexpected result, as well: the kids who have more trouble writing exact, concrete imagery seem to be freed by this writing idea. I don't know why, but the environment of nonsense words seems to help some of them see more clearly what they describe.

Salmon, red, salmon, orange.
Red and orange.
Salmon, red and orange.

Its name is Fish of the Sea.

Shobop beebop shobop beebop
shobop beebop shobop beebop
shooooooooooooooobop

He flows into the center of the sea.
He flows there to catch his prey.
In the center of the sea,
to catch his prey.

The Fish of the Sea is red and orange.
Shobop beebop shooooooobop
To catch his prey in the center of the sea.

The Fish of the Sea swims fast and steadily.
The Fish of the Sea goes
to the center of the sea,
to the center of the sea,
to catch his prey.

—*April Lowenthal, fifth grade*

Kids whose native language is not English also have special fun with this technique. Maybe the pure sounds somehow connect them with their native languages. Marwan is Iranian:

Eeeeeeeeeeeeeeeee
bom bom bom bom

The horse is black.
His neck is blue.
He jumps like a train.
He jumps like a rabbit.

Eeeeeeeeeeeeeeeee
bom bom bom bom

—*Marwan Younis, fifth grade*

★   ★   ★

The second model poem I use is the flipside of the first. Guillen invades sense with sound and rhythm. Michael McClure, in his *Ghost Tantras*, tends to invest pure sound with sense. At first, I used this idea only with pullout groups, fearing the wildness that all the sound might invoke. Lately, I've found that it works well in full classes, too.

5

BRAHHNG! KROOOR BRATOOOOOOTH-MAR
GRRRRRRRRRAHH! GROOOOOOOR!
Swow mownarr grah roooooooh muhr
zneeeeeeeeeeeeeeesweeeeeee bwooooooooo
BWEEE NOOOOOOOOOO!
GOOOOOOOOOOOOOOOOOOOOO;
sweeepie joooo nahg gar drrrrr twi
chengreeoooo grrrrrrrrrrrr gowld snarr
mroooooooooooooo-wub
WUB
WUB
WUB
WUB
WUB
WUB
WUB
bweeeeeeeeee.

★   ★   ★

15

THE TREES ARE ELEPHANTS' HEADS.
The brown whorls of hair at the top of your head.
The trees are gray-green grooooor greyeeee.
AMM SOOOTEEE AIEE! GAROOOOOOOOOOH.
Gragg. Hrahhrr mok now-toony. Bwooooooh.
Grooooor. MARRRR! GROOOOH! Grooooooor.
GARHOOOOOOOOOOOOOOOOOOOOOOH!
GAHROOOOOOOOOOOOOOOOOOOOOH!
MOMM.
Hraghhrr.
GROOOOOOOOOH!
Mowk-towr-nnowth-own-eii!
FACE,
TUSK,
WHAHHH!
GAHHROOOOOOOOO!!
LUKK!

When we write poems based on these, I ask the kids first to imagine that they are ghosts, spirits, or some sort of immaterial creature.
This imaginary being's language directly shows how it feels, without

any need for a dictionary. Every once in a while, however, the spirit appears in the world of people, and then, for a line or two, it speaks in English. The first of these I ever received was by a shy sixth grader. It blew me away.

Grough. Grough! Eeeeooo. Eeeeood. Whidyaaa.
Sschwiraaya. Greeayaa. Oooeeeod o o o o.
The pussywillows are knots on a rope to the sky.
Uhgaraaa. Eeeoooo. Teeawaaa. Sweeooooo.
Grough. Grough! Whidayaaa. Eeeeoooo. Whiyaaaaa.
The lightbulb is a piece of the sky caught in a trap.

Mrowaoo.

—*Krista Bray, sixth grade*

Krista was so startled by what she'd done that she refused to read it. When she finally did, however, her pleasure, and the class's, were palpable.

I have also found the ghost tantras to be a good way to put life into ideas that might otherwise evoke hoots and yawns. For a May parade at New York's P.S. 84, I tried to find ways that the kids could write about spring. The tantras freed us very quickly from the inevitable tulips, or rather, they put energy into the usual imagery:

Flooooooooooooooooooooo
bweeeeeee flaaaaaaaoo
Shnnuuuuuuuu meeeeeeeeee
mroooooooooooo mub
BUB
LUB
BUB
LUB

See the life come
off the trees Bweeeee
See the treeeeeeza
Fly Flyaaaaaaaaay
The flowerzzzzza fieflyfleefly
BooooooooooooOooooooooOoooooOa
Seeeeao flafla
See the trees!

—*Raquel James-Segarra, fourth grade*

Everyone in Raquel's class did his or her own spring sound-poem. In the end, we held an informal reading. They never read with more expression.

Bibliography

Nicolas Guillen. *Sóngoro cosongo*. Buenos Aires: Editorial Losada, 1952.

Michael McClure. *Ghost Tantras*. San Francisco: Four Seasons Foundation, 1969.

William Bryant Logan

Verbs and Whitman

My third and fourth graders are addicted to the verbs *go*, *do*, *say*, and *be*. I use Walt Whitman's "The Sleepers" to get them inspired about other action words. The poem is full of sleep: everyone and everything sleeping, and the poet able to sense and see the sleeping of them all. My students and I write poems that, like "The Sleepers," repeat one strong verb in many different ways.

When I work with "The Sleepers," I use most of the first thirty-one lines down through "And I become the other dreamers." The constant repetition of the word *sleep* (in lines 12–23) is delightful, and my students and I talk about how a rhythm is created by that dependable word returning in line after line. We notice how full and exact the lines are, including everyone from the peaceful husband and wife to the condemned murderer. I also discuss the poet's mind, not only his sympathy for everyone, but also the openness of a mind that, when it doesn't know something, asks a question about it: "And the murdered person . . . How does he sleep?"

Next, we make a list on the blackboard of all the actions that we might want to see the way Whitman sees sleep. It's fun, almost a poem in itself: jump, laugh, yell, roll, fly, command, flip, dance, giggle, fish, run, walk, swim, whisper. . . . All by itself, this list gives us an entrance into Whitman's paradoxically full but always spacious world, a world of action and possibility.

Because this poem uses line-by-line repetition, it's a natural to try it out first as an oral collaboration. Sometimes I write the children's lines on the board, sometimes just let them flow by. When all the children's minds are working together, the results are strange and beautiful. Here, for example, is "The Swimmers" (the Spanish in the last line means "Come here"):

The red bugs are swimming.
Mrs. Glenn is swimming in the Bronx.
Animals are swimming in the sea.
Mr. Logan was swimming at the beach with a crab monster.
Bruce Lee is swimming, swimming in the Pacific Ocean.

Swim, swam, swum. . . . Where is the bum?
My brother, he swims, swims, swims. . . .
President Gorbachev is swimming in the classroom.
A sound. Is it swimming in my ear?
My mother swims in the hot blue water.
The seahorse . . . it dies, it comes alive and it swims in the sea.
My guitar is swimming in the sea.
"Ven aca!" it sings.

Whitman wrote that he wanted his poems to express the fullness of his own personality. It's interesting to see that, imitating him, third and fourth graders can give such a full portrait of their own wishes, wonder, cantankerousness, affections, and fears.

If the collaborations reflect the personality of a class, the individual poems let the students take what tone and attitude they will. I ask each of them to choose one action word—either from the board or not—and to use the word as much as they can to make a poem that is full of the action. The variety of results is surprising. One student, obsessed by questions, wrote a whole scary poem of questions about hanging, beginning, "Does the girl hang peacefully by her ponytail?" Melody Prosser stuffed her poem full of forms of the word *giggle*. Another student wrote about a foot race between Carl Lewis, a goldfish, a dolphin, and a lamppost. Tanya James wrote an extraordinary poem about her jumping heart and jumping frogs. Occasionally, students elect to use all the words on the board, like Makeda Benjamin did in her piece below about crazy action.

More than most imitations, these pieces seem to belong to the kids, since Whitman's breathless way of writing is similar to the way children think when they're excited. I find that the kids not only enjoy writing these poems, but that they enjoy performing them for the class as well. The oral energy is already in the poems, waiting to burst out.

My mommy is a giggler.
My father is a giggler.
Sam's a giggler.
Buck's a giggler.
The man of my dreams is a giggler and a giggler.
The frog is giggling.
I don't know if the pig is giggling.
Ronald Reagan. Is he giggling?
Even I giggle and giggle and giggle.

—*Melody Prosser*

*   *   *

My fingers are playing football with each other,
and my nose is dancing, and my toes are playing handgames,
and my heart is swimming in my veins.
My lips are smacking.
My teeth are having lunch and turning yellow.
Shoes are running down the street.
And the fruits are jumping into people's mouths.
It was raining clocks and plops on my block.
And the crayons are scribbling graffiti on the subway . . .

　　—*Makeda Benjamin*

*   *   *

My heart jumps every time I breathe
and jumps faster every time I run.
And every time little girls jump and sing
my heart goes the same beat.
Frogs jump into a blue pond,
and my heart jumps into a red pond
that's inside me. It seems
like my heart tells them to come to me.
They're jumping into each other's ponds,
because they're related to each other.
My heart jumps into the frog's blue pond,
and the frogs jump into my red pond.

　　—*Tanya James*

Phillip DePoy

Saying What Can't Be Said
Three Startling Poetry Exercises

If poetry is an attempt to say something in words that can't be said in words, we must make a deliberate effort to break students of poetry from linear, normal thinking patterns. In order to write poetry, a student must first be escorted out of the frame of the classroom and into the formless ether of inspiration. Here are three particularly good exercises I've developed, along with examples of the resulting work by my often reluctant, always surprised students.

Exercise 1

This exercise consists mainly of telling the students to think of a question that has no answer. Thus no question can be wrong, but some ostensibly unanswerable questions ("How far is it from here to the next galaxy?") actually do have possible answers. I encourage students to think of questions that are deliberate nonsense ("How far is Up?"). When the students have each written an unanswerable question, I tell them to write an answer to the question. I assure them that, since the question doesn't have an answer, any answer is correct (the answer to "How far is Up?" could just as easily be "Blue monkeys" as anything else). The question can serve as the title of the poem, and the answer (at least four lines) can become the body of the poem.

Aside from being tremendous fun, with no possibility of anyone's being wrong, this exercise has produced some remarkable work. Here are some examples from Rabun County, a mountain region of Georgia.

How Far Is Heaven?

What does it look like,
what do angels wear?
Ballet clothes—
or suits of bright aluminum?
Do they have wings—

can they fly—
do they die, bleeding thought?

   —*Arlene Rice, ninth grade*

Arlene had never read Emily Dickinson's "What is Paradise," but the ideas and the structures are similar. Arlene's is one type of response to the assignment: to answer an unanswerable question with more questions. The notion, however, that angels don't bleed blood but bleed thought is a transcendent idea that intrigued and delighted both the poet and her audience, exactly the feeling often elicited by good poems.

What Is in the Mind?

In the midst of the hollow,
something scratches as though it were the wind,
beating the door, tearing the soul.

Like a sealed box:
nothing may enter,
nothing may leave.

Like an empty skull
it pulls the sea.

   —*Rhonda Webb, tenth grade*

On a somewhat darker note, Rhonda seems to be trying, in some meditative way, to answer the impossible query. This is a second kind of normative response to the exercise: sincere, often quite profound, introspection leading toward self-awareness or even enlightenment. When Rhonda read her work to the class, she read it as if someone else had written it, and even weeks afterward told me she was still thinking about it—and writing more poetry at home.

What Is Music, That We Should Hear?

A golden note struck
by a falling sphere,
or a window struck
by a shining tear.
The aching sound
between things torn,
or a single note
from a golden horn.

   —*Dawn Watson, eighth grade*

A few students, such as Dawn, know they're in class to write a poem, and that's what they set out to do. These students scarcely need the encouragement of an exercise like this one, but they can use it as a tool to create great work. Every student writes at least something in response to this idea. Some responses are quite odd, many are hilarious, and all seem to succeed in cracking the student's shell, letting out the thing that flies.

Exercise 2

This exercise asks the student to describe an impossible object: a one-sided coin, a book with no beginning or ending, a mirror made of the sky. Sometimes the objects are people: a woman with eyes made of the wind, a man who eats air. Sometimes the objects are completely fanciful inventions: a machine that runs the sun, an envelope big enough to send the earth through the mail. Once again, no response is "wrong," but a bucket with a hole in the bottom isn't as useful as a bucket full of angels. Once an object is conceived, it becomes the title, and the description of the object is the body of the poem. As always, following the instructions for this exercise too closely could be detrimental to the poem. This is a basis, not a strict pattern.

An Apple of Air

I see an apple,
it's big and round.
I stared at the apple,
it fell on the ground.

Take it to my wooden chair.
How does it taste?
It's an apple of air!

I loved it so,
but now it's gone,
I felt it blow.

My apple of air
has turned into wind
and flown over there.

—*Keri Oliver, fifth grade*

Keri's poem is less a description of an impossible object than a description of the wonder that the object inspires; in any case, she has invented an amazing image. Often the student's response to the challenge of the exercise is to create an image out of juxtaposition, and the resulting images are striking and strange.

Shadow Stair

The shadow is rising,
the wolves climb the sky.
After the wind,
we knew it would come.
We no longer saw
the wings of eagles
in the east,
no longer heard
the whispering of the sea.

—*Laura Lee, ninth grade*

Laura was moved by the strangeness of her original concept. More a metaphorical image than an actual description, the object (a stairway made of shadows) appealed to her, but she wanted to wait until the mood of the rest of the work was correct. It took several weeks for her to complete this poem. The power of the poem was worth the wait.

Angels

Ghosts from the inside in,
a glow like the solemn beam of light
in a cave image of the mind.
I was not afraid,
I was filled with wonder.

They played a nameless song,
the song sang itself,
the last note was sorrow.

I began my way home
in the cold and black
on a blanket of snow
from the new-fallen tears.

It was a nameless song
that played itself,
welcome without answers.

These, my soul,
they might have been angels.

—*Lee McClure, eleventh grade*

Personally, I'm stunned by this piece, especially the last couplet. Some students choose impossible animate objects, objects that already exist in the literature of the unconscious: minotaurs, gnomes, angels. Lee has created a Wallace Stevens-like description of not only the look, but the content and even the aura of angels—no small feat.

Exercise 3

This final exercise is fundamentally the contemplation of infinity. It works best with sixth grade students and older, but it's even been successful with second graders on occasion. An endeavor of this sort prompted Einstein to theorize curved space, Bertrand Russell to find useful mathematical concepts, and Schopenhauer to find God—not a bad day's work for a classroom assignment.

Students who are especially interested in science and mathematics seem to be prompted more by this exercise than any other exercise. The idea is to sit comfortably and imagine the infinite: sizeless size, endless space, eternal time. What can be visualized or imagined beyond the farthest reaches of the mind? The image of infinity is presented in the poem's title, and the description of the image is the poem.

Medial Eternity

Figures move silently,
space is the sunny world stepped outside.
Characters struggle to entertain.
Continually, characters tumble:

5——2——4——7——46——11

Freedom arrives, the dark shield,
traveling into the brighter world.

Electromagnetic forces pull
and steal away the light

The slate is clean.

—*Tracy Hogan, eleventh grade*

Tracy was a star student in mathematics and not really interested in writing poetry until this experience. She's now written a series of one hundred poems about mathematical concepts called *The Universe Explained*.

You Stand on the Bank of a River

You stand on the bank of a river.
The river runs perfectly straight
with no curves or angles.
Brilliant white light is reflected from the water,
but there is no sun in the sky.

There is a waterfall in the river,
25 feet down. It drops away
at a 90 degree angle
barely splashing at its base.

There are no animals, there are no plants,
and the only sound is the orderly splash
of the falling water.

All of this is enclosed in a metal box
a mile square
floating at the edge of an unknown galaxy.

—*Michael Dean, eleventh grade*

Some students enjoy the experience of the journey beyond their ordinary conceptual framework; it's just great fun to travel. Once in the outer reaches, Michael realized that he was experiencing realities within realities, a particular kind of infinity. (The relationship between the product of this exercise and the "impossible object" exercise is apparent here.)

The White Albatross

I fall into the water of life.

The white albatross dips
into a blood-red sky.

Waves of comets star my sightless eye
with visions of the past
flowing sideways.

—*Melissa Noblet, eleventh grade*

Picking a mysterious image to solve the problem of describing the indescribable, Melissa has expressed an experience of standing outside herself to watch the flow of eternity. This poem embodies the aim of the exercise: to experience the indescribable, and then describe it in original language.

★   ★   ★

At heart then, these three exercises could be described as answering the impossible question, describing the impossible object, and contemplating infinity. If an aim of poetry is transcendence, then the first step toward it would seem to be a step away from the boundaries of conventional thought. These heady exercises are designed to usher or jolt the poet out of the desk and into the ether.

Jane Augustine

The World of Color

The following exploration introduces students to the power of colors as image-enhancing, visually exciting, and capable of conveying symbolic meaning through their emotional associations. I always give each student a copy of this poem, then read it aloud with the gusto that William Carlos Williams must have felt in writing it:

Primrose

Yellow, yellow, yellow, yellow!
It is not a color.
It is summer!
It is the wind on a willow,
the lap of waves, the shadow
under a bush, a bird, a bluebird,
three herons, a dead hawk
rotting on a pole—
Clear yellow!
It is a piece of blue paper
in the grass or a threecluster of
green walnuts swaying, children
playing croquet or one boy
fishing, a man
swinging his pink fists
as he walks—
It is ladysthumb, forget-me-nots
in the ditch, moss under
the flange of the carrail, the
wavy lines in split rock, a
great oaktree—
It is a disinclination to be
five red petals or a rose, it is
a cluster of birdsbreast flowers
on a red stem six feet high,
four open yellow petals
above sepals curled
backward into reverse spikes—

Tufts of purple grass spot the
green meadow and clouds the sky.

Rather than attempt to tell the students what they experienced in
reading this poem, I ask them to tell me. I ask a simple leading question, for instance: what does yellow really mean to Williams?

A: Lots of things . . . summer . . . how can it be pink fists? How can
   yellow be a hawk or bluebird?
Q: Is yellow just a color then?
A: No!
Q: You can't have a color that isn't part of a thing. These are all
   things, but they are not all things we usually think of as yellow.
   How come?
A: Yellow reminds him of these things . . . no, these things have
   yellow on them . . . it's summer. . . .
Q: What do you think of when you think of yellow?
A: Sunshine . . . a banana . . . warmth . . . lemon, lemonade.
Q: You *see* things that are yellow.
A: Yellow makes you feel that it's light or warm . . .
Q: . . . and so it carries that feeling over to other things. What is the
   yellow thing that starts Williams off on this whole trip through a
   summer's day?
A: ??
Q: The title?
A: Oh, a primrose. He's thinking about a primrose. . . .
Q: Which isn't a rose, by the way, and he's not thinking about it, he's
   actually seeing it. He's out in the country and he's telling us
   exactly how it looks, at the end of the poem especially. But the
   yellowness of the primrose is so overwhelming it colors everything
   else he sees around it in the country that day.

You can write a poem like this just by thinking of something that
has a very rich distinctive color, and letting the color of that thing—
and its shape, smell, size—carry your mind off in any direction, or all
directions. Williams found that yellow became summer, paper, bird,
tree, rock, children—much more than just a big yellow flower. Take
out a piece of paper; think of a color you like—you'll find you're
thinking of a thing that has that color actually, or several things; you'll
find you have feelings about that color and those things. The feelings
may remind you of something that happened that made you sad, happy,
curious, or revolted—write them all down. You can start simply with
a first line like Williams's: just say "red, red, red, red" and then go on:

"it's not red, it's a valentine, a bleeding heart, sorrow of love," without worrying about whether the thing is actually red or not. Let the color's feeling attach itself to anything in the whole world, even to other colors.

The beauty of this exploration is that it can embrace both concrete objects and unconcretized feelings; color always has a visual impact and is always interesting in any context. Students sometimes ask if they can use two colors. Of course they can. I've found, however, that poems should not start from a multicolored object, e.g., a rainbow, since there is no focus of feeling then in the "warmth" or "cold" of the single color, and no identification with a season of the year. I have also used this poem idea (without the model) with retarded and disabled students who couldn't read or write, as a collaboration.

Mary Swander

About a Wolf Maybe Two Wolves

Lockers banging. The squeak of the lunchroom door and clank of dishes and trays. The swish of basketball through hoop. The revving of the school bus engine pulling out of the lot, gravel grinding under the tires. The gravelly voice of E. T. phoning home. I was spending another autumn day with sixth graders in Clinton, Iowa, in a Writer-in-the-Schools residency, and the sixth graders' noises were all around me. *Coming not from the objects, but from the students.* These students were naturals at sound effects. The previous week when I had visited these classes, in preparation for a writing exercise, I'd done some storytelling about the migration of snow geese. And *whap, whap, whoosh*, right away the students accompanied my tale with the sounds of the geese. *Honk, honk, honk.* They knew these noises. They lived on the Mississippi Flyway and had watched the dense flocks head south in the fall. Some had hunted the birds with their parents. *Ka-blam.*

So the next week I returned to the classroom with an idea for using these students' good sense of sound. I gave each student a translation from Jerome Rothenberg's *Shaking the Pumpkin*, a Seneca piece called "A Poem about a Wolf Maybe Two Wolves." (I have found that kids this age respond to the direct syntax, the simple word choice, and the gentle humor of Native American poems.) Before I could even read the poem aloud, wolf howls were echoing up and down the aisles. The classroom teacher glanced up at me a bit skeptically and I wondered if I'd let loose more than I'd planned for, but soon I gained control again. And enthusiasm for the poem was running high. I read it aloud, sentences first, then the howl:

A Poem about a Wolf Maybe Two Wolves

"Do you think the poem should be read that way?" I asked, and suggested that perhaps the piece was meant for more than one voice. I asked the students to help me read the poem. This time, I read the sentences, and the students sustained the call throughout the piece. A chorus of thirty voices joined in one long eerie wolf howl.

Then we talked about the poem. "Why," I asked, "does the howl wind down the page the way it does? Did this influence the way you read the noise? And what about the title? Why does it say the poem's about a wolf, then hint that maybe it's about two wolves?"

A student suggested that there were two "clumps" of words and perhaps each clump belonged to an individual wolf. This led us into a short discussion of the word "stanza" and the idea behind the term. Another student suggested that there could be two wolves because there were two "yowee's." Another insisted that the poem was about only one wolf—a wolf who was running across the field in the beginning of the poem and up a hill at the end of the poem. From there, we talked about a poem's story or plot, and about the fact that in a poem, as in a story, something usually happens.

Finally I asked, "And what about the feeling you get from this poem?" Spooky. Faraway. Lonely. "But notice that nowhere in the poem do we find the words *spooky, faraway, lonely*. What things do we find in the poem that show us these feelings?"

A student suggested that the lonely feeling came about because you can see this single wolf out in the field all by itself. It might be winter. Snow all around. Another student had the idea that the poem took up a whole page by itself. The poem looks "all alone" out there on the paper. And another student felt that the faraway, spooky feeling comes from the howl—the way it was loud at first, then faded into the "eeee" sound.

"Okay," I said. "Let's try writing a poem like this together. Give me the name of something that moves and makes a noise."

"Does it have to be an animal?"

"No, not at all. It can be anything you want."

"How about a sportscar?"

"Fine." I wrote on the blackboard: "Poem about a Sportscar," and asked, "What kind of noise does a sportscar make?"

Tongues pressed against teeth and the whole class downshifted, then rounded a curve with the sounds of a hot rod.

I wrote: "N-n-n-ner-r-r-r-er-n-n-n-n."

"Now if we wanted to put this noise into some kind of shape that had something to do with a sportscar, and then we wanted to show the reader how we wanted the sound to be read (just like the poet did the "yow-ee-yow-ee"), how would we place it on the page?"

Hands shot in the air and I invited one student up to use the chalk. In a few minutes, our sound looked like this on the board:

"So, if at first a wolf 'comes running' across the field, what would a sportscar do?"

"It'd race."

"Good. Race where?"

"Race on the track."

"Then what would it do?"

"Glide up on two wheels."

"Good. Now we're ready to write out stanzas. But where shall we put the writing? Remember, we can put the writing anywhere on the page."

"Let's put it on the top."

"No, on the bottom."

"No, inside."

"Inside the wheels?"

"Yeah."

"Yeah."

Soon, our poem looked like this:

"Now, let's look at the poem and see if we're happy with everything about it. How about this word *race*? It's a good verb. But when you think about it, don't most sportscars 'race'? Could we pick another verb that would make the action a little more specific? So that we could see what is really happening to the car?"

"Zoom."

"Yes, that's good."

"Tromp."

"Good."

"Peel."

"Yes. Which of those words do you like the best?"

"Peel."

"Yeah, peel."

After our revision, we agreed on a final form for our poem:

Poem about a Sportscar

Next, I asked the students to try their own poems—poems about something that moves and makes a noise. And, in the end, a poem that gives us some sort of emotion or feeling—but doesn't name that feeling in the poem itself. The students quickly went to work, some writing two or three poems before the period was over. Here are some of their pieces:

Fall Poem

They fly through the air effortlessly going South.

QUAAAAAAAAAAAAAAAAAAAAAAAAAAAAAAAAAAAAK

QUAAAAAAAAAAAAAAAAAAAAAAAAA

They fly through the air gracefully

　　　　　　　　　　　going South for the winter

　　—P.G. and B.K.

★　　　★　　　★

A Cymbal

tist　tist　tist　tist

tist　tist　tist　tist　tist

tist　　A drummer hitting　　tist

tist　his cymbal and grabbing　tist

　　　it to make an interesting

tist　　　　beat　　　　tist

tist tist　tist　tist tist

　　—B.E.

★　　　★　　　★

Donkey Kicks

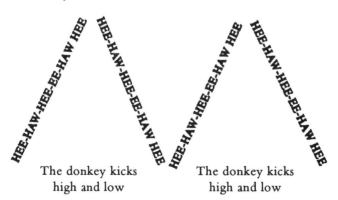

The donkey kicks
high and low

The donkey kicks
high and low

—*Sandy Cody and Tammy Schurson*

★   ★   ★

The next day I went to the Clinton Public High School where there was plenty of noise in the halls, but little in the classroom. I was teaching poetry to an Advanced Composition class of seniors and it was the time of year when the senior class pictures were passed around—those hairsprayed, necktied images forcing their smiles against pale blue backgrounds. During my class the previous week, the photos had been shuffled, dealt, traded, and passed up and down the aisles and the students had been reluctant to break their poker-faced trance to verbalize their ideas about poetry. So this time I brought in some photos of my own, slides I'd taken of Clinton landmarks and characters: Ed's Fruit Stand, Smitty's General Store, Carl Bengston, the blind welder, St. Boniface Church, Harry Carpenter's Bait Shop.

"Hey, I know that place. It's Harry's—up in Lyons."

"Isn't that where they sell all those Christmas trees in the winter?"

"And watermelons in the summer."

"And bait. I heard old Harry cuts his worms in two, so he'll have more."

"But what does he do with all those tires? Does he ever sell any? They just pile up higher and higher."

"You know what he says, 'Never know when a guy might come along and want to buy a tire.'"

"He does fix radiators, though. And sells gas. Cheapest prices around."

"Yeah, if you can find the pumps."

The students seemed to know Harry's in detail. The photo called up visual, tactile, olfactory, and auditory images, and since we'd been working with these kinds of images in haiku in previous sessions, I hoped the students could play with their knowledge of Harry's in a short, imagistic poem. The week before, I'd ended the class by passing out a haiku by Gary Snyder:

A great freight truck
     lit like a town
through the dark stony desert

I asked the students to look at the poem again. First, we focused on the main image, how the use of the simile allows the poem its swift leap—the freight truck suddenly becomes the town, glowing in the dark. We discussed the way the image of the town—surrounded by nothingness, or the desert—shows the singleness of the truck, pointing toward the isolation of the man driving. Then we talked about the sounds of the poem and the way they reinforce the main image: the repetition of the long *a* sound with the *r* in "great freight truck" lets the reader imagine the roaring of the semi's engine, while the repetition of the *t* toward the end of the poem slows it down to the point where the roar becomes more like a wail.

But most of all, I tried to show how every word in the Snyder poem matters, how every word adds one more element to the scene, something that can be seen, heard, smelled, tasted, or touched, how there isn't room for fancy adjectives and adverbs, abstraction, and general observation. Yet, each well-chosen word works with the preceding one to create an image that resonates with some feeling or meaning. This poem is more than just a good exercise in image-making.

With the Snyder poem in mind, I asked the students to write a short poem about Harry's. No, they didn't have to worry about counting syllables and lines, but I did want them to concentrate on word choice. And I encouraged them to try for a simile that surprised yet gave the reader some insight into the human emotion behind the description. (If it didn't work, they could always throw it out. It needn't be forced.) And yes, they could team up with a friend.

Chairs scraped together, pencils ground through the sharpener, and pieces of paper were ripped from spiral notebooks. I flashed the slide on the screen again and the students' heads bent over their desks. The classroom teacher and I circulated about the room, providing encouragement and suggestions when needed.

A group of three waved me over. They'd begun by jotting down some details: rusted radiators, blue roof, gray walls, brown windows, window shades, gas pumps.

"Now what do we do?" one of the students asked, pushing the piece of paper toward me.

"How about some action?" I said.

"Action? There's nothing happening in the slide."

"But the poem doesn't have to match the slide exactly. The poem can have its own story. You can make it up. Or make up an action for one of the objects. What do the rusted radiators do?"

"They just sit there."

"Sit and wait. . . . Oh, yeah, I see."

The student started the poem: "Rusted radiators wait. . . ."

"Now what?"

"I'd like to do something with Harry," another student said.

"What's most interesting about him?"

"The way he talks."

"The way he chews tobacco."

"The way he's been in that same shack all these years."

"His face. I think it's his face. He must be ninety. His face is a mass of wrinkles."

"How about using Harry's face, then, as the central image in the poem? Let your other details build up to that image, and let that image convey the emotion of the poem."

"Huh?"

We all laughed, but the students said they had the idea, and went to work again. I directed my attention to another group; after a while, the first group waved me back and handed me their poem.

"Great. Now how about a title?"

"Like what?"

"Well, something to indicate where we are, perhaps. Something to locate the poem immediately."

After a couple of minutes, the students had their title and finished poem:

Harry's Palace

Rusted radiators wait
with piles of tires . . .
A black eye in the corner. Blue roof, gray walls, brown windows
brightened by yellow gas pumps.
Window shades drawn like old Harry's face.

—*Pat Ribar, Keili Paaske, and Katie Halbach*

The students were pleased with their piece, especially the last line. They'd successfully made the leap from the words to the human detail, from the outside to the inside, from concrete detail to emotional resonance. Other students were equally successful, so we tried a couple of other slides together. Here are some of the results:

A Clinton Porch

On the steps

The fat man stands waiting,
Watching . . .

The sun beats down
And sweat pours from his face.
Slowly, he turns and pulls out his handkerchief.

—*Brent Dirks and Charles Davis*

*   *   *

Ed's Fruit Stand

For days
His acorn squash, pumpkins, watermelons
And gourds wait.
As the sun sets, he feels like a
Train depot no longer in use.

—Steve Knight, Gary Soderstrom, and Paul Schnack

*   *   *

By the Tracks

His face is twisted into a constant smile
As he sits among the autumn vegetables.
Pumpkins, gourds, acorn squash
Surround him like the ancient train tracks.

—Jim Watson and Brent Woods

*   *   *

General Store

Boxes and baskets, trunks and washtubs
hide the walk in front.
Smitty's looks as though nothing is ever sold.
Inside, stocked shelves sag from the weight
of dog collars and leashes hanging from the ceiling.
Sometime
Someone
will want to buy something.
The rooms wait.

—Mark Leonard and Chuck Harris

*   *   *

Smitty's

My family of junk
In front
Greeting you.

I'm the wicker basket
Alone in the corner,
My top blown away in the wind.

　　—*Brian Schaefer*

★　　　★　　　★

The Blind Welder

For years
the tools were used.
The fire burned day after day.

But now he sits,
Dark glasses over his eyes.

　　—*Julie Johnston and Debbie Gaulrapp*

★　　　★　　　★

St. Boniface Church

After confession

Sin lingers on the front steps of the church,
the blackness of the railings, of the lamp,
the glass on the door, the boy's shirt.

　　—*Chris Kinkaid*

I was excited about the precision, the focus, the emotional impact of these poems, the lack of bald statement common at this age level. The students were excited, too. I remember a conversation with one of them following class.

"Hey," she said, "that poetry stuff is kind of fun. I don't usually like it. Always before I'd written all that mushy stuff, you know, 'Love is . . .' jazz. But this poetry was about things and places I know."

And that's what I'd hoped for. Students writing in their own voices about things from their own environment. I knew that not all their poems would be great, and I knew that these students wouldn't necessarily keep writing poems. But I attempted to leave the students with two things: first, I hoped that both of these groups, sixth and twelfth graders, would look at their environment differently, that the sights, sounds, textures, and smells of their everyday lives would open up new possibilities, new perceptions; second, I hoped that these new perceptions might spill over into their regular classroom writing. A good essay seems to deal with the same things that a good poem does—how to make an idea concrete, and how, in an interesting way, to lead the reader to a new insight.

In both approaches—using sound with sixth graders and sight with twelfth graders—I tried first to set up a clear model and then encouraged the students to begin writing with literal, concrete facts and to allow the more abstract "meaning" to emerge from there. Although hesitant at first, the students (especially the older ones) learned to trust their subconscious, to allow the right sides of their brains to go ahead while the rational left sides were given a rest. The students delight in this sense of play and are relieved of the pressure of coming up with something "profound"—the kind of profundity that often ends up in "mush"—as they see an image drawn from common experience come to life on the page.

Jeffrey Schwartz

Renga
Teaching a Collaborative Poem

In 1969 four poets descended into a hotel basement in Paris for five days to write the first Western renga, a chain poem invented in Japan around the eighth century. From Italy, England, France, and Mexico, the four poets worked simultaneously in four different languages on one collaborative poem. Each worked in view of the others, constantly sharing words, ideas, and sensations. In his description of the experience, Octavio Paz, the Mexican poet, writes about feeling alternately ashamed and voyeuristic to be sharing such a private act as writing with his fellow poets. He also writes about how the Japanese renga clashes with the Western Romantic tradition that focuses on the writer or the subjective "I" behind the poem. The renga, on the other hand, focuses on the work itself. The "I" is obliterated and replaced by the collective consciousness of a small group working as one.

For anyone not used to writing with others, collaborative poems are as frustrating as they are fun and challenging. To a degree each writer must sacrifice his or her individuality in order to write the part of the poem that will conform to and extend the stanzas that came before. For students used to writing solely about their own experience and from their own point of view, writing a renga is one of the best ways to snap into a different perspective. As the renga grows, the writers must fit themselves into the points of view of their fellow collaborators, scrutinizing the poem for patterns and directions, struggling to add their individual touches to the group work.

The renga works very simply and can take as little time as a class period to as long as six weeks to complete. Normally when I teach it to college students, I have them work on a stanza per day so that the first draft is completed in one week and revised in the next. After giving the students some background on the renga, I ask them to bring in a stanza the next day. I tell them the stanza can be any length, though they must consider that whatever form they initiate, everyone else will have to follow. No revisions of other writers' stanzas are allowed at this point. Students work in groups of five so that each completed renga will be five stanzas long, one by each group member. Although they know whom they are working with, I try to make the process as anonymous as possible by asking them to leave off their names until the end and also by arranging the order so that they "pass off" to a different collaborator each time. At the end of the fifth day, the completed renga goes back to the originator for a title.

Between working on each stanza, we discuss the kinds of constraints each writer faces and how they differ as the renga progresses. Students become aware of how much more difficult it is to develop someone else's idea. When we write poems, our notion of what's to come doesn't halt abruptly when we reach the white space between stanzas. Students find that their choices for where the poem may go become more and more limited as stanzas are added. In addition to developing the subject matter of the poem (which soon begins to have a life of its own), each writer must concentrate even more closely on particular elements of craft—the number of lines, line length, punctuation and capitalization, diction, imagery, tone, point of view, and especially syntax—to continue the pattern set by the first stanza. Here are two renga with a lot of surprises, but with a lot of coherence, too, because of the way the writers use plot. Notice in "Take Two" how enjambment invites the next stanzas.

Take Two

Into the vestibule
you came carrying two bottles of wine
a perfect dinner guest.

Wearing a pin-striped suit
wide yellow tie
and yellow-striped socks

you were meticulously dressed
and walked the stairs to my door.
Wine tucked under your wing

you proffer Golden 100s and silver lighter
to my lipstick smile.
Fumé blanc and Chianti are set aside

the taste lingering
as I gladly
help loosen your tongue and tie.

—*Alice Alfonsi, Anna Coleman, Louise Crocoll, Gina Fleitman, and Judith Maiksin*

As the suspense story unravels in "The Risk of Poker," there's an unusual coordination of flashbacks, association, points of view, and the languages of both description and instruction.

The Risk of Poker

Graffiti on the walls
An ominous ticking.
Cigarettes, matches
Deck of cards
Top the nightstand.

"Drive 75 miles south
Past Alberta, find
The Bates Motel,
And wait there."
That's all they said.

Room 14 ticks.
Clock says 11:15 P.M.

AT MIDNIGHT, OPEN
THE MEDICINE CHEST, ON
THE LEFT SIDE OF THE BOTTOM SHELF
ARE THE BLUE PILLS, DROP THEM
IN A GLASS OF WATER, AND DRINK

I drink, and like Alice,
Fall into Wonderland where
I stand outside my body
Lying next to a dog-bitten
Flea collar & the Queen of Hearts.

—*Susan Bossi, Julie Harris, Rod Packard,*
Marge Palcsey, and Jeffrey Schwartz

When Paz and his collaborators wrote their renga, they chose the Western form of the sonnet as the chain in order to approximate the original Japanese tanka or haiku chains. When I teach the renga, I concentrate more on the idea of collaboration than on the form. Students' own forms will be strict enough and will raise the same issues of group writing that the traditional sonnet or tanka would raise. Here are two renga where I think the writers have worked successfully within the formal limits initiated by their precursors:

Four that's dots enough
a piddle of hearts or a pot

of lame spades always
making for matches in cards
what is red as points
Plays as four in a pack
Five what's riddle of suit
black lain up on pile jokers red
darkens score or air
what is not hearts knows that
what is red as points
plays as four in a pack

Six who's jokers triddle
on the club of spaded hearts
gathering midnight fog
of shade no pair can secret keep
what is red as points
plays as four in a pack

Seven it's said almost dead
reach to find blood stain mark
no longer fiddle black
even shaded cards reveal in time
what is red as points
plays as four in a pack

Eight where's leopard spot
thirteen in plastic pile
rearranged by fingers
set up even straight
what is red as points
plays as four in a pack.

—*Scott Allburger, Tom McCarthy, Andrea Olsheskie,*
Kathy Phillips, and Debbie Small

        ★   ★   ★

About Pittsburgh

Below Pittsburgh,
yesterday's coal galleries
undermine today.

Around Pittsburgh
depleted mines, idle mills
become handicaps.

Above Pittsburgh
rusted smokestacks seem immortal
thrusting into clouds.

Inside Pittsburgh,
buildings hang over people
in heavy depression.

But beyond Pittsburgh,
natives recall their rivers and hills,
their beer, ethnicity, even their bridges
with pride.

> —*Susan Bossi, Julie Harris, Rob Packard,*
> *Marge Palcsey, and Jeffrey Schwartz*

Though our discussion of the renga starts after reading Paz's introduction to *Renga (A Chain of Poems)* by Octavio Paz, Jacques Roubaud, Edoardo Sanguineti, and Charles Tomlinson (New York: George Braziller, 1971), I make it clear our rengas will be different from Paz's experience in France. We won't lock ourselves in the basement of the Ramada Inn for five days or write in four different languages, but we will write a unique collaborative poem that will stretch our imaginations in a way we haven't written before. I often write with my students, too, which gives me an inside perspective on their struggles and teaches me what kinds of poetic constraints to pay attention to. When finished, we have a set of poems that each of us has shared in producing, and though we can sometimes identify individual voices in the poem, we read the renga as a whole.

With the anonymous but familiar pieces before us, we look for surprises in the poems and talk about how they succeed and how we read these group efforts differently than single-author poems. To get the students to appreciate even more what Paz calls the "crisis of the notion of the author," I ask each of them to revise the particular renga he or she started. In that way, they can see how the poem changes under one person's editorial control. They are free to add, delete, or change the direction of the poem. Essentially, I am asking them to shape the group-written renga into a more traditionally defined coherent whole and to pay closer attention to their choices and constraints in writing.

The renga is a very good assignment to follow the reading of almost any contemporary American poets, since many poets these days emphasize writing from experience and often blur the line between autobiography and poetic subject. The renga, on the other hand, can take the writer's experience as a starting point, but must always reduce that individual's experience to suit the poem. More gets imagined (as opposed to borrowed from real life) in a renga, and students learn to discover unexpected meaning by following the language of the poem.

Grady Hillman

Writer's Block

Poetry-in-the-Schools in Prison

After two years of conducting creative writing residencies for Texas school districts as disparate and distant as Terlingua and Beaumont, I had developed my pro-poetry patter to a finely tuned sales pitch. All I needed was a dubious look from parent, teacher or principal and the tape plugged in: ". . . generates enthusiasm for writing which extends into regular curriculum . . . got to know the rules of grammar before the students get their poetic licenses . . . even the football coach at UT uses imagination exercises to improve his athletes' ability to execute plays. . . ."

For the kids I had other tricks in my bag. Just standing in front of a class, a flesh-and-blood poet, was generally astonishing enough to get their attention. They'd reasoned from the poetry they'd been exposed to that the human species *Poeticus* had been exterminated around the turn of the century by some strange malady, probably consumption. Since they were curious about what I might do, they were open to instruction.

My defensiveness about my profession was gradually causing me to become jaded to the joy of my craft. Constantly defining it in conventional and palatable terms was removing the mystery and magic. My muse wasn't looking so hot anymore.

But my Artist-in-Education vehicle took a sharp turn in Huntsville, Texas, where I agreed to conduct GED writing workshops for the Texas Dept. of Corrections in the Windham School District, a nongeographic school district. AIE funding would be possible.

I am now in the middle of my second ten-month contract and have managed to visit only fifteen of TDC's twenty-two prison units. There is a school in each penitentiary, with a total enrollment of 14,000, out of 34,000 people incarcerated in the entire system. Each person entering prison passes through the Diagnostic Unit where his or her level of educational competency is determined. The average educational level of all TDC inmates is fifth grade, though the average years of attendance in the public school system is eight. In terms of IQ, they are the equal of their "free world" counterparts.

When I accepted the job, I requested that I be able to organize a couple of weekly writers' workshops for prisoners, who could use the sounding boards of fellow writers and an opportunity for uncensored discussion. Windham agreed, but said that it would ultimately be up to the unit wardens.

I cut my hair, put on a tie (really), and shuffled my way under those gun towers and through four hissing gates to meet my first warden. He already knew about me. I'd worked with his daughter at the local high school. "Be happy to have a workshop. Set it up."

The second warden was only slightly less congenial. I hadn't worked with his daughter, and he thought I might be a "writ" writer instead of the creative kind. Once I'd assured him that my only legal experience constituted ignoring parking violation tickets, he Boy Howdyed me and we were set.

★ ★ ★

I was forced to take on a third workshop under duress. This last warden found out about the other two, and he was not going to be left out. Considering I was in his office at the time, behind his walls, with sunlight nowhere around, I thought it best not to argue.

The wardens' positive attitude amazed me. Nobody has ever accused Texas of running "country club" prisons. It was supposed to be much harder than that. I later learned that Texas prisons, like those everywhere else in the country, are severely overcrowded. Traditionally, rehabilitation has come via the handle of a hoe with a shotgun-toting guard for quality control. At many prisons, inmates are being laid in (confined to their cells) during workdays. This means a lot of tension and, concomitantly, trouble. Here I was, offering a program which could provide diversion, and those wardens recognized it.

Initially, it wasn't easy getting on a "unit" to work with a GED class. At each unit, my first trip was always to the warden's office to get permission to come in. Once they gave me sanction, and the radio pickets (the guards in the outermost entrance) got to know me, I could come on and off without too much difficulty.

Another wrinkle in the residency came with the scheduling of classes. With rare exceptions, students attend class only one day a week, and since they were on a self-paced program, they might be promoted at any time to a higher level. I resigned myself to three or fewer visits with any specific GED class, since with more visits I saw an increasing number of strange faces. Match that with transfers to other units, bench warrants, paroles, and discharges, and in three months' time I would have a virtually brand new group.

Some of the classes began at 5:30 A.M. so the inmates could be through by noon and get a half day of work in. The only problem that presented was with the artist. Conducting a writing workshop two hours before sunrise at a prison a long way from home can be quite a disorienting experience, especially if I haven't had an adequate coffee ration.

The students have been enthusiastic about the program. A great advantage, similar to one I enjoyed in the "free world" schools, is that I am not a teacher but a temporary consultant, therefore essentially free of the stigma of being an authority figure. That is vitally important considering the adversarial relationship of prison personnel and prison inhabitants. Being an employee of TDC would be sufficient grounds for mistrust among most of the inmates.

During the years I was a "free world" artist in public schools, I devised a creative writing curriculum of sorts, a set of exercises for every grade level. In the beginning of my Windham residency I was apprehensive that these activities might be perceived as demeaning to an adult class. What I discovered through practice was that there was nothing intrinsically insulting about teaching a group of middle-aged men how to write poetry unless I approached them with a superior attitude and talked down to them.

Windham's GED program is broken up into three levels: Phase 1 is the approximate equivalent of first through third grades; Phase 2 fourth through sixth; and Phase 3 (or pre-GED) seventh through ninth. My first task was to explore my curriculum for exercises that dovetailed with GED instructional objectives. I was compelled to teach specific language arts skills through everything I did in the class; though I have had the support of many fine teachers and administrators, the exclusive fostering of student creativity was an ambition I held alone.

Walking into my first Phase 1 class I was apprehensive at how I would be received. "Hardened criminals" would have to be sold on poetry, right? Wrong. Since that day I've determined that thirty to forty percent of the inmates write poetry. Those who can't either pay somebody else to do it for them or rip poems out of the library books and copy them over. The reason? Most inmates have spouses or lovers in the "free world" who are going to exist without lovemaking for a long time; so hopes the inmate. To insure a minimum of wandering, the exiled lover has to get across that what's behind bars is a whole lot better than what can be found outside, even if it requires some waiting. It takes a poem, nay, many poems to achieve that end. Suffice it to say, my reception, even among the illiterate, was enthusiastic.

An important part of the Phase 1 GED curriculum is instruction in consonant recognition, rhyme, syllable slicing, and vocabulary development. No problem here. My first session with a class would be devoted to reading poems to the class and having them listen for alliteration and rhyming words. In the "free world" that end could be handily achieved with poetry by Shel Silverstein. In prison I use poems by Etheridge Knight, Michael Hogan, and Ricardo Sanchez, all former prison inmates who have achieved literary recognition and have easily accessible publications. I select poems that they've written about their experiences in prison that are heavy on lyric elements. Knight's "To Make a Poem in Prison" has never failed me. Hands shoot up immediately at the completion of the poem while the sounds are still fresh in the ear. Even two words in close proximity starting with the same letter do not pass unnoticed. The discussion of alliteration easily lends itself to the introduction of the concepts of assonance and dissonance, and how certain feelings and places can be associated with a type of sound. (In prison poetry hard *c*'s dominate when it comes to describing penitentiaries.) My students also recognized the rhymes used by the authors in the poems, but were often confused by the placement. It amazed them that rhymes didn't have to come at the end of the line but could be located internally to pace the rhythm, either speeding up or slowing down the tempo.

Spontaneous blues songs are a tradition in agricultural prisons, long narratives to be created spontaneously and sung while working on the line. But in TDC that tradition takes on greater meaning with the legendary Leadbelly, who sang his way out of prisons in Texas and Louisiana. My class at the Central Unit outside Sugarland was quite impressed when I informed them that the song "Midnight Special" was written about their prison. At a different prison, the Wynne Unit, I was working with a Phase 1 class, talking about rhyme, when this old fellow who could've been a contemporary of Leadbelly spoke up saying he didn't know how to read or write but he knew all about rhyme. I gave him a line and he returned it immediately with a blues counterpart complete with the appropriate number of beats. I responded and we went back and forth for a few lines before I opened it up to the class, which jumped in with gusto. In fact I had to quash their volume a bit to keep the guards from coming down to visit us.

With this under our belts we proceeded to actual writing. I pulled from my bag of tricks the good ol' standby, haiku. I explained that in poetry writing they needed to be efficient. It didn't matter how many words you used, so long as you used the right ones. I told them that the Japanese were so adamant about this that they restricted their poets to a specific number of syllables. I moved to the board and wrote a couple of haikus of my own to get the formula across, and then I asked for offerings from the class. Someone would throw out a line, I'd chalk it up, and the class would pare or expand as the situation warranted. Some preferred working alone and would proudly call out haikus of their own after we'd finished one as a group. One group haiku that came out of a Phase 1 class at Wynne has stuck with me. That prison unit, just outside Huntsville, looks over the municipal airport. The prisoner who started this piece lives in a cell with a view of the runways:

> Sitting in my cell
> Cold, dark wind blowing through bars
> Watching airport lights

The class recognized this as a good poem not for what was said, but for its ability to capture a feeling with an image, the beauty of haiku.

I began my Phase 2 and 3 classes in much the same way as I did Phase 1: by reading poems about prison from successful inmates. I'd also relate a list of famous writers who'd spent time behind bars, such as Dostoevsky, Wilde, and Texas' adopted son, William Sydney Porter, alias O. Henry. It's a little-known fact that Porter founded one of the first prison writers' workshops ever, the Sunday Recluse Club, a weekly gathering in his Ohio penitentiary. This brief bibliography and reading raised the class' self-esteem. It helped them to hear about peers who'd managed to transcend prisondom while doing time.

After readings and discussion, we immediately moved into writing. I began with another old standby, the first memory. This exercise opens them to the concept of imagery (and simultaneously, descriptive writing for the GED curriculum). The power released by the reading aloud of their efforts was overwhelming. Tears and tremors would unexpectedly rock a class as a "hard case" would relate an instance of child abuse or unreturned love for a parent. I was amazed at how many in prison are the victims of painful, terrifying childhoods. Since I read their work anonymously at the front of the class, they could express sentiments and feelings in their writing without fear of peer reprobation. All who are in prison wear emotional armor to some degree to protect them from others, but also to shelter them from self-destruction. This "open" reading allowed for a sharing which had a tangible therapeutic effect. Some tension always dissolved between the time they entered and the time they left the class. They would tell me this, but I could feel it myself.

Another good feed-in for my upper-level classes was the task of relating dreams on paper. Unlike my "free world" students who oftentimes could not remember their dreams, prisoners live for dreams. It's the only time they can visit the outside. There is only one specific type of poem that is indigenous only to the prisons of the world, and that is the dreaming-"free-world"-waking-up-in-prison poem. Here's an example:

Such a Dreamer

I'm riding in my new Ford pick-up
Cathe sitting so close I can smell her hair
I love the smell of her clean freshly shampooed hair

Wind along the river
blows freely through our souls
It's spring
and spring invades our every fiber

I make plans
Cathe mischievously smiles
and her eyes sparkle brighter with my every word
can't help but laugh
She knows I'm such a dreamer

Mile upon mile
We're really not going anywhere
just going together
past cane pole wielding children
past river camps
past the dotted farms on the Mississippi bottoms

past our every fear
past our every worry

WATER TIME 5 HOE yells the prison guard

I come back back
to this prison farm
back to this cotton field
and back to reality

I lay down my hoe on the row I'm working
and walk past the horse-riding guard to my water

I'm smiling

Don't go away Cathe dearest I'll be right back!

—*Joseph M. Depauw*

Many inmates use their poetry and short story writing in much the same way Depauw uses the convenient daydream: for escape. For a brief spell they can be any place their imaginations conjure up. I once asked a class why they chose not to write about their prison experiences. A few responded that they were afraid of official retribution if their journals ever came to light, but the overwhelming response was: "I've got to live in this place. Why the hell would I want to write about it?" Science fiction and fantasy are very popular in the prisons of Texas.

I did encourage journal writing with all my classes and workshops, emphasizing a writer's need for self-reflection as well as the description of emotional and physical environments. This hit home as well. I found that every compositional tool introduced was eagerly grasped or was already in vitally useful practice. One of my best workshop poets told me that he could not survive without his journal. In a world that dressed him in white, stamped a number above his heart, and gave him a boot camp appearance, it became increasingly difficult to recognize himself. His journal was his last and greatest defense against institutionalization. It salvaged what was most vital in his identity, and most important, it kept his memory intact. After years in prison, the memory begins to fuse with the mind's imagination zones and the past becomes dreamlike, surreal. The journal is the very best means available for documenting the past and sorting it out later.

★ ★ ★

Creative writing has some more mundane and practical uses as well. Institution Program, Inc., the agency that provides fine arts residencies for the federal prisons, brought in an independent evaluator to judge their programs' effect on the inmate participants' behavior, and found that "the incidence rates dropped from over ninety to fifty-seven percent during program participation." ("Incidence rate" is a prison term for inmate misbehavior.) This decrease in misbehavior brought about by arts residencies ought to interest some "free world" educators. The analogy of prison to public school has often been made. And in some school systems, violence is a fact of life.

Creative writing is meat and potatoes for people in prison. It is a tool for survival on every level. I've rarely had to explain to convicts or educators "why" we should introduce it to the correctional classroom. It's always been "how." And isn't that what an Artist-in-Education is for?

Alan Ziegler

Writing about People

I once wrote a poem about someone named "Mr. Gutman." There was no real Mr. Gutman, but the poem needed one, so I made one up. I showed the poem to David Ignatow, my teacher at the time, who read it and said, "Now, if you had showed this to William Carlos Williams, he would have said, 'So, you *know* Mr. Gutman? Well, then *tell* me about him.'" Truth was, even though I had invented Mr. Gutman, I didn't really know him.

In graduate school, I was in Kurt Vonnegut's fiction workshop. He read a story I was working on and started asking me about the characters: what kind of people they are, what they like to do, and how they'd react to certain situations. As we discussed them as people, the characters began to grow, becoming more than functionaries programmed to perform fictional tasks. Ironically, the more dimensions they acquired, the better-equipped they became to perform their tasks, and new, interesting tasks materialized. Vonnegut started talking in the voice of one character speaking about two others: "Yeah, they're lousy guys. Fire them." I was about to defend their worthiness as characters, when I remembered he was talking about them *as people*.

In order for a reader to find a character convincing, he or she must perceive that character as a whole iceberg, not just a tip. The writer must give the reader enough information to convey the essence of a character without loading the reader down. (Often, it's through the process of telling that the writer will get to know the character.)

I begin class sessions on characterization with a discussion of how people are differentiated from each other. For starters, there are physical differences. Some of these are genetically determined (height, facial features, eye color, etc.), but people have control over some physical aspects (the way we dress, how we wear our hair, etc.) and varying degrees of control over others (facial expressions, body shape, etc.). In addition to physical features, people are differentiated by how they act, how they react, what they say and how they say it, how they deal with other people and ourselves, habits and ways of doing things, and so forth. Some people put ketchup on almost everything they eat, or we can tell when they are about to enter a room by the sound of their footsteps and the way they knock. I know someone who, when he is on the phone, paces back and forth, extending the wire to its limits. If I were to write about him, I would surely use this detail to help the reader get a sense of who he is, and as it happened, in creating a character recently I used this trait because it seemed to work. A writer usually warehouses such observations for future use; it's like having money in the bank.

All of the qualities that differentiate people should be kept in mind when writing about people. Writers who can detect and express these traits have a head start in developing characters who breathe. It is crucial that the reader *care* one way or another about the people in a story or poem, and it is easier to care about someone presented in a tangible way.

I have students do "portrait exercises" in order to give them a feel for characterization, as a foundation for future writing. What follows are exercises in self-portraits, fictional portraits of famous people, and other portraits. In all cases, the writer is free to invent and exaggerate to make a point.

Self-Portraits

Many kids are used to reading about (or seeing on TV and in the movies) extraordinary people—superheroes and the like. But writers and other artists also deal with "ordinary people"; a good writer should be able to present a common person as a unique character. Since it is helpful to know the character you are writing about, I've found that a good place to start is with oneself. Most painters try their hand at a self-portrait (for one thing, the model is always available). In this writing exercise a self-portrait is made with words. "Who am I?" may be too large a question for a short poem or prose piece, so it is easier for the students to think in terms of components: "What are some things that contribute to making 'me'?"

The main idea is for the students to isolate various aspects of themselves—to put together a series of statements that will result in a sum greater than its parts. Good writing has a lot to do with selectivity; out of all the things you could say about yourself, pick a few that seem to reverberate. The aim is not to compile a thorough profile, but to practice projecting a person on paper. In the following "sketches," emphasis is on behavior patterns rather than physical description.★

★ All student material in this article, unless otherwise noted, is from fifth graders at P.S. 173, Manhattan.

Me

Pulling up My Sleeves:
I always seem to pull up my sleeves hot or cold even in snow it never
  fails me I pull up my sleeves

Putting on My Watch:
Every morning when I get up I put on my watch even if I'm not
  going anywhere I put on my watch

Combing My Hair:
I always comb my hair when it's neat I still comb it twice in the
  morning, twice in the afternoon and twice at night I comb my
  hair

Leaning Back in My Chair:
Every time I sit down I lean back in my chair even in a formal place I
  lean back in my chair even at my house I do it I lean back in my
  chair

I Always Want to Punch Someone:
I seem to do it playing or not I ask to see if they'll do it playing and if
  they don't I punch anyway

—*Daniel Hano*

★   ★   ★

Who is this?
He walks with no sound
He never fights
With a bang of his feet
He's off again
Who is this?

I try to do homework,
Then I stop.
And stop and stop and stop.
I always get distracted,
I don't think but I walk.
Up and down, down and up.
Until I get the answer.

During the night
I hope and pray
That I'll make it till the next day.

When I buy
A pack of slightly overpriced baseball cards
My brother rants and raves
"Too expensive
Back to food, shelter, and water
Nothing else"
And caps it off with a big:
"Don't spend money!"

　　　—*Michael Sid*

　　　　　　★　　　★　　　★

I try to do something
Then I learn it,
I do it for a few days
Then I can't.

I'm busy working
And I get a great idea
For something to do later
Then I can't remember it
Till I'm busy again.

There's nothing in my way
But I think there is
But I go ahead anyway.

The day is dragging on
I feel like it's never
Going to end
But when it's over
I wonder where the
Time went.

　　　—*Pamela Schwartzman*

　　　　　　★　　　★　　　★

I laugh so funny
People think it's a joke.

I mostly read at night
And never in the day.

I sit so close to the
TV set that I can

Strangle my eyes.

When I answer the
Phone I just say,
"Hi. How are you? What's new?"
And then give it
To my parents.

Every time I see somebody
I hardly know
I get shy.

— *Sophia Tarhandis*

Fictionalized Portraits of Famous People

Donald Barthelme's book of stories, *Unspeakable Practices, Unnatural Acts,* contains a piece called, "Robert Kennedy Saved from Drowning," in which the author weaves a compelling portrait of Senator Kennedy with a series of vignettes and quotations. Each section is individually titled, including: "K. at His Desk," "Described by Secretaries," "Attitude toward His Work," "Dress," "Gallery-going," "K. Puzzled by His Children," "A Dream," and "K. Saved from Drowning." Barthelme presents these scenes in such a convincing way that many people have taken them all to be true. He uses a variety of vantage points for establishing his version of Kennedy: what Kennedy says, what others say about him, Kennedy in various contexts (with employees, family, strangers, etc.), how he dresses, what he dreams, and so forth.

I read a class excerpts from this story and suggest they take a well-known person and write a portrait, trying to show the private as well as public side of the person. The objective, as with other portraits, is to shine the spotlight on telling moments.

Here is a portrait of President Carter that uses short vignettes, and one of Gilda Radner, in one longer vignette:

President Carter

President Carter is at the grocery store with wall to wall people around him. Trying to get out, moveless, not knowing what to do. One person says, "Don't ruin his beautiful suit, or most important his shiny shoes." So finally the owner of the store pushes everyone away and President Carter is free to go.

President Carter is at his home town and everyone treats him like anyone else. Everyone is glad he is the president now. He just wants to rest and read his newspaper. He has on slippers, a white short-sleeve shirt, summer pants, and a gold belt. He decides to walk down the street and say hello to his old friends. Now if President Carter walks around his friends just say, "It's nice to have you in town!" But his best friend calls him "short stuff." I don't think he minds what he calls him, but if everybody else does I think he would get mad.

President Carter is invited to a luxury restaurant and when he is going to sit down other people stand to salute him. When he sits down they give him champagne. The waiter says it's from a man across the room that thinks you are doing a great job and paid for your champagne. President Carter gets up to thank the man and asks him to join him and his family at their dinner table.

President Carter is at the White House. He is mad because he doesn't know what to say for a speech at a very special meeting. His daughter asks him to help her project for school and he says, "NOT NOW, YOU CAN DO IT YOURSELF!" So her mother helps her and calms President Carter down. He says "sorry" and everything's back to normal.

President Carter is in the Big City, New York. Everyone's glad to see him. He is going down the street shaking everyone's hand. They tell him their problems and he tries to help them. He cannot help all of them, but he will try hard to make them happy. President Carter is a person, too! He doesn't like being screamed at or people to complain a lot. When he comes home he sits down angrily and once more his wife calms him down.

President Carter is at a party. Everyone is offering him a drink, and he is covered with people. On the other side of the room there are people that don't like Carter, and they try not to look at him. All around him there are people that like him and people that don't. But he tells his friends he will not pay any attention to the others. All people don't have to like him.

—*Lisa Bracero*

★　　　★　　　★

Gilda Radner

The lady with humor dressed in a summer dress walks into the Washington Square Restaurant. She sits at a table politely waiting. A waiter comes to give her a glass of water and a menu. He doesn't realize who she is.

By accident she spills the water and another waiter recognizes her, rushes over to her. Meanwhile she is wiping the wet table. The waiter says, "I will clean it, Miss Gilda Radner. You might strain yourself." She says, "It's okay. Thanks." "No, no, no, no, I will," says the waiter. "Will you please stop treating me as if I were some kind of queen. Can't I walk around without people trying to help me with things, can't I?" she shouts at the waiter. "But I just love to watch you, Jane Curtin and

John Belushi on 'Saturday Night Live,'" the waiter announces. "I don't care. Now excuse me for ever coming here." Gilda walks out in a hurry.

Gilda says to herself, "Why me? God, why me?" People behind her say, "Oh, look, there's Miss Radner. Doesn't she look divine." "Oh my, yes." Gilda is frustrated by now. Her stomach is rumbling, so she goes to Blimpie's.

She decides to order a hero to go instead of eating it there with people talking to her. So she goes home to eat there. She goes to the refrigerator, gets out a Pepsi, gets a glass and pours it in the glass. She puts the soda back.

She sits down with the soda and opens the hero. She takes a bite of the hero and the mayonnaise drips down her mouth. She doesn't feel it dripping because she is daydreaming.

—*Christine Mitsis*

Other Portraits

In the following two pieces of writing, the authors use exaggeration to convey their perceptions of their characters.

My Friend Chris

Chris and his friends walk
into the restaurant.
He flashes his money around,
He shows off to his friends,
They try to ignore him.

He's wearing expensive clothes,
He buys everything he wants,
He owns all sorts of things,
He also shows off.

We're in the restaurant,
He orders three large pizzas,
He buys ten sodas,
We sit at the biggest table,
We wait for the food.

The food comes,
It won't fit on the table,
Chris gets up and looks for another,
He finds a big one,
He sits down and tells us to bring over the food.

We finally bring the food,
We see Chris resting in his chair,

He's asleep.

We don't want to wake him, but a strong force pulls us toward him,
We wake him.

We start eating,
I see Chris eat five slices of pizza,
He drinks my soda,
I tell him to buy me another soda,
He buys me three sodas.

We're finished eating, Chris leaves a big tip,
I see him lay down the green paper,
He puts more and more,
I want to go out.

We're finally outside,
A car comes to take us home,
Chris sent it here,
He gets inside the car,
He asks us to come,
We decide to walk home,
He drives away,
We sigh with relief.

The next morning he calls me,
He asks me to come over,
I say I'm busy.

— *Michael Bromley*

★   ★   ★

Joggers

They run all day, they run all night. They don't stop until their knees
are down to their bones. They never eat, or smile. They stay silent until
they stop running. Sometimes I wonder how they live by just jogging.
One wears a cap, one wears a tie. Their shirts have holes in them, their
pants are up to their knees. Their shoes are worn down to their toes.
Their hair is over their shoulders. One has a mustache, one has a beard.
They run as fast as deer. They bite their nails like candy because they
are so hungry. They run when it's raining, they run when it's snowing.
They don't even stop for cars to go by.

One day when I was outside, I saw them. They stopped running for
the first time! Their house was an old one, sort of grayish. They went
inside. They didn't come out for a long time. I began to wonder what
had happened. I went inside and saw them lying down as if they were

dead! I left them so they could rest. They didn't come out of the house for a year!

—*Theresa Hanna, West End School, Lynbrook, N.Y.*

This one captures a character through the use of imagery. In just nine lines, we get a picture of an intense, explosive person:

A person who is partly happy,
with a memory of her father's death
blocking the way
to total happiness.

A firecracker in its last second
of silence.

A cheerful girl jumping rope,
turning the rope so quickly
that all you see is a blur.

—*Pamela Schwartzman*

Here's one about a local neighborhood character, known to many of the kids in the class. Although this piece is not as developed as it could be, it is useful in that it demonstrates how a resourceful writer can find a "story" in places where others have looked but not noted.

Circles?

Who is Circles?
Circles is a bum that sleeps in Ft. Tryon Park. We call him Circles because he's always in circles. For instance, he's always walking up to 218th St. and back down to 168th St. Circles has a lot of friends.

What Does Circles Look Like?
Circles looks like an ordinary everyday seventy-year-old man with a bald spot and white hair. You will probably never find him without a cup of soup, a can of soda, or a cup of coffee.

Circles Meets New People
Wherever Circles goes he always meets new people. In the parks he sets dates to meet his friend at a certain place and time.

What Does Circles Talk About?
I've always wondered what Circles talks about. One day I overheard him talking to a lady's baby. Then he started talking to the lady and telling her how quiet and pretty the baby is. He also started to tell her how nice the weather is and how he wanted to be a weatherman.

Circles in J. Hood Rite Park
A few years ago Circles spent one summer's month in the park. One Saturday my friends and I were skateboarding down the back hill and when we got to the bottom we saw him feeding the birds. He has a lot of friends in the park. On weekdays sometimes he plays chess and sometimes he plays checkers.

Circles Stays Uptown
Circles used to come back and forth. When Nancy and I went to 181st St. I'd point Circles out to her. Now it seems to be Circles is staying uptown. I wonder if he'll ever come back down?

—*Jeannine Budikas*

High school student Nanci Siller used carefully selected memories to create a harsh portrait of a cold, ungiving person. The remarkable image in the first stanza ("Legs that ended in claws") sets the tone. We learn about the aunt not only by what she says and does, but also by what she doesn't do.

Aunt Elsie

Once I had sat
cross-legged by your feet
studying the grooves and carved bottom
of your chair.
Legs that ended in claws.

My father's aunt
who never baked me cookies
ignored me because I asked too many questions
made me cry for asking your age.
My father's aunt
who always bought me slips
(the wrong size)
for every birthday and Christmas.

You were the house in Fairhaven
and the dark-walnut chair.

They took you away.

Sold your house
and gave your chair to a stranger
who smiled

On Christmas

I did not visit you
in the cold white room
with metal chairs
where they said you lived

and when you died
I did not cry.
There is no mourning in death
the second time.

— *Nanci Siller, Finkelstein Memorial Library*

These are two family portraits. The first is straightforward, and the second uses visual imagery.

My Father

My father likes to work a lot so he got a job on April 15, 1968, in New Jersey. He works putting boxes in certain places and shipping them. He likes to talk a lot with the people that work there in that same department.

Once when he was working, a box fell on his shoulder and he was injured and did not get to work for six months and four days. He was very sad because for six months and four days he did not get money because he was not working and because my mother had to make all the payments on the house.

The place where my father works has a big garden full of flowers and grass all around the garden. The company is divided into three departments, three cafeterias where the employees go to eat lunch or drink coffee or anything they want. They also have fire drills to test how fast they could react if a real fire were burning the company.

My father is five feet eight inches, has black hair and brown eyes. He is very active. He likes to walk and run. He always goes to his sister's house to go out with his nephews. They go out to lots of places around the area. He likes to watch television programs every night and loves to watch baseball and boxing.

My father likes to do things like going bowling with his friends, and he likes to take me on my bike to the park in the summer.

When he is alone and does not want to go out he opens the window, looks out, smokes a couple of cigars and then just sits with a can of soda watching television.

— *José Tavarez*

★   ★   ★

My brother plays football like a pro and he throws like a clock going very fast. When he moves it's like an ape when he eats a banana, something looking so easy like making a line or falling asleep. His face has at least ten freckles on each side and his hair is like long thin strings hanging from his head. His hair waves back and forth when he moves his head—it looks like a weeping willow when the wind blows the leaves back and forth. He doesn't stay still, it's like a bear was running after him. His sneakers are white and get ruined very easily.

—*Karen O'Connor, West End School, Lynbrook, N.Y.*

A final selection: I've told classes that when you are stuck without something to write about, the answer is sometimes at the tip of your fingers.

Mister Ziegler

He walks around the room helping, talking to children about people. My friend Ale asks, "How do you suck air?" Mr. Ziegler says, "Like this, sllllllllurp!" Ale says, "Oh, that's how."

Mr. Ziegler's green eyes pop looking at the papers. While he looks he reads every single line. He stands up holding the paper and saying, "That's very good." Other times he says, "It's good but . . ." and other times he says, "You don't need this."

As he leaves with his brown bag he says, "Have a nice weekend." Next week he comes and we all cheer. He saves us from our math. He asks us what "isolate" means. No one knows. He reads a part of an image from a blue book.

He always waves his hand when he reads or talks. Whenever he comes he always walks around the room, looking, staring, talking. When the children do something wrong he corrects them. Whenever he goes by me he laughs because I am writing about him.

I think when he goes home he reads our poems and writes his own poem. Then he picks a book from his book rack and reads it. I think he's the best.

—*Antonio Gonzalez*

Meredith Sue Willis

Writing Dialogue

In my own work I am constantly drawn to the writing of dialogue. It is one of my primary points of departure for the exploration of character and it is frequently my choice for presenting the dramatic climax of a scene.

The very first words I ever wrote except for schoolwork were the conversations between characters in my homemade comic strips. My first literary models were comic books: *Uncle Scrooge in the Klondike* and a version of Zane Grey's *Riders of the Purple Sage* were my all-time favorites. I began writing, then, in the same genre I liked to read.

There were also deeper reasons for my attraction to dialogue. I was a great fan of radio in the years just before television came—the bodiless voices running on with their various stagey accents fed my imagination. I go back even further. I am on the patio in the dark with my mother and father, sitting on someone's lap, and I can't see much, but my parents' voices go on and on around me. Sometimes we sing hymns, sometimes they just talk on and on about everything, making a warm nest of language around me.

About a year ago I taught some creative writing workshops on dialogue, and was pleased by the number of children who seemed to respond well. It seemed unusually successful with the children who weren't doing very well in the language arts curriculum. When I began this fall at P.S. 321 in Brooklyn, though, the first teacher I worked with had a class of academically advanced fifth graders who were already doing a lot of creative writing. These were children who could already write long pages on command, but their prose was sometimes flat. I noticed some of them reading adult books for their own entertainment. I decided to begin dialogue writing with them by offering some short reading selections that I considered worth emulating for one reason or other, because I suspected they were already emulating something.

As an experiment, I chose a short selection from *Yonnondio* by Tillie Olsen and the opening of Federico García Lorca's play *Blood Wedding* as texts to give out in class. The Tillie Olsen piece is about a

Depression-squashed family and the texture of their unhappiness. It is written with conventional quotation marks, and includes an impressive number of novelistic devices—some description by simile ("the dark walls of the kitchen enclosed him like a smothering grave"); some non-metaphoric slice-of-life description ("There was a sour smell of wet diapers and burned pots in the air"); and even a little internal monologue ("You hear, he reiterated to himself, stumbling down the steps, you hear, you hear."). The selection from *Blood Wedding* is written in dramatic dialogue form, of course, but the style is spare and suggestive even for a play. I liked this little piece for its mystery and atmosphere. The Tillie Olsen piece gives a whole picture, compactly but richly; the Lorca drama hints and leaves much unsaid.

> . . . No one greeted him at the gate—the dark walls of the kitchen enclosed him like a smothering grave. Anna did not raise her head.
>
> In the other room the baby kept squalling and squalling and Ben was piping an out-of-tune song to quiet her. There was a sour smell of wet diapers and burned pots in the air.
>
> "Dinner ready?" he asked heavily.
>
> "No, not yet."
>
> Silence. Not a word from either.
>
> "Say, can't you stop that damn brat's squallin'? A guy wants a little rest once in a while."
>
> No answer.
>
> "Aw, this kitchen stinks. I'm going out on the porch. And shut that brat up, she's driving me nuts, you hear?" You hear, he reiterated to himself, stumbling down the steps, you hear, you hear. Driving me nuts.
>
> (*from* Yonnondio *by Tillie Olsen*)

★   ★   ★

(*A room painted yellow*)

BRIDEGROOM: (*entering*) Mother.
MOTHER: What?
BRIDEGROOM: I'm going.
MOTHER: Where?
BRIDEGROOM: To the vineyard. (*He starts to go*)
MOTHER: Wait.
BRIDEGROOM: You want something?
MOTHER: Your breakfast, son.
BRIDEGROOM: Forget it, I'll eat grapes. Give me the knife.
MOTHER: What for?
BRIDEGROOM: (*Laughing*) To cut the grapes with.

MOTHER: *(Muttering as she looks for the knife)* Knives, knives, cursed be all knives and the scoundrel who invented them.
BRIDEGROOM: Let's talk about something else.
MOTHER: And guns and pistols and the smallest little knife—and even hoes and pitchforks.
BRIDEGROOM: All right.
MOTHER: Everything that can slice a man's body. A handsome man, full of young life, who goes out to the vineyards or to his own olive groves—his own because he inherited them . . .
BRIDEGROOM: *(lowering his head)* Be quiet . . .

(from Blood Wedding *by Federico García Lorca)*

I doubt that many fifth graders will read the Lorca or Olsen in their entirety, although there is no reason they shouldn't. I doubt children really get much pleasure out of tragedy, though. I merely wanted writing that I respect, that could be excerpted, and that had enough excitement to interest young students. In the current cases, a good family argument and hints of violence to come. To a teacher interested in getting ideas from this article, however, I would not necessarily insist on these texts or others like them. It would be much better to find your own—a bit of dialogue from a book you really love. Later in my work with the advanced fifth grade class, I brought in a piece of *The Maltese Falcon* by Dashiell Hammett for slightly different purposes, but the conversation in the selection is a wonderful demonstration of character exposed through different styles of speaking:

The fat man raised his glass and held it against a window's light. He nodded approvingly at the bubbles running up in it. He said: "Well, sir, here's to plain speaking and clear understanding."
They drank and lowered their glasses.
The fat man looked shrewdly at Spade and asked: "You're a close-mouthed man?"
Spade shook his head. "I like to talk."
"Better and better!" the fat man exclaimed. "I distrust a close-mouthed man. He generally picks the wrong time to talk and says the wrong things. Talking's something you can't do judiciously unless you keep in practice." He beamed over his glass. "We'll get along, sir, that we will. . . . I'll tell you right out that I'm a man who likes talking to a man that likes to talk."
"Swell. Will we talk about the black bird?"

Later I read a whole story that is almost entirely dialogue, Hemingway's "The Killers," and also a wonderful, powerful long scene from Maxine Hong Kingston's *The Woman Warrior* in which an elementary school girl tries to force another girl to break her self-imposed silence and talk. In this scene one character never says a word, but there is a dialogue just the same. I read my selections from Lorca and Olsen to my fifth graders on the first day I met their class. My journal entry for that day reads:

September 28

Pretty much a stinkin' perfect lesson! These were the so-called smartest kids in the school and I definitely felt it. They already do a lot of creative writing. I began by asking for a volunteer to write on the board and got a chubby blond girl named Elizabeth. The board writer's job was to write What Happened. I then got volunteers for instant improvised sketches: a cop and hooky-player, three girls in a schoolyard and a new girl, two kids deciding who should wash dishes, a couple of strangers bump on the street. The class loved the acting, lots of liveliness, instant goodwill. Elizabeth meanwhile was supposed to be writing what happened. We discussed what she wrote, which turned out to be headlines (OLD LADY AND BOY COLLIDE ON SEVENTH AVE.)—her own idea, but just perfect for what I wanted to get at. When I started asking for more detail about what they had seen in the actual sketches, the tones of voice people used etc., poor Elizabeth threw up her hands indignantly and protested that I hadn't given her time to do any better. I explained that she did exactly what I wanted, that I had *wanted* the barebones assertion of the event. Then I handed out my samples, the stuff from *Yonnondio* and *Blood Wedding*. The class really liked talking about them, got my little pedagogic point about the difference between stating that an event happened and fleshing it out to cause the reader to experience something. They immediately picked up the differences between the two selections too, both formal things like the dialogue form versus the direct quotation, and the more subtle stuff. I asked which they preferred and there was a general agreement that the Tillie Olsen piece was better because it was more realistic. Oddly though, I had felt as I read aloud that the class was more spellbound by *Blood Wedding*. They wanted to act out the selections, which I let them do, and then I gave the assignment: continue one of the selections in the same style, or, if you prefer, write what happened before the excerpt.

Interestingly enough, most of the class chose to write more of the *Blood Wedding* piece, even though they said they didn't like it as well. Was it only that they found the form easier to imitate (and it is a far clearer system than quotation marks) or was it that something of the unfinished quality of the excerpt made them want to complete the action, get rid of the uncertainty for themselves? Here are a few of their continuations:

(*The Bridegroom goes to the vineyard*)

BRIDEGROOM: Oh, what beautiful grapes! (*The Bridegroom yells, Mother yells out to him to be careful.*) I'll cut two bunches of grapes off for breakfast. (*The Bridegroom cuts one bunch down but he cuts himself on the finger.*) OW! (*Bridegroom is bleeding.*)

MOTHER: What's the matter?

BRIDEGROOM: Bring me a towel quick! (*Mother runs to aid the Bridegroom.*)

MOTHER: I told you to eat breakfast, but you had to eat grapes like a fool!

(*Mother brings him to the house.*)

—*Chun Liu*

      ★   ★   ★

MOTHER: You shouldn't use knives.

BRIDEGROOM: Please.

MOTHER: Please me, nobody pleases me.

BRIDEGROOM: Good-bye.

MOTHER: Come back here.

BRIDEGROOM: What do you want?

MOTHER: I don't like knives.

BRIDEGROOM: Good-bye.

Act Three (*3 hours later*)

MOTHER: Where is he? That damn knife. (*Calling*) Son, son where are you?

BRIDEGROOM: Mother, here I am.

MOTHER: What happened, son?

BRIDEGROOM: Big man kill with knife.

MOTHER: Oh my son!

BRIDEGROOM: Mother, help me.

BRIDE: Oh my darling, what happened?

BRIDEGROOM: Help me to a chair.

MOTHER: Oh my god he's dying.

BRIDE: Darling, don't die.

BRIDEGROOM: (*His last words*) I love you Mary Jane. . . .

MOTHER and BRIDE: Oh God.

—*Justine*

      ★   ★   ★

The Novel: Beginning

"You're fired," the boss shouted angrily at him. "And you're a dang fool who ain't got no sense!" Those were the words Andy Cobbale had heard, but that was an hour ago. He had been roaming the streets wondering how he would face his wife. He was in debt and he would have to get a new job to support his family. He started home and soon noticed Jake. "Jake!" "Oh, it's you, Andy. I heard you got laid off." "Yep, I sure did and I don't reckon he'll give it back." "Oh well, so long Andy." Andy started going down the rough gravel road. In a distance he heard Bess. He sighed and continued on his way. . . .

—*Susy Ashton*

★　　★　　★

It's a Hard Life *(Continuing the Novel)*

. . . He stomped down the path on to the dark city streets, the overfilled garbage cans disappearing into the darkness of the evening sky! His stomach was growling, but he couldn't go back inside, not yet at least. He faintly heard the sound of Bess's crying. "Damn that brat always getting into trouble! Always wetting or other disgusting things like that," he mumbled to himself. The door opened, Anna walked to him. "You missed dinner," she whispered sweetly.

—*Julie Arenson*

These students were able to get very close to the original style of the selections I gave them. Susy Ashton even put the dialogue in a theatrical but closely observed poor white dialect ("Dang fool" and "I reckon"). Other students went off in their own directions, many picking up the violence in *Blood Wedding* and nothing else, introducing police and underworld gangsters and pitched battles with submachine guns and bazookas. Elizabeth, the girl who wrote on the board, turned *Yonnondio* into a farce:

Nut Driving

As Bill was outside he spilled ketchup on himself and fell asleep. Three hours later Anna called wearily, "Dinner." Ten minutes later when he fails to appear, Anna (carrying Bess) with Ben next to her, screams "He's dead!" Bess finally shuts up and Ben vomits on Bess making her cry again, which immediately wakes Bill and he screams seeing Anna and Ben on the floor, waking them. Then Bill and Anna get all kissy and mushy and Ben finally says, "Let's go eat." Now this time Bess hides, after countless minutes looking for her, Anna hollers "AAAA" and faints. Ben and Bill together call "Not again" and faint. Then Bess comes too and whispers, "My plan worked," and walks away.

—*Elizabeth R.*

The following week the class had a substitute teacher and I commented in my log, "Teacher absent—with the group 'cutting up' but never forgetting for long they are supposed to be good students. Read (to great guffaws) their writings from last week. Then ten minutes of writing overheard conversations and finally read aloud some of these pieces." The writing that day tended to be short and aimed at entertaining the other students, with several kids making conversations consisting of elaborate curse symbols ("Why you son of a ✶✶&¢%!" "How dare you call me a ✶✶&¢%!"). Everyone loves those symbols; graphically they make a paper so striking. In spite of the general festivity over having a substitute and a creative writing teacher all at once—absolute dispensation to goof off—there were still a lot of interesting pieces written. This time I was surprised by the range of what the various children chose to report from their lives, everything from the curse fests and other fights to family conflicts and interaction with pets.

Phone Conversation

FRIEND: So how are things in Park Slope?
ME: Boring.
FRIEND: My school is so modern. God. I swear!
ME: Did you make any new friends?
FRIEND: Yes, some but they're really strange. They've all got these accents and funny ways of talking.
ME: Maggie. . . .
FRIEND: Oh, you know, we have this really fancy elevator in my new building.
ME: Really? How's your mom?
FRIEND: Fine. Ya know. . . .
MOM: Julie, get off the phone!
ME: Okay. Bye Mag, I miss ya. Bye.
ME: Oh Mag. . . .
MAG: What?
ME: Forget it.

　　—*Julie Arenson*

✶　　　✶　　　✶

Hi Nancy How you doing there. Fine. Guess what? What? My grandpa died. My grandmama cried to death. Want to go to the funeral with me? Yes, but what color do we have to wear? Any color you want. I'm wearing violet. What color are you wearing? Pink. Guess what my grandmother said before she died? Cod bless America Amen. Ha ha ha ha ha. Nancy: Bye. Debbie: Bye.

　　—*Gwen*

At about this time I began work with another fifth grade class at P.S. 321, Mrs. Eisenberg's. This class was described to me as academically behind the one I'd been working with, and I was eager to try some of my same assignments on a new set of students. Mrs. Eisenberg runs a rather tight ship, but at the same time there is a lot of room for hugging and joking between her and her kids. The first session caused me some worry, though, because she and I seemed to be at odds over whether or not the kids were carrying out my instructions. When I give an assignment, I have definite goals and pedagogical points in mind, but I am usually willing for the kids to get something different out of a lesson than what I planned. My assignments are meant in the broadest way to get kids started writing, and when they go off in their own directions, I generally don't mind. I want above all for them to have a positive experience with writing. My teaching journal says:

> Lovely, lively kids, mostly black, a few from P.R., a Chinese girl, two or three white ones. I did a "What is a Conversation?" acting out thing—followed by an assignment to write an actual conversation they have heard. They loved the acting of course and certainly understood what is a conversation or dialogue. I even wrote a short sample on the board, mostly to demonstrate the name-of-speaker-colon form of writing dialogue. It seems easier than quotation marks. I was praising the kids right and left, including those who didn't follow instructions precisely, and then I realized that at the same time Eisenberg was going around the room correcting those same kids. Some of them got discouraged—or was it confused over the different responses from two teachers?—and balled up their writing and threw it away. They were writing narratives, not dialogues, and I was just letting them go, glad to see them writing because it was obviously difficult for them. So painful to me. I am in trouble, not a good teacher, making kids feel dumb and confused instead of making them feel good, etc., etc., etc.

It should have been a good class, too, that day, but I was so eager to make a success for me and for the kids that maybe I wasn't asking enough of them. I wasn't sure about Eisenberg either—was she angry with me or was she worried rather that the kids were shaming themselves and her in my eyes? My next journal entry for that class shows a complete change in mood:

> Eisenberg was very complimentary to me! She wants me to continue with her whole class, is surprised by how well they are doing, she says, and says they looked forward to me coming. I was thrilled. I like the feeling in this class a lot, and they are quite successful with the how-people-talk aspect of dialogue. I must type up and make copies of their

work. Their own words reproduced on mimeograph paper is a real necessity if they are to make the connection. I intend to do some acting with them (of their own dialogues), next I'll give them the sheets of *Yonnondio*. Their reaction to *Blood Wedding* today—how were they different from the other class? Probably reacted a little more concretely, fewer kids got involved in the discussion, but not substantially different. No one said "This is a mysterious piece of writing," but on the other hand, no one said, "This is junk." They listened very carefully, were a responsive audience to my reading aloud.

The dialogues they wrote (observed conversations from real life) tended to be short, and they did a lot of mother-child conversations because that was what my example happened to be. They felt less free to experiment with the written word than the other class. For example, they rarely did playful things like writing an important word in fat shaded letters; they didn't do the asterisk-dollar sign-ampersand curse game either. Written language is, for most of them, a minefield of rules. But oh they were thrilled when I handed out the long mimeographed sheets with their work typed on them. I was asked once, twice, six times if they got to keep the papers. I used to do more typing up of kids' writing, feeling it to be vital to demonstrate to the children that what they write out of their own lives is the same sort of thing as what appears in printed books—the enormous, beautiful idea that writing is a place to hear what people have to say, and also a way to talk yourself. Mrs. Eisenberg's class needed to see their work. I read *their* dialogues aloud with the same expressiveness I gave to the selection from *Blood Wedding*, and they discovered that the voices in their handwritten dialogues could be transferred to typed pages ("Did you type *every one* of these?" asked Armando. "You mean you typed thirty of these? Didn't that take a long time?"), and then, through reading, be transferred all the way back to the spoken word again. This was what I wanted them to see: that what is thought can be spoken and written, and that what is written can be spoken and felt.

In their pieces I was pleased to see them transferring the constructions of their spoken language to the written, even when those constructions and locutions are not standard English, because until they can truly grasp the connection between the spoken word (and the spoken word has to be the word as they speak it) and the written word, they will fail to become fully at ease with written language of any kind. Reynando, for example, was a boy who was just learning English, and it seemed that every week I came into the class his spoken English was improving immensely:

JACK: Hello, Mom.

MOTHER: Hello, son, now why did you come late from school?

JACK: I was playing baseball with my friends.

MOTHER: Go to your room.

JACK: Okay, Mom.

MOTHER: I am going to tell your father at what time you came today.

JACK: Please, Mom, don't tell father that I was playing baseball.

MOM: Okay, I won't tell your father because I don't want your father to hit you with the belt.

JACK: Thanks, Mom, you are my best mother.

MOM: If you do that again, I'll tell your father.

JACK: I am going to school, Mom, okay?

MOM: Don't you dare come late.

JACK: Okay, Mom, I will try to remember.

   —*Reynando Taveras*

           ★   ★   ★

MOTHER: Eat your breakfast now.

ARMANDO: No! I want to go to my friend's house.

MOTHER: Only for a little while.

ARMANDO: I wish you was asleep for a day now!

MOTHER: But I'm lucky I ain't asleep. Don't say that again.

ARMANDO: I going now! But I ain't coming back!

MOTHER: If you don't I will hit you hard.

ARMANDO: So!! So!! I will not come back here . . . Mom, I'm sorry. I forgive you, Mom. I'll eat my breakfast now. But can I go to my friend's house when I finish?

MOTHER: Yes you could, and listen to me from now on.

ARMANDO: I'll listen to you for my life.

   —*Armando*

Armando is a really lovely kid, very bright and easy with words. When I read the story "The Killers" to the class a few weeks later he kept throwing up his hand and when I called on him he would grin with cunning and say, "I *think,* I think I know what's going to happen," and then share his theory about the outcome of the story. Others became braver because of him and raised their hands with ideas. Thanks to Armando, my reading generally became full of participation from the class. I like Armando's writing for the same reason. His personality comes bursting through. In his short piece here he shows a boy going through changes. I especially liked his cheerful offer to forgive his mother. After seeing this typed up, Armando became very interested in writing, and every time we wrote, he told me how good what he wrote was, and how he wanted to be sure it got printed in the next class publication.

After I read *Blood Wedding*, some of the class continued their observed conversation pieces, and others tried to continue the play:

MOTHER: Son, eat your breakfast.
BRIDEGROOM: Mother, I said I'd eat some grapes.
MOTHER: All right.
BRIDEGROOM: (*Goes to the vineyard*) Hi Jack, do you want some grapes?
JACK: Okay, but just some.
BRIDEGROOM: Okay, come on and eat.
JACK: I'll cut some for my mother.
BRIDEGROOM: Okay.
(JACK *kills the* BRIDEGROOM. MOTHER *sees the* BRIDEGROOM *on the ground. She cries and cries.*)

    —*Semsija K.*

Others in the class struggled to write even something short in the style of *Blood Wedding*. They seemed to be striving more to follow my instructions than the style of the piece. They became very involved in time-consuming tasks such as printing out the name of each new speaker and making big fat colons. Others wrote essentially realistic, modern conversations that had little to do with the selection I read them.

Frequently what might have developed into something powerful would be curtailed because the student ran out of energy or realized how slow it is to write down the words in his or her mind. And yet, perhaps because so much of the time was spent in dramatic readings by me and acting out their own work, they didn't groan over the assignments to write. This was the most exciting thing to me. The academically advanced fifth graders had complained when the time came to stop talking and acting and write; this class seemed to be enjoying it. I had a suspicion, which is only theory, that they found the writing time to be when they could do something of their own, just their own, something communal and private at the same time. Some few were even doing writing during the week that they brought to me on Wednesdays. To combat the slowness of their writing, I didn't insist that they finish an assignment in one session. For those who did, I had a new assignment, but I allowed the ones who wanted to continue last week's to do so. Ignacio, for example, spent the better part of two sessions on the dialogue with his mother. It is not a sophisticated piece of writing, and when I read it I am dissatisfied in a lot of ways—it leaves out many things that would make it more vivid and dramatic than it is.

This was partly due to that basic drawback of the dialogue form—the lack of description—but in spite of that, I would submit that Ignacio used the narrow focus on just the words to his own advantage. He manages to get a great deal of the fond relation between him and his mother into this piece, a city boy's idyllic fantasy of a picnic:

MOM: Let's go to Prospect Park.
IGNACIO: Okay.
MOM: First do the sandwiches.
IGNACIO: Let's go now to Prospect Park.
MOM: Okay.
IGNACIO: I'll take the sandwiches.
MOM: Let's go to the corner for the bus.
IGNACIO: Let me get my half a dollar.
MOM: Look and see if you see the bus.
IGNACIO: I see the bus in First Street.
MOM: Get on the bus. We will get off at Flatbush Avenue.
IGNACIO: I see the park.
MOM: We get off the next stop.
IGNACIO: Mom, I am going to play ball with my friend.
MOM: Okay, but be careful!
IGNACIO: I will be careful, Mom.
MOM: Come and eat a sandwich.
IGNACIO: But I am not hungry, Mom. When I finish playing ball I will come and eat a sandwich.
MOM: So I will save you a sandwich for later.
IGNACIO: Okay.
MOM: Come and eat your sandwich.
IGNACIO: Okay, I will eat my sandwich.
MOM: I lost my ring.
IGNACIO: Mom, I found the ring. It was in my sandwich.
MOM: We got to go home.
IGNACIO: What bus will we get on?
MOM: We will take the 41.
IGNACIO: Okay.

—*Ignacio*

Yvelissa, on the other hand, did try to get everything into a breathless narrative of something important that happened to her. She seemed a fairly capable writer, so after I read her story, "A Bloody Day," it occurred to me that what happened was more striking and important to her than the flat description made it appear, so I suggested that she write the same story again in dialogue form. I was expecting more terror and pain, but in fact her dialogue presents the experience as amusing, and her own character as far tougher and more wry than she appears in class:

Two Versions of "A Bloody Day"

1. One day in my house I was playing tag and my little brother dropped a glass and it broke and I ran over it and I did not have shoes and I got cut real deep and my mother took me to the doctor in the ambulance and the doctor took me to a room and took me thirteen stitches and that hurt me.

    And this is true.

2. (*One day I was playing tag and my brother dropped a glass.*)

BROTHER: Oh my God, Mom, I dropped a glass.

ME: Oh I cut my foot and I'm bleeding a lot, Mom!

MOM: Oh my God I have to call a cab you could bleed to death.

SISTER: Oh that looks ugly.

ME: Don't be stupid, it ain't going to look pretty.

BROTHER: Oh I'm sorry, I did not mean it.

ME: That's okay.

(*And my mother took me to the hospital.*)

DOCTOR: She is badly hurt.

ME: How many stitches?

DOCTOR: Thirteen.

ME: Mom, how much days do I have to stay in bed?

MOM: A week or so.

CARMEN: How are you?

ME: Fine and goodbye.

(*And I got to play and now I feel good. And this is a true story.*)

—*Yvelissa Torres*

As the weeks went on, even though I continued to work with the whole class, it seemed to me that more and more of the children's personal outlooks slipped into their writing.

One day me and my sister were going to the store and I got hit by a car. My sister said, "Oh oh, my brother!" The man gave my sister a lollipop. She said, "I am not a baby. You trying to bribe me. No you don't!" My sister kept crying, "Mama!" So the man gave her a card. So the next day she went to the bank to get the money.

—*Frantz*

★ ★ ★

I have a friend named Rommel.
He is a sick boy now. He's not in school
because he don't feel well.
I wish he feel well soon
because he said to me
he wants to learn more.

I am scared that my father might
have a crash with his truck. I
am scared that he might get killed.

—*William*

With Mrs. Eisenberg's class I have stayed with the dialogue form because it is something they can succeed in using for themselves. After I read them "The Killers" by Hemingway, I asked them to write another dialogue, either observed or made up, with a conflict or fight in it. Conflict gives, in essence, a means of organizing a piece of writing by building tensions toward a climax. Making something exciting happen sounds like a fictional device, but in fact nonfiction writers use something far more similar to that in their writing than to the topic sentence type of paragraph construction we used to be taught in school. Rhetorically sophisticated writing or speaking builds to something dramatic for its convincing power.

Conflict between a Man and a Woman

The man went out on the woman. This is taking place in the living room. Red sofas.

The lady said, "I'll punch you in your nose." The man said, "I dare you," and she punched him, and he was bleeding. She said, "I'm not going to tell you sorry, because you went out with another woman." He said, "I'll buy you new furniture." "No, I already have furniture." "So your bed is broken. You need a new bed. And you need panty hose." "I don't want nothing. Now that you went with another woman, buy it for her. Anyway, you can't afford the money for it."

—*Wanda*

★   ★   ★

Between a Girl Chair and a Boy Desk

Once there was a girl chair named China and a boy desk named Japan. Japan liked to look at beautiful China. Japan asked China if she would marry him. She said yes. At the wedding.

You may kiss China.

For their honeymoon they decorated the house. China wanted the kitchen yellow and green.

Japan wanted it white.

China said, "I hate you because every time I ask you about something you say white."

Japan said, "Shut up before I kill you."

"No you be- be- be-"

"Please please please."

With a big scream "OH OH OH."

—*Karen D.*

Dialogue, then, seems to me an ideal entry into written language for beginners. It can be written by a child able to do little more than write "Okay" and "No," yet it also can be used by Tillie Olsen, Hemingway, Hammett, and Lorca with great effect. Especially good for working with younger students is the ready-made interplay between acting out and reading aloud and the dialogue form. At any point an interesting dialogue can be more fully dramatized by an individual or a small group and turned into a stage play or tape-recorded radio drama. Using comic books is another way to teach dialogue.

I also want to reemphasize that students who are writing dialogue should also constantly be reading poems, plays, and fictions where the spoken word has also been selected, transformed, and intensified in exemplary fashion. There must be the connection to the performing, entertaining arts; there must certainly be the connection to the spoken language; but there must also be literature.

Bibliography

Hammett, Dashiell. *The Novels of Dashiell Hammett*. New York: Alfred A. Knopf, 1965.

Hemingway, Ernest. "The Killers," in *A Pocketbook of Short Stories*. Edited by M. Edmund Speare. New York: Washington Square Press, 1967.

Kingston, Maxine Hong. *The Woman Warrior*. New York: Alfred A. Knopf, 1977.

Lorca, Federico García. *Three Tragedies of Federico García Lorca*. New York: New Directions, 1955.

Olsen, Tillie. *Yonnondio, From the Thirties*. New York: Delacorte Press/ Seymour Lawrence, 1974.

Walter Dean Myers

Maria

"Maria" is a chapter from Walter Dean Myers's Sweet Illusions, *an interactive novella for young adults.*—Editor

> *I have struggled so hard for this girl, so hard. How can I write to my mother in Ponce and tell her this thing? What kind of a father will she think I am? I cannot look at Maria without a pain in my heart. When I lay down at night I can't sleep. She lived in my house and is flesh of my flesh but I don't know the girl. I don't know my own daughter.*

—Hector Rojas, the father of Maria Rojas

Mrs. Robinson, the head of the Piedmont Counseling Center, asked me to wait around until she was finished talking to the new girl and I said yes. I knew Bobby's band, The Sweet Illusions, was practicing and I wanted to hear their new song. I was hoping they didn't practice the new song first.

Actually, I wanted to meet the new girl. I wanted to see how she was handling things. It's like I wanted to see how other girls who were pregnant acted so I would know how to act myself. It's easy to see what's right or wrong with somebody else.

I remembered when I first came to Piedmont. I had seen a brochure about it on the wall of the guidance counselor's office at school. Sometime between the time I found out that I was pregnant and just after I had decided not to kill myself I went to the office and took down the address. Actually, I went to the office twice. I had to go twice because I was waiting for a time when the guidance counselor wasn't in her office. I didn't want her to know that I was pregnant, either.

The way the place looked helped a lot. The center was in a nice brownstone with trees in front of it. The offices had casual furniture that made it look friendly, more like a home than a place for the kinds of hard decisions the girls were making in it. The first floor was all offices in the front, and an examination room in the back. Two doctors came in on Wednesdays and you could talk to them if you had a medical problem.

One of the floors above had places girls could stay if they were put out of their own homes for some reason. There was also a lounge that we could just hang out in if we wanted to. It all helped. There were times when we needed hanging out.

Mrs. Robinson had spoken to me, too, the same way she was speaking to the new girl. It was two weeks after my eighteenth birthday and I was so scared I couldn't even see straight. I hadn't told my father I was pregnant yet, either. Mrs. Robinson had helped me through that period, had shown me that I wasn't alone. So when she asked me to talk to the new girl, to help her, I was more than glad to.

"Maria, I'm glad you stayed." Mrs. Robinson came out of her office with this girl that looked so white I thought she was dead or something. "I thought you and Jennifer could have tea."

"Sure," I said. I flashed my best smile at this chick Jennifer and she looks at me like I'm going to bite her or something.

"You going to be at the meeting tomorrow?" Mrs. Robinson was slipping into her coat.

"What meeting?"

"We're going to decide about a Christmas party."

"Sure, I'll be there."

Jennifer looked about eighteen, maybe even nineteen. She sat down on the couch and looked down at her hands. I watched the door close behind Mrs. Robinson and then I sat down.

"We have lousy instant coffee and pretty good tea," I said. "And when the soda machine is working we have sodas. Right now the soda machine is working."

"I'll have the tea," Jennifer said. She was a little overweight but she had a nice face. Her eyes were a grey-green and I thought she would look nice if she wore liner.

"I'm just starting my eighth month," I said. I took some tea bags out of the can and put them into the cups.

"I'm four months. . . ." Jennifer kind of mumbled to herself.

"Let me tell you something about myself," I said. "We're all different, but we're not that different. When I first came here I had the same talk with Mrs. Robinson that you had. Then I came out here and sat on that same couch. Only I went for the lousy instant coffee."

Jennifer smiled.

"The whole thing is that Mrs. Robinson doesn't want us to feel alone," I said. "You know, when you feel alone you can't think too well. I don't know how well I think anyway, but—"

"—Are you married?" she asked without looking up.

"No. Only a few of the girls that come to Piedmont are married. Some of us wear wedding rings because the guys who hang around outside the place give us a hard time. We take care of ourselves, though."

"I'm not married, either," she said.

"How did you like Mrs. Robinson?" I asked, pouring the tea.

"She's nice," Jennifer said. "I don't know if I can remember everything she said."

"You don't have to," I said. "She's got booklets and things all over the place. And most of the girls who've been here a while can tell you where to find out what you want to know."

"You like this place?" she asked. She looked right at me like she was really going to see if I was telling the truth.

"Yeah, I like it," I said. "Mostly because everything is right up front. They'll give you all the information you want about everything dealing with having a kid or not having a kid. But you have to decide what's best for you, nobody pushes you into anything."

"Wish I had decided what was best for me about four months ago," Jennifer said.

"I know what you mean," I said. "But we got to live in the here and now, not four months or eight months ago. You live with your parents?"

"My mother," Jennifer said. "They're split up. She's been okay about it, really."

"My mother's been okay, too," I said. "She cried when I told her, and I knew she was hurt. But it was like she reached inside of herself and pulled it all together and said she was going to stick with me. You know what I mean?"

"My mother took it hard, too," Jennifer said.

"My father had a fit. He's from some other time or something. He keeps talking about being from Puerto Rico, as if that makes a difference. I think the real difference is what he thinks I should be, what's in his mind. He's got this thing, I don't know. I think if I was married he would have hired a twenty-piece band and have me marching down Fifth Avenue. All my life, ever since I can remember, he's always been talking about his grandsons, what he was going to do with them."

"What's he say now?" Jennifer twisted one hand in the other.

"Now is not so bad. Now he doesn't say anything. Now he sits in front of the window and looks down into the street. He doesn't even pull the curtains back.

"But when I first got pregnant—no, when I first told him—I thought he was going to have a stroke. He's got this way of thinking that a girl is either a virgin or a whore. I know he was very hurt. He wanted to kill Bobby."

"Bobby's your boyfriend?"

"Yeah, he's got a band. It's a combo, really. Bobby plays trumpet, José Aviles plays *timbales,* Chico plays keyboards, and a guy named Carlos plays guitar."

"Sounds nice," she said.

"It's okay," I said. "Sometimes I think Bobby likes the band more than he likes me, though. You don't use sugar in your tea? How can you drink it like that?"

"I'm just not thinking," Jennifer said. "You know, Mrs. Robinson asked me what I wanted to do about the baby. I never thought about, you know, having a choice."

"Sometimes it's easier not thinking about it," I said. "But Mrs. Robinson tries to make you come to some kind of decision. None of it's easy."

"When I first found out I was pregnant I was so . . . so messed around. I missed three periods, I had morning sickness, everything. . . before I even admitted to myself that I was pregnant. Can you believe that?"

"Can I believe it?" I looked at her. "When I started getting big I prayed it was a tumor. I figure, a tumor, at least everybody's going to say 'poor Maria.' You say you're having a baby and everybody hits the ceiling."

"When Mrs. Robinson asked me if I were going to keep the child I wanted to run out of the office but my legs didn't move." Jennifer was crying. She wiped at her face with her sleeve. I gave her some napkins. Sometimes a good cry helped.

The clock on the wall pointed at four-thirty. Bobby's rehearsal started at four. Even if I had left right then I wouldn't get uptown until five-thirty and the rehearsal would probably be over.

"Are you going to keep your baby?" Jennifer asked.

"Yes," I said. "I have a dream about something happening with me and Bobby. Sometimes I think it will and sometimes I don't think so. I used to always think that if you had a baby there were things you had to do. You had to get married, you had to get an apartment."

"It doesn't seem to work out that way," Jennifer said.

"Are you tight with somebody?"

"This tea is awful," she said.

"That's because you haven't tasted the coffee," I said. "You taste the coffee and you're going to love the tea."

"Does it sound stupid to say that I don't have a guy even though I'm pregnant?" Jennifer seemed more relaxed.

"I talked to a lot of girls here at Piedmont, baby," I said. "Nothing sounds stupid. You hang around here a while and you're going to hear stories you wouldn't believe, only you'll know they're true."

"There's a guy, his name is Harry. I met him once and one thing led to another and we ended up in bed. None of it made sense. It just didn't make any sense at all. I keep thinking back on it, trying to put the pieces together, but it doesn't help."

"It makes sense," I said. "You know all the biology, and all the 'how comes' and everything, so it makes sense. It just doesn't make the kind of sense that makes your life any easier."

"You want to know something else?" Jennifer had a twisted smile on her face. "I told you I only met the guy once? Well, I even forgot his name. I had to call my girlfriend later on to find out what his name was."

Jennifer and I talked for a while and I let her put her hand on my stomach when the baby kicked. When she felt it, she pulled her hand away real quick. She smiled, though, and I could tell she was more relaxed. She asked me was I nervous and I said yes, a little. I was nervous and I was excited. I just wished I was married to Bobby. Then I could have the rest of it, too.

"Piedmont helps," I said. "Because what you need is a place that doesn't dump on you. Mrs. Robinson never looks at us or says anything to us about 'making a mistake' or anything like that. She just keeps telling us that we have to make decisions, and take control over our own lives."

"I think you're okay," Jennifer said. "I really appreciate you talking to me."

It was five-thirty and I had to go home. I knew my father left home at five-fifteen. He'd be gone by the time I got home.

In a way he was gone even when he was there. He didn't say anything to me, or even look at me. He hardly even spoke to my mother anymore. It was as if she was responsible, too. She wasn't, just me.

When me and Bobby were younger it didn't matter about sex. We were supposed to be boyfriend and girlfriend and everything was cool. We used to talk about going places together. I always wanted to go to Puerto Rico and he always wanted to go to California.

When we got older and he started The Sweet Illusions band and got a van, then the girls started coming around. I knew he was fooling around with some of them. I tried to make believe it didn't bother me, but I guess it did. Sometimes I used to hear girls talking about doing it, and it was like they were talking about having a slice of pizza or something. After a while I figured I was the weird one because I wasn't having sex with Bobby.

The first time it happened was at Bobby's house. I made believe that it wasn't going to happen. He was fooling around with my clothes but I took my mind off it. I told myself that we were just going to be kissing and hugging, the way we always did. I even asked him what he was doing when he started making love to me.

Afterwards I never went for birth control stuff because I kept telling myself that it wouldn't happen again. I told myself that, every time it happened.

"Hi, Mommy." I kissed my mother when I got home and she patted me on the shoulder the way she did sometimes.

"You want something to eat?" she asked.

"Sure," I said. "Daddy went to work?"

She nodded. I knew he had been giving her a hard time again.

She fixed me a plate of chicken and rice with a side dish of black bean soup. I loved black bean soup, but with the baby it made me have too much gas. I ate it anyway.

"What did Daddy say?"

She didn't look at me. She started putting rice on a plate for herself and then scraped it back into the pot. "He wanted to know where you were going to live when the baby came," she said.

"I'll find a place," I said. I tried to smile but I couldn't get it out, so I just went in and sat on the couch.

How could I be so different? One day I was Maria Rojas that everybody loved and the next day I was something different. How could I be so different?

I didn't hate my father. I knew how he felt. I knew that he wanted good things for me and that he was disappointed, but I wasn't the first girl in the world to get pregnant. Why couldn't he just be my father again? That's all I wanted from him.

I was sixteen and I felt like I was a hundred years old already. How could I be so different?

The TV sports news was on and I curled up on the couch and fell asleep. When Mommy came in to tell me to get up and go to bed, the dream I was having was so real. I had to tell someone.

In the dream, there was a. . . .

Pretend you are Maria. (It doesn't matter whether you are a boy or a girl.) Put yourself in her place. You have come back from the clinic, had a bite to eat, and fallen asleep. You have a lot on your mind. You have this dream. It can be a very strange dream or a very ordinary one. What happens in this dream? You decide. Write down your dream.

Meredith Sue Willis

Deep Revision

When revision is working best, it is as experimental and exhilarating as learning to walk and talk. One day the toddler stands upright for a surprised, balanced instant, then falls on its well-padded behind, laughs at the sensation, clambers up again and adjusts its balance just enough to stay upright half a second longer before being brought down again by gravity. I believe that the revision an adult writer does is on a continuum with the child's teaching itself to walk. Our lives are full of revision, conscious and unconscious. Revision is a form of learning: it pushes us farther into experience, which alters how we perceive the past and prepares us for the future. I don't mean to describe revision as extraordinary; on the contrary, it seems to me one of the most ordinary of human activities.

★   ★   ★

As a child, when I had worked as much as I wanted on a given piece, I simply laid it aside and went on to something else. This can be viewed as one form of revision, particularly suited to very young writers: when you've gone as long as you can, you stop, and start something else afresh.

I remember in second grade reading over what I had written the previous year:

> Fredy is a cowboy
> Fredy eats beans
> Fredy is a cowboy
> Becaus his teth gleamz

I had no interest in revising "Fredy," but my new writing had a relationship to what had gone before. In the second grade I wrote stories rather than poems, and they were longer, in script, and had more models from literature because I was reading more books from the library. I was making constant starts, trials, experiments, and the revision was centered not on any particular text, but on my whole relationship to literature. The old saws may be rusty: *If it's worth doing, it's worth doing well.* What if it's not worth doing but it takes doing it for a while to find out? Who's to say what doing well is? Sometimes we polish highly, sometimes we simply check for the most egregious spelling errors and send it off. *Don't start something you can't finish.* Why not start something to see if you want to finish it? What is finishing anyhow? For a six- or seven-year-old, finished is when you're done with it.

For an adult writer too, there are times when the initial flash of insight or inspiration will be enough. Or perhaps a piece is best left as a fragment. Coleridge's "Kubla Khan" exists as a fragment of a dream he could not fully recapture. Or, you actually might hit it right the first time. We need to have different revising strategies, depending on the task or inspiration at hand. There are many adult writers who, like children, do not revise—at least not on paper—or who revise very little. Ironically, I consider it a form of self-discipline *not* to revise certain things I write; that is, I am so accustomed to long bouts of polishing that it's difficult for me to figure out when to stop making changes. At the same time, elementary school children *can* begin to learn to go back and *see again*.

★   ★   ★

As students get older, revision can be presented to them as an activity done by professional and creative writers. The idea of writing as a profession didn't occur to me until I was well into my teens. I had no models of adult writers; I certainly knew nothing of the business and industry of book publishing and selling. But I did begin to recognize certain writers' names and to associate power with their invocation: Shakespeare! Tolstoy-and-Dostoevsky! Margaret Mitchell! I read articles about writers, and even began to play at being a writer myself. One summer, having read in *Reader's Digest* that great writers spend an hour a day or more (!) at their desks, I committed myself to being at the typewriter one hour each morning, rain or shine. I remember, one extremely hot summer morning, sitting on the rough home-poured concrete of our little patio with my mother's old black Underwood typewriter on a stool in front of me. How could anyone really do this? I thought. An hour is so long! It's so hot. I'm not cut out for this.

Then I learned that Great Authors revise over and over again. With a new self-awareness, I began to look at the stories and personal essays and poems I had been writing for my own entertainment. I found that making word choices was actually fun. Crimson? Scarlet? Incarnadine? I imagined the Great Author in a room lined with bookshelves, with one large powerful hand clutching his hair while the other fingered his words as if they were old coins. He held them to the light as if candling eggs, he sniffed them as if they were little vials of perfume. I saw him in my mind, and simultaneously I saw myself in my attic room at my small student desk. I saw myself as from a distance, and tried to revise myself into this revising Great Author. I didn't look like him, but I tried at least to do what I imagined he did: I looked at my story word by word. I had written: "I was insulted that he thought no more of my power." I scratched out the word "power" so that the sentence read: "I was insulted that he thought no more of my abilities." A page later, I had written: "Then in spite of everything, I slept." I changed it to: "Finally in spite of everything, I did sleep."

Were the changes an improvement? It depends on how you look at it. I cannot say they are the changes I would make today. "Did sleep" seems fussy, as if I wanted to make the tone of my story more genteel or to show off my knowledge of complex past tenses. If I had been that fourteen-year-old girl's teacher, I would probably have been pleased mostly by the sheer bulk and ambition of the forty-page story. I might have felt duty-bound to point out that "in spite of everything" is a phrase that needs to be set off by commas at both ends. But I think I would have appreciated the experiment in tone that is represented by "finally" and "did sleep." When I scratched out "that" and replaced it with "the" or changed "lice or fleas" to "some horrible parasite," I was teaching myself that words are malleable.

Should a teacher or reader faced with such a student writer suggest that "lice or fleas" is more concrete and thus more vivid than "some horrible parasite"? My instinct is not to intervene too much with any-one who is—for himself or herself—playing with words. I would rather give models of the best literature and trust the student to discover the power of plain, concrete speech later, although over against this is my belief that any respectful response, no matter how detailed or strong, is useful to a young writer. Writing is not, after all, a sacred ritual that can be done only one way without angering the gods. Nor are young writ-ers such frail beings that they cannot bear some contradictions and varying opinions. The most important thing, it seems to me, is a sense of respect on the part of the teacher for the student's own ideas and projects—and it's sometimes difficult to learn to participate in the younger writer's process of writing without taking it over. But this sense of respect is vital to the art of teaching.

Revising as a Response to Literature

Even in our earliest efforts at writing we are always consciously or un-consciously imitating. We learn to structure our ideas about writing from literary models—the story the teacher read the class or the comic book our big brother gave us. Our first forms are the ones that seem simply to be there. A boy who is engrossed in the origin of superheroes and decides to create his own superhero doesn't agonize over how to begin, any more than I agonize over filling out a subscription coupon: he knows that you start with the superhero's super-characteristics, just as I know what to write in the space labelled "name." In other words, we have conventional structures in our minds even before we read and write, and conventional structures are often exactly what is needed. Thus one thing a teacher can give students is familiarity with and practice in such forms. This can be done only through wide reading and lots of practice.

"Conventional" structures and "creative" writing are by no means antithetical. I love the fresh, the new, and the original, but making a fetish of it is a twentieth-century quirk. In the sixteenth century, mastery of the conventions of sonnet writing was a desirable accomplishment. Variations were of course necessary, but the main project was to master the form with its exact number of lines, its set rhyme scheme, and the tropes that were appropriate to it—just the way a great basketball player does not make up the art of dribbling, but embellishes and perfects it.

My son Joel was assigned his first homework composition in the late winter of first grade. The assignment was to write something about the season, and he sat down and rapidly wrote a little half-poem half-essay about snow and children sliding and sledding. Not only did the piece sound nothing like his speaking voice, but we had not even had any snow yet. My satisfaction was in the beginning of his mastery of forms and levels of discourse. It was his idea of what he thought appropriate for a seasonal composition, his maiden voyage on the ocean of formal writing.

Some of my own earliest efforts at writing were imitations of popular culture. My poem about Fredy the Cowboy was essentially a commercial jingle. I turned to the funny papers and comic books for my models, because those were my first forms of literature. I carefully drew blocks, made pictures, squeezed words into the balloons—and one day discovered that if you write the words first and make the speech balloon afterwards, you don't have to squeeze. This was a technical breakthrough—the beginning of my taking control of conventions and forms.

As I got older, I would write my own version of whatever I read or saw. After the movie version of *Old Yeller*, I wrote a story called "The

Yaller Dog." My version was not plagiarized, but something much less civilized: I wanted to get inside the story and eat it from the inside, like a voracious little larva working its way out of a fruit. In my version of the dog story, the dog doesn't die at the end. This doesn't mean that I hated the original or was traumatized by it, only that I wanted to do it my way.

One theory of literature states that what is written is only fully realized when a reader receives it, that the reader is, in a way, the true creator of a text; a poem or essay or novel or news article does not really exist until the reader has filled in the gaps with his or her own experience and knowledge. The psychology of the author and the author's intentions are nothing compared to the activity of the reader, who by recognizing conventions and transforming them with his or her own perceptions and beliefs creates what *is* on the page through the activity of reading it. As one theorist says, "The whole point of reading . . . is that it brings us into deeper self-consciousness, catalyzes a more critical view of our own identities."[1]

While I don't embrace this theory entirely, I am struck by the idea that a textbook, a story, a poem, a newspaper article, or a magazine essay is not something to be treated with exaggerated respect. This idea is of enormous practical value for those of us who teach.

• *The next time you read something leisurely—the sports page,* TV Guide, *or an article in* People *magazine—write a quick response to your reading. Include whatever is on your mind, even if it doesn't seem to be on the subject. Write about how hot the weather is, or your concerns for your team's standing in the league, or whatever. Do this over a few days with the same type of reading material. When you have three or more entries, revise them into an essay in the form of a feature article or review, such as an essay on Ann Landers or this season's Cleveland Indians.*

Writing can thus be a way of making what you read your own and altering what you read to make it fit yourself. Some years ago, I was teaching a required first-year literature course at Pace University. For many of the students, this would be the final go-round with the standard English literary canon, and—to add insult to injury—this class met on Friday afternoons. We had some good times in that class, although attendance was always sporadic. When we came to the required grappling with *Hamlet,* a number of the students were willing to try anything rather than actually read the text, and when they did read it, they seemed at a loss as to how to talk about it. I typed up some of the more famous monologues ("How all occasions do inform against me" and "O, my offense is rank, it smells to heaven!") for closer study, and then asked everyone to choose a character in the play (excluding Hamlet himself) and write a prose or poetic monologue. To my surprise, several students tried something in blank verse, and most had a better grasp of the character they chose than I would have expected. Overall, I felt each of the students was able to think better—and consequently learned more—about the play through the revision exercise than they would have in class discussion alone. To speak analytically about literature requires a kind of training that these students had not had and might never have, but writing these pieces allowed them to meet the literature on their own terms, and showed me that they really did understand the play.

• *If your students are studying* Hamlet *(or some other famous work), have each of them write a dramatic monologue for a minor character. This is meant to be an exercise in capturing tone and meaning, in imitating a form—the dramatic monologue—and in revising the text by imagining its events from a different point of view.*

> I, Laertes, despise the wretched Hamlet.
> Such a fool as he deserves no kingship.
> No true king would allow the transparency
> of marriage to obstruct divine ascending
> to the crown as did Claudius to Hamlet.
> His soul is a flicker where mine flares.
> That king fool we have now
> who thinks from his groin
> would never have eliminated his predecessor
> were it not for my connivance.
> Yet I still have no power;
> I'll seek Fortinbras in this matter.
> Now with my father dead,
> his spirit rises with opportunity;
> opportunity in the guise of revenge.
> To kill Hamlet with the poison sword
> Claudius shall give me!
> Upon Hamlet's death, there shall be great mourning,
> a nation in distress.
> It is then that I shall expose
> Claudius and his foul plans.
> Revolutionary upheaval will follow,
> and a divided Denmark will surrender

to Fortinbras's invading armies,
and I shall have power.

—*Tom Wright, first-year college student*

★   ★   ★

Claudius

I am now dying—and what for I ask. Here I have the throne and a beautiful queen. I have power throughout the land and am very happy. Why must I die by the sword of such a brash young prince? Life has finally been good to me, till now.

True, I have deeply sinned. I killed, manipulated, and schemed to get to the top. If only I could have done away with Hamlet sooner. I knew that crazy fit by Hamlet was an act. He always suspected me of killing his father.

It is so sad it has to end this way. I was just getting used to the idea of being the one with unchecked power and the final say in stately matters. It is a shame that I was outwitted by such a young prince like Hamlet. And yet he dies too. Now that is indeed sweet revenge. All I can say is, at least I made it to the top.

—*Wayne Hugar, first-year college student*

• *If your students are studying a particular period in history, find a poem or two written at the time, and have students pretend to be the poet and write another poem about some other event or theme of the day, imitating the form and style. You can try the same thing using a news article from the actual period, a short story, or—perhaps best of all—a journal entry or letter.*

Writing your way into literature by making your own versions can include both direct imitations (such as the Shakespearean dramatic monologue) and more playful exercises (such as writing anachronistic news reports about the events surrounding Hamlet's death). In both kinds of writing, the student changes the existing literature in order to get closer to it, deeper inside it. This approach to studying literature works as well with modern literature as with older literature. Monologues are particularly good for getting inside characters. I asked my college students to write pieces based on "Cutting Edge," a story by James Purdy about an unpleasant confrontation in a family when a son comes home with a beard and his mother wants him to shave it.[2] One student wrote his piece from the young man's point of view:

She is so blind. She can't possibly see beyond this beard.

I know that trying to change our damaged relationship is not likely but I want her to accept me as who I am and start building our relationship.

I am a new man now and unless you accept me and the things that are in the present, we won't get anywhere. I can't believe that she will refuse to accept the past.

What do you think of my face that's naked in its raw form? This beard is clothes for my face. What do you want? Nude? Or clothed?

There's no hope. We are finished as a family. I don't want to see you again. It's quite clear that you don't want to see me.

—*Jae Song, college junior*

These next examples were written by high school students. I had them read one of my short stories, "Evenings with Porter."[3] The story is about two characters who meet at various points in their lives. The male character is about to go overseas as a pilot in the Vietnam War, and the female narrator tries to convince him not to. I then had the students rewrite one of the scenes from the male character's point of view:

Just came back from Blair Ellen's grandmother's store. I was there for a long while. Hangin' out and drinkin' pop. I went this afternoon. It's now past dark. I remember walkin' in to the store. Blair Ellen sold me a pop. She looked kind of cute, I mean for twelve. After my pop, I hang around a little longer, we, Blair Ellen and me, went out on the porch to talk. We talked of the town boys and such. After a bit, her grandmother was rustlin' about the kitchen makin' noise. I guess Blair Ellen had chores to do or had to attend to her grandmother 'cause she said good night and left. We cut our talkin' kinda short. I'll prob'ly go back tomorrow.

—*Kate Renlow, tenth grade*

★   ★   ★

Now, I'm flying all alone, I'm fighting for my country. I'm very scared, even though I told her I wasn't. I wish I would of listened to her, and flew up into Canada. Why can't I just turn around now, and go back and be with her? Well, I gave my devotion to the Air Force and this is where I'm going to stay. I just hope I'll stay alive, so when this is over, I can see her again. Now as I reach Cambodia, I'm even more scared, but I'll be all right, won't I. . . .

—*Rick Raymond, tenth grade*

The thing that pleased me about this exercise was how much in tune the students seemed to be with the story. They chose to go into it at various points, but in each case I found myself believing their interpretation. This piece also reaffirmed my sense that often a so-called creative or reader-involved response is the best one to literature for non-specialized students. When the student can take something he or she is reading and revise it, there is likely to be much more real understanding of its shape and texture. I am certainly not suggesting that there should never be critical writing about literature, but that critical writing should be only one of several ways of engaging students in literature. Personal involvement through revising literature should always precede critical thinking, because it is extremely difficult to think deeply about a work of art with which you have never really been connected.

• *After reading any story or novel (preferably one in the first person), write one scene from the point of view of a character other than the narrator. Do this by assigning parts before the class begins reading the novel so that each class member has one character to follow and study throughout the work.*

One quick way of using an author's writing to get a feel for its shape is through copying and dictation. I am always collecting samples of fiction to use with students and in my articles and books on writing, and I have typed many paragraphs by my favorite authors, poets and nonfiction writers as well as novelists and short story writers. It's a great feeling to have someone else's words go through your body—learning what the rhythm of those words feels like, the shape of the paragraphs or the length of the lines. Imitating and copying should be, it seems to me, among our regular language arts activities.

• *Find some poem or paragraph that you admire and copy it longhand. If you are a teacher, bring in a piece that you admire and ask students to copy it over. This can be followed by the writing of an imitation or a continuation.*

• *Try the same exercise through dictation, having someone read aloud while the rest write it down.*

• *Do this with a poem, and then compare how you broke the lines with how the poet did it.*

• *After using copying or dictation, turn the paper over and, without looking, write down as much of it as you can remember. Compare the two pieces. Do you like your own remembered version better? Try writing it again a week later. The point is not to get a headache trying to remember, but to see what your memory adds and changes.*

• *Type a sonnet or other fairly compact poem, or a dense paragraph of prose, leaving out most of the middle, keeping just the first and last lines, or sentences, or perhaps the final rhyme scheme if it's a sonnet. Duplicate and distribute, and have everyone fill it in with their own versions. Depending on the students' ages and your own style, you can do this either by requiring the poem to be completed with the exact same number of lines as in the original poem (as in the example below, based on a James Wright poem) or by letting the middle part be as long or short as the students want.*

Over my head, I see the bronze butterfly,
Asleep on the black trunk,

_____
_____
_____
_____
_____
_____
_____
_____
_____
_____

I have wasted my life.[4]

• *Pass out the opening paragraph or line of some famous prose work, and have everyone continue the story. For some real fun, see what younger students can do with "Call me Ishmael" or "It was the best of times, it was the worst of times."*

• *Instead of starting with the words, give the plot of some famous story: married woman falls in love with other man, destroys her marriage, in despair kills herself. (That's Tolstoy's* Anna Karenina.) *Flesh it out.*

Kids imitate whether you want them to or not—in fact, we all do, in life and in writing. For me, writing comes out of the experience of daily life (including all our language and mental imagery) and from literature. For many students, of course, literature (and much life experience) has been replaced by television and, to a lesser extent, the movies. It seems to me only fair and realistic to make a space for imitating models the students already have and are comfortable with. Thus student writers should get a turn at writing music lyrics or television scripts. Of course, there is a job of analysis here too—to understand the forms that are used by professional songwriters and television writers.

I observed writer-in-the-schools Josefina Baez working with eighth grade students at the Bergen Street School in Newark, New Jersey. The class was a small group of eighth graders, and Josefina perched on a desk, with the students arranged in a horseshoe open to the blackboard. The classroom teacher was sitting at her own desk. Josefina used the students' own choice, rap poetry, as a means of working through the process of revision. The poems sprang from the students' ideas and themes, which included drugs, pollution, and getting a paycheck versus getting a welfare check. The students first wrote their verses—which they discovered took more effort than they expected—then they transcribed the lyrics to the blackboard one at a time. Everyone helped ensure that the mechanics were right. After making written revisions on the board, the students then read the poems aloud in various styles: as sentences; as poetry; as rhythmic rap. One boy said, "Hey, mine could be a slow song, too," and proceeded to sing it, and the teacher said, "Why, that could be blues—" and then *she* took a turn singing the student's lines. It was a great atmosphere for showing how words can be changed and exchanged.

After this group session, the rap poems were revised individually by the students, typed up by Josefina, and prepared both for performance and for inclusion in a written anthology. Josefina's students learned a number of things simultaneously: how they can use one another's critiques to make changes, as well as individual revising and editing under the supervision of adults; that their poems can cross into other media—printed in a booklet and performed for an audience; and that songs do not appear magically in a music video. Much work precedes even a popular form.

• *Have your students choose any song form that they like. Depending on geographic location, you might get country music, rap, heavy metal, or something I've never heard of. What is essential here is that the students choose their music, whatever it is. Have them transcribe lyrics, and then write their own, using the form as you've analyzed it from the songs they bring in. Next, discuss how accurately the pieces followed the form, and how to make them better.*

• *Try the same thing but with a television or movie script. Again, decide together what the elements of a television drama or, say, a horror movie are.*

• *Choose a poem or song that you like and ask everyone to write an imitation of it. Have the students write before any discussion, so that they can discover the elements and form on their own. (Later, when they discuss the poem and compare their imitations, they will pick up more elements and figure out more about the form.) After one draft of writing, read aloud, discuss what people chose to imitate, and then have them do a second draft, giving everyone the opportunity to imitate further, or add further elements or stylistic devices. There are a number of excellent poems that lend themselves to imitation by children of different ages. Look through any good anthology for poems that appeal to you.*[5]

Revising previous works of literature is another approach to writing fiction. For example, some years ago I read the *Confessions* of Saint Augustine in conjunction with a biography of him. Augustine mentions his concubine of many years—mother of his son—but never tells her name. I had many reactions to reading Augustine and learned a great deal, but this particular fact stuck in my craw, and I wrote a short story called "Sermon of the Younger Monica," which was from the concubine's point of view. This was a deeply satisfying exercise for me, as were other stories I wrote, including a revision of Shakespeare and a couple of Biblical revisions. In my version of the Adam and Eve story, I embedded sentences from the King James translation of the Bible as well as a fragment of Milton's description of the serpent in *Paradise Lost*.

Revisionist literature has a very long and venerable tradition: Aeschylus's *Oresteia* uses material from Homer, who borrowed from previous stories of the gods and heroes. Eugene O'Neill wrote his own version of the same material in *Mourning Becomes Electra*. Parodies and travesties are time-honored literary forms, and science fiction includes a whole sub-genre of writing about what would have happened if history had been changed. A few years ago, a science fiction editor solicited stories that answered the question, "What if, at each presidential election in the history of the United States, there had been a different outcome?" What would have happened if Lincoln had lost his election? If Richard Nixon had become president in 1960 instead of in 1968? Judy Moffett wrote a story that had Davy Crockett defeat Andrew Jackson with positive results for the United States government's policies toward Native Americans. Beryl Bainbridge has a mainstream novel called *Young Adolf* about a visit Adolf Hitler may or may not have paid to England in his adolescence, when his brother lived there, and Leon Rooke's novel *Shakespeare's Dog* revises history from a canine point of view.

• *Write a poem or story from the point of view of some minor character in literature—someone whose life was affected by the hero, but who did not* necessarily see things the way the hero did. This can shed new light on the story, perhaps from a comic point of view.

• *Try writing an imitation of some brief passage or short work, such as a parable. Write it in such a way that you critique the original or give a different emphasis. This parable from Franz Kafka is followed by a high school student's revision of it:*

A Little Fable

"Alas," said the mouse, "the world is growing smaller every day. At the beginning it was so big that I was afraid, I kept running and running, and I was glad when at last I saw walls far away to the right and left, but these long walls have narrowed so quickly that I am in the last chamber already, and there in the corner stands the trap that I must run into." "You only need to change your direction," said the cat, and ate up the mouse.

—*Franz Kafka*[6]

*   *   *

"Help!" the mouse yelled. He stood caught in the trap and had no means of escape. "Surely," he thought, "one of my many friends will rescue me before The Cat comes." He waited and waited and yelled and yelled, yet no one came. Finally, he saw a mouse running to him. "Mother!" he yelled. "You could be killed. The Cat will surely be here any minute! Please, save yourself and allow one of my many friends to save me," he pleaded.

"No, I will save you my son," she said.

"But mother, why is it none of my friends came?" the little mouse asked.

"Son, it is true, you have many friends and you have chosen them well, but only one is your mother," she said as they ran together back into the wall, just as The Cat lunged for them.

—*Billy Maris, tenth grade*

Billy captures the style very well, but revises the ending to fit his own world view. This "answering back" to literature and other arts is one of the things that writers do all the time. Filmmakers use showers and towers and crowds of birds and dozens of other images that allude to Alfred Hitchcock; Anthony Hecht revises Matthew Arnold's "Dover Beach" in a humorous poem called "Dover Bitch."

• *Write a modern version of some other parable or fable. Aesop's are good models, as are the parables of Jesus.*

• *Write your own Zen parable, using the brief, surprising forms that the Zen masters use to make their students think in new ways.*

Learning to Be Silent

The pupils of the Tendai school used to study meditation before Zen entered Japan. Four of them who were intimate friends promised one another to observe seven days of silence.

On the first day all were silent. Their meditation had begun auspiciously, but when night came and the oil lamps were growing dim one of the pupils could not help exclaiming to a servant: "Fix those lamps."

The second pupil was surprised to hear the first one talk. "We are not supposed to say a word," he remarked.

"You two are stupid. Why did you talk?" asked the third.

"Ha! I am the only one who has not talked!" concluded the fourth pupil.[7]

This process of using existing literature to form your own literature can be done directly, through imitation, or through the answering back of parody and rewriting, and also through something I call embedding. Embedding consists of incorporating a previous piece in a new work. One particular embedding exercise is one of my all-time favorites. It works at many levels of age and competency. I especially like to do it once with total open-endedness, then have a discussion and send students back to have another go at it.

• *Here is a Skeleton Story. Copy these words on your paper with at least three spaces between each line.*

Hi.

Hi.

Where were you?

Nowhere.

Take these words and do anything you want to them to make the story longer and more interesting. Add, change, reverse, cut.

"Hi," said Jessie, her blonde hair bouncing up and down.

"Hi, it's nice to see you again," said Samantha, struggling to hold her duffel bag.

"Where were you?" Jessie wondered, eyeing her duffel bag suspiciously.

"Nowhere," said Samantha, thinking how nosy her friend was being.

"Well, you had to be somewhere if you weren't home last night when I called!" she said, anger sparkling in her wide blue eyes.

"You don't have to know everywhere I go," said Samantha, thinking about how much fun she had last night when she slept over at Kelly's house.

"Well, then, goodbye," said Jessie, stomping off gruffly.

—*Erika Robinson, sixth grade*

After everyone writes for five or ten minutes, have a short discussion and read a few pieces, to show different ways the students handled the assignment. You might brainstorm a list of ways people made their boring conversation interesting: by adding gestures, narration, and setting; describing people, specifying tone of voice, etc.

• *Do the same exercise, requiring that everyone write for at least ten minutes (or whatever length you choose). This generates more details.*

• *Go out on the street or to some public place and collect fragments of dialogue. Bring them back and write up just the words, then try to reconstruct a whole scene from memory.*

• *Do the same thing, but by making up the scene, rather than by remembering it.*

• *Do the same thing, but exchange skeletons with someone who wasn't in your group so that everyone has a bit of dialogue to use that is new to them.*

In one of my novels, I wrote a scene that I realized was very much like a particular Kafka parable. I tried typing and embedding Kafka's words as a focus for my visualization of the moment of crisis in my novel. Kafka's parable "The Vulture" ends with:

Falling back, I was relieved to feel him drowning irretrievably in my blood, which was filling every depth, flooding every shore.[8]

My scene ends as follows:

She laid her hands on her thighs and stared at her fate, at the embodied shriek that plunged and plunged, plunged deep into her throat. She felt it fill her depths, flood her shores.

I should note here that this is not plagiarism because the original material is altered so much, and also because I am not trying to pass off an entire work by someone else as my own. Jane Wilson Joyce does something along these same lines but much more extensively in her beautiful poem-saga of the Oregon Trail, *Beyond the Blue Mountains*.[9] She uses passages of diary entries of real individuals who went on the Oregon Trail in their covered wagons, and reorganizes and embeds those bits of diaries and journals in her narrative poem, hangs her work on these structuring elements, these bones of found language. Here is one poem from her book:

> Not a tree,
> not a stone,
> nothing
> but flowers and grass.
> We women
> spread our skirts
> for one another,
> spread them wide as if about to
> curtsey, plain
> wool and figured
> calico, overlapped,
> a courtly dance of
> modesty.[10]

She is able to pinpoint her sources for this poem: all from *Women's Diaries of the Westward Journey*: "Not a drop of water, nor a spear of grass to be seen, nothing but barren hills, bare and broken rock, sand and dust" (p. 207) and "Passed what is called the fort, chimney & other bluffs, in appearance resembling castles, capitals of cities" (p. 65), along with introductory material about women's need of each other for keeping their modesty while attending to bodily functions.[11] She describes the process of putting together her book:

> Looking back at the process [of writing *Beyond the Blue Mountains*] now, I'd say there are probably five basic methods:
> 1. Straight found poems (ex. "Oh my dear Mother")
> 2. Pastiche found poems (ex. "Pressing On")
> 3. Photo-based poems (ex. "A company of emigrants")
> 4. Incident-based poems (ex. "Accident")
> 5. Free inventions (ex. "We passed a rosewood/spinet")
> There are mixed methods within poems, too. The main thing is that I immersed myself in Lillian Schlissel's book. There was a time when I could lay my hand on any phrase in its 200+ pages. . . . Another hidden resource is, of course, my personal stock of memories and experiences and impressions.[12]

• *Take a journal or letter of your own, or perhaps better, of your parents or some ancestor, and choose phrases that move you. Use these as structures for a piece of prose or poetry, fiction or nonfiction. Let them form the posts you hang other material on.*[13]

• *Copy a poem, preferably one from previous centuries or otherwise difficult, then write your own paragraph, short essay, dramatic scene, anecdote, or whatever you want based on that poem. Change it as far as you'd like, perhaps in the end leaving no more than a few choice verbs.*

Consciously, unconsciously, and self-consciously, we are always using previous literature when we write: we imitate what went before us; we sometimes react against it; once in a while we make something genuinely new of it.

Notes

1. Wolfgang Iser, as quoted by Terry Eagleton in *Literary Theory: An Introduction* (Minneapolis: Univ. of Minnesota Press, 1983), p. 79.

2. Reprinted in Janet Burroway, *Writing Fiction: A Guide to Narrative Craft,* 2nd ed. (Glenview, Ill.: Scott, Foresman, and Co., 1987).

3. Meredith Sue Willis, "Evenings with Porter," *Pikeville Review* (Humanities Dept., Pikeville College, Pikeville, Ky. 41501), Spring, 1988.

4. These three lines are from James Wright's "Lying in a Hammock at William Duffy's Farm in Pine Island, Minnesota" in *The Branch Will Not Break* (Middletown, Ct.: Wesleyan Univ. Press, 1975).

5. One particularly useful anthology of contemporary poems by adults and children is *The Poetry Connection* by Kinereth Gensler and Nina Nyhart (New York: Teachers & Writers, 1978).

6. As translated by Willa and Edwin Muir in Franz Kafka, *The Complete Stories of Franz Kafka* (New York: Schocken Books, 1971).

7. This parable appears in Paul Reps, *Zen Flesh, Zen Bones* (Rutland, Vt.: Tuttle, 1957).

8. Translated by Tania and James Stern, from Kafka, op cit.

9. Jane Wilson Joyce, *Beyond the Blue Mountains* (Frankfort, Ky.: Gnomon Press, 1992).

10. Ibid., p. 26.

11. *Women's Diaries of the Westward Journey,* ed. Lillian Schlissel (New York: Schocken Books, 1982).

12. Jane Wilson Joyce, in a private letter to the author.

13. See also William Carlos Williams's long poem *Paterson* (New York: New Directions, 1963), which incorporates previously existing material.

Peter Sears

Learning Language by Invention

As we English teachers move from relative pronouns to the business letter to the topic sentence, we can't help but wish for our students a bold, far-reaching view of language. Since from their standpoint, they already *have* their language, new approaches should interest them. A good way for students to see language as an instrument of social discourse is for them to actually *create* language. Here is a program that I have used with tenth graders that improves language competence by involving students in the making of language.

My starting point is something students like and can make: codes. The first exercise for each student is to invent a code, send a message to someone who understands the code, receive and decipher a message from this person, and, lastly, try to decipher a coded message in an unknown code, namely, a message between two other people. Here's a message to decipher: 8-5-12-12-15/6-18-9-5-14-4. Since the highest number is less than 26, the student checks to see if the numbers directly parallel letters. They do. The message is "Hello friend." Here's a reply: 13-1-11-5/1/8-1-18-4-5-18/3-15-4-5/6-18-9-5-14-4.

Cracking a code is translating a secret language into a public language—in our case, English. How this public language works is what English teachers try to convey. Can working with codes help English teachers? Yes. English is based on conventions; altering these conventions is a way to create a code; therefore, codes can be used to teach the conventions of English.

Before showing you a code for students to crack, let me specify what I mean by conventions. The conventions of a language are the culturally agreed upon practices for writing. They are the "given" of the language, the starting point preceding even grammar (the rules of which are also conventions).

The alphabet is the first convention of written English. Second is word formation: letters are combined to make words and the beginning and ending of a word in sequence is signaled by a space. The third convention is direction: English "reads" from left to right and top to bottom. Fourth is syntax: meaning is determined by a word's location within a series of words, as well as by its literal meaning. The fifth convention is the signaling devices of punctuation and capitalization, which further qualify meaning.

Now for a code for students to crack. I gave my tenth graders a message in code based on three alterations of English conventions: reverse direction, drop the signaling device of punctuation, and use only capital letters. The message THE MAN GIVES THE WOMAN THE TREASURE MAP BUT DOESN'T TELL HER THE CODE becomes EDOC EHT REH LLET TNSEOD TUB PAM ERUSAERT EHT NAMOW EHT SEVIG NAM EHT. Fairly easy? Had I reversed the direction of the letters too, it would have been a breeze; and it would have been harder with the altering of a fourth convention: for word formation, the last letter of each word moves to begin the next word, except for the last word. EDOCE HTR EHL LETT NSEODT UBP AME RUSAERTE HTN AMOWE HTS EVIGN AME HT. The newly encoded message is harder. Yet once students crack the code—the repetition of "the" helps—the teacher is in a position to introduce the idea of language conventions. A student's saying "All you did was write it backwards and move the last letter of each word over to the next" allows the teacher to ask, "What if I had written the message from top to bottom instead?" Discussion of what makes a good code provides the teacher with the opportunity to ask the students, "Are there other conventions, besides direction and word formation? Let's make a list so that you can experiment further in your code invention."

The logical conclusion of this work with conventions through code making is for students to invent their own language. If this idea sounds like courting chaos, take heart, it's manageable and it's most interesting to them and to you. Still, at least one more step is advisable. Students like the idea that rules of language are conventions. So the timing is good to introduce the notion that conventions are needed to assure that a meaning can be reliably conveyed. I try to demonstrate this principle by showing them lousy writing and asking them to decipher it:

> It is obvious from the difference in elevation with relation to the short depth of the property that the contour is such as to preclude any reasonable developmental potential for active recreation.

Students enjoy criticizing "adult" writing, and they may notice such phrases as "It is obvious from," "with relation to," and "is such as to." As the students struggle with this overwritten passage, they may give up on working word to word and go directly for the overall meaning. As Stuart Chase says in his helpful essay, "Gobbledygook," "Seems the plot was too steep." (Another essay loaded with examples students delight in translating is George Orwell's "Politics and the English Language.") The teacher can ask, "Is the passage hard because it is profound or because it is badly written?" Once students translate a bloated, syntactically flabby passage into a terse, lucid statement, they can better avoid such flaws in their own writing. They begin to appreciate, from first-hand experience, that conventions—rules if you wish—are for the purpose of clarity.

An optional exercise I use is to have the students look at other languages before trying to invent their own. Does Spanish, for example, have the same conventions as English? A line of Spanish full of cognates with the translation beneath it surprises students who assume that all other languages are indecipherable. But on the other hand, what about Hebrew or Arabic?

הלחלון ל־ד׳ י׳עשבה ה׳ א

| to the window | next | sat | she |

In relation to English, this line of Hebrew may be indecipherable, but with the translation, students can see that the line is to be read from right to left—a shock to some students, who ask, "How do people decipher languages they don't know?" "Just like they decipher a code," you can answer. "But a code," an unsatisfied tenth grader may say, "is based on a language and a language is based on its conventions, so how do you translate a passage without knowing the conventions of the language?" Good question! As complex as it is, the question is directly connected to cryptography—to the Rosetta Stone, to archeology, and to ancient languages. "You mean there are languages that no one can read?!" Of course! This fact sends students scurrying to the library, where they may try their hand at ancient Aztec. It also leads to the best question of all: "How did language begin?"

This, of course, is the essential question of my approach and, ideally, should precede their inventing their own languages. Before telling them the usual theories—the keeping of records, for example—"How boring!"—and showing them "word signs" (as the writing from Uruk of 3000 B.C. is called), I ask them to come up with their own theories for the invention of writing, along with an example. If they invent a series of units each of which has a meaning and the meaning is visually represented, they are on their way to inventing Chinese, not English—

they are inventing a pictorial as opposed to an alphabetical language. This difference is important. It raises the question, "Is there a way to make a language other than by means of an alphabet?"

I am glad if my students grapple with this question before trying to invent their own languages. My tenth graders came up with "pictures," then "picture ideas, like symbols." I showed them the symbolic drawings of the Hopi Indians, the three stages of Egyptian writing, and finally Chinese. Then I asked them if they wanted to try to invent their own pictorial languages. Many fast starts but many fades. Inventing a pictorial language is hard to do. Yet some students particularly enjoy the effort: they become so involved in creating elaborate systems of pictorial symbols that they almost come to think the English alphabet is boring. In any case, they all come to understand what a remarkable invention the alphabet is.

Inventing languages is extremely helpful in developing students' language skills. Language making consists of first deciding on the conventions, the five fundamental ones listed earlier, and then deciding on further conventions, which students know as the rules of grammar. (Some students invent tense and personal pronouns before they invent nouns and verbs!) When they're ready, I give them a simple sentence to translate into their languages. Whoever cannot do it needs only to invent a rule whereby he or she *can* do it. The farther they go, the better they come to understand English, for it is against English that they are testing their creations.

★   ★   ★

After inventing their own written language, can students read English better? I'm convinced they can. The second part of my approach is to have students read a passage as coded information and try to decipher it. I choose passages that look hard, and I say, "Try to crack them." Students like the challenge, and thus challenged, they are not intimidated by "difficult literature." Instead, they see the writing as just something to decode. When they are successful—which is frequently—they like saying that "advanced writing" isn't so hard. Some students even get interested in the literature for its own sake. I begin by writing these lines on the board:

> Whan that April with his showres soote
> The droughte of March hath perced to the roote,
> And bathed every veine in swich licour,
> of which vertu engendered is the flowr.

I then ask my bewildered students, "Does this passage follow the conventions of English: alphabet, word formation, direction, syntax, and signaling devices? Can you decipher it? Think of conventions as the code of the language."

The class works as a group on the passage line by line; I write the suggested translation possibilities. The syntax is straightforward and the new words fairly easy to guess. After we do the four lines, I give them copies of these four and the next ten and ask them to translate the lines on their own. Despite a few snags, they are usually able to "translate" the basic meaning of the fourteen lines. For the most part, the fact that these lines are the opening of Chaucer's prologue to *The Canterbury Tales* doesn't interest them. The concept of Middle English, however, does. "Is there a Beginning English or Early English?" "Yes, it's called Old English." "What does it look like?" At this point I sometimes ask them to invent their own Middle English, to write an imitation of Chaucer. Some students view this as silly and write something careless, but most don't, and the point is that by writing an imitation of each passage they decipher, students become more sensitive to language.

The next passage I give them is lines 33 through 84 of Book I in *Paradise Lost*. Heavy going? To a literature class, perhaps. To code-breakers, not necessarily. The English is "easier and more modern" than the Chaucer, even though the passage is harder. "It's not the words that are hard," students say, "it's the sentences." To avoid bogging down, we skip the first sentence:

> . . . Him the Almighty Power
> Hurled headlong flaming from the ethereal sky
> With hideous ruin and combustion down
> To bottomless perdition, there to dwell
> In adamantine chains and penal fire,
> Who durst defy th' Omnipotent to arm.

The main problem for one group of my tenth graders was the last line. Where do you put it? They solved the problem by moving the line up between "Him" and "the Almighty Power." Tying the lines together like this was harder than paraphrasing them. So they learned firsthand the syntactical complexity of Milton's poetry. Yet they liked it. I was surprised. I feared they would find Milton more pretentious than glorious. Their pleasure in reading Milton was evident in the imitations they wrote: they picked up on his rhythm and his rich cadences.

A Shakespearean sonnet is next, and then I move to the final challenge: do you think you can decipher a passage that breaks from the conventions of English, if it does so systematically, like the codes you

invented? While they are pondering this question, I give them a copy
of the final lines of Joyce's *Ulysses*, beginning with:

> they might as well stop the sun from rising tomorrow the sun shines for
> you he said the day we were lying among the rhododendrons on Howth
> Head in the gray tweed suit and his straw hat the day I got him to pro-
> pose to me yes I first handed him the bit of seedcake out of my mouth

How does this passage follow or not follow the conventions of
English? Most students enjoy these questions: they like the break with
the convention of signaling devices. They also like the passage, and
they enjoy writing imitations—amidst their jumbled writing may be
some lovely prose. As with Milton, it's a matter of rhythm. Next come
two poems by E.E. Cummings:

Beautiful

is the
unmea
ning
of(sil

ently)fal

ling(e
ver
yw
here)s

now

          ★   ★   ★

l(a

le
af
fa

ll

s)
one
l

iness

Students have fun deciphering these ideogrammatic poems by re-
assembling the words, and they enjoy seeing that the poems are better

not re-assembled. They contend that the word play of the last two lines of the first poem is impossible to render aloud. (They're right.) They also see that, besides "snow" being broken into "s" and "now," the word "everywhere," broken across four lines, produces "here." The last two lines of "here" and "now" echo—in a way students like— a central idea of the poem. In the second poem, Cummings also merges form and meaning. The central idea or image of oneness occurs eight times in nine lines if one counts the "a" of line one and the word "lone-liness."

Then we talk about these poems before taking on the question of how Cummings breaks the conventions of English. He retains the alphabet and the direction from left to right and top to bottom. One student disagreed, saying that these poems read dramatically from top to bottom and only slightly from left to right. A valid distinction— what creates this vertical effect is Cummings's breaking with conventional word formation. With some prodding, students see the connection between Cummings's syntax and his handling of punctuation. Cummings suspends our expectations by using phrasing within parentheses, which adds to the impression of falling—as do the parentheses themselves. So, in fact, Cummings breaks, at least in part, with most of the conventions of English. "But does this make the poem hard to read?" "No, not really," the students answer. Then we each write an imitation of Cummings.

Then I read them this final example, just for fun:

'Twas brillig, and the slithy toves
Did gyre and gimble in the wabe;
All mimsy were the borogoves
And the mome raths outgrabe.

Students know this sounds like nonsense, but at the same time they see that it does follow the conventions of English. One student said that the conventions make it "pretty easy." Others agreed: "It's not hard to make up a meaning for invented words." "'Slithy,'" a student offered, "sounds like 'slimy.' And 'wabe' is close to 'wave.'" The point is not to translate for meaning but rather to demonstrate that meaning is suggested by context. Most nonsense verse has some sense, not no sense. Students have little trouble grasping this.

The purpose of scrutinizing these "Jabberwocky" lines is not to translate the "untranslatable," but to allow students to establish meaning in their own way. They experiment with different words and phrases and then integrate these pieces to come up with a meaning for the whole poem. This means, in essence, that they are exploring the syntactical structure of English. In the process, they learn that no passage following the conventions of the language can be entirely devoid of meaning. Grasping this fact allows them to realize how deeply ingrained in us is the habit of reading for meaning. Their success in translating "difficult" passages from literature and in writing imitations helps them realize that language is more interesting than they thought and that they are "better at it" than they thought. Their new ideas excite them. Inventing their own languages provokes their imaginations and challenges them to understand a system; they may find themselves delving into computer languages, Chinese calligraphy, cryptography, or the genetic code.

Bibliography

Burgess, Anthony. "Creating a Language for Primitive Man," *New York Times Magazine*, November 15, 1981, pp. 102–109. The author of *A Clockwork Orange* tells how he "invented" a language for primitive European man in the movie *Quest for Fire*.

Chadwick, John. *Decipherment of Linear B*. Cambridge, England: Cambridge University Press, 1970.

"Communing with Chaco Canyon's 'Ancient Ones,'" *New York Times*, October 26, 1980, Section 10, pp. 1, 12, and 13. This article about our oldest major primitive settlement includes a picture of a petroglyph.

Gelb, I. J. *A Study of Writing* by New York: Phoenix Books, 1963.

"Genetic Gibberish in the Code of Life," *Science 81*, November, pp. 50-55. Genetic "messages" are written out here as sentences in this article about the new wrinkles in the effort to crack the genetic code.

Herndon, Frank. *How to Survive in Your Native Land*. New York: Simon and Schuster, 1971. Beginning on p. 26, the author describes his excitement as a teacher when he joins his students in making up a pictorial language and sending messages to other classes.

Hofsinde, Robert. *Indian Picture Writing*. New York: William Morrow, 1959.

James, Norman. *Ancestral Voices: Decoding Ancient Languages*. School Book Service, 1975.

Kahn, David. *The Code Breakers: A Story of Secret Writing*. New York: Macmillan, 1967.

Kohl, Herbert. *A Book of Puzzlements*. New York: Schocken Books, 1982. Contains an entire section on pictographic writing and codes.

Laffin, John. *Codes and Cyphers: Secret Writing Through the Ages*. New York: Abelard, 1964.

Lysing, Henry. *Secret Writing: An Introduction to Cryptograms, Cyphers, and Codes*. New York: Dover, 1974.

Norman, Bruce. *Secret Warfare: Battle of Codes and Cyphers*. Washington, D.C.: Acropolis, 1974.

Sanderson, James, and Gordon, Walter, eds. *Exposition and the English Language*. New York: Appleton-Century-Crofts, 1969. This fine collection of essays includes those mentioned in this article: "Gobbledygook" by Stuart Chase, "Politics and the English Language" by George Orwell, and "Revolution in Grammar" by W. Nelson Francis.

Schlauch, Margaret. *The Gift of Tongues*. New York: Modern Age Books, 1942. Still an excellent survey of writing systems and languages.

Waters, Frank. *Book of the Hopi*. New York: Penguin Books, 1977. Within this book about the fascinating Hopi Indians are explanations of the meaning of their drawings or "picture writings" (e.g., pp. 61 and 78).

"Wisdom of Ancient Egypt Comes to Life as Limericks," *New York Times,* August 25, 1981, pp. C1 and C4. The first evidence of the genre of limericks, with examples from Egyptian hieroglyphics.

Wolf, James. *Secret Writing: The Craft of the Cryptographer*. New York: McGraw-Hill, 1970.

Wolff, Dianne. *Chinese Writing: An Introduction*. New York: Holt, Rinehart and Winston, 1975.

Priscilla Alfandre

Inventing Primitive Languages

October 6

Because my third–fourth grade class is studying early man this year, it is a perfect time to study the history of language as well. Today we started with a half-hour discussion about how language might have originated.

I began by saying that (so far as we know) human beings did not always talk, that it is probable that initially they communicated by using gestures and simple sounds, but that as time went on the intricacy of their lives and survival techniques called for the development of words. I asked the children to think about what events or things early man might need words for. They were so excited by these ideas that they all wanted to talk at once. Alan was loudest and quickest, however, and my seizing on his answer made the other students focus on what he said. "To communicate!" was Alan's triumphant contribution. To this I responded, "Yes, indeed! But what would they communicate *about?*" "You'd have to *warn,*" Paul said thoughtfully. "About what?" I asked, and then hypothesized (dramatically) a mother who, twenty-five feet away, saw a cheetah about to leap down from a tree onto her child. If she couldn't indicate what the danger was, she might not be able to get him to run. We imagined ourselves as early nomadic hunters and speculated about the dangers we would have to name in order to save other people's lives: predatory animals, poisonous foods, traps, storms, unexpected abysses, and so forth. (This led to a lengthy discussion about snakes and how it came about that people knew certain animals or foods were dangerous.)

As we talked, I wrote on the board "To communicate about danger" and underneath listed the dangers we had come up with. "What *other* things would have to be communicated?" I asked them. Emily pounced: "To get food!" "Well," I said, pantomiming, "does that mean you'd pull on someone's arm and say, 'Get food! Get food!'?" There was considerable hilarity about this, but Malcolm interrupted by saying,

"You'd have to be able to tell the rest that there were animals nearby which the people could kill for food, and you'd have to tell them where they were. Otherwise you might not get there fast enough with the right weapons." So I added this second category, "getting food," and under it wrote "locating animals" and "the right weapons." Next I suggested that if early people had had to depend on nothing but meat, they might have starved to death when they couldn't find any animals to kill. What else did they eat? Seeds, grasses, fruit, nuts, and roots were suggested, and we decided that these also would have to be located by use of speech, and that some instruction was needed as to how to pick, carry, and store such foods. We returned to the concept of "danger" and concluded that warnings about poisonous foods or dangerous thorns or spines would be an important part of the instruction to others about foods they might gather from plants.

We then considered another exciting and intriguing source for words—weapons and how they were made. Anna Maria observed that life would be a lot easier if they had verbal ways to instruct each other about the best ways to make effective weapons—slingshots, bows and arrows, arrowheads and spearheads, snares and traps. I added that if each person had to figure out how to make each kind of weapon, the process would be very time-consuming—how much better to have an expert *tell* him! This prompted Diana to speculate about the need for communication: cave people must have needed to communicate because they could work more effectively in *groups* than they could on their own.

I pointed out that today we had discovered a lot of reasons why early nomadic hunters would need words and terms—to warn, to locate, to instruct, and to explain. I noted that human beings have always been (glorious new word!) "gregarious," and probably also wanted words to explain how they felt. The children immediately came up with "happy," "sad," "angry," "friendly," along with a whole list of expressions and gestures. Emily mentioned sickness: people would have to express *how* they hurt or felt ill. She asked whether they had any medicines; they would also have to be able to tell which herbs or roots or bindings would be helpful and where to find them.

Time being short, I moved the children on to consider what language would be necessary to the first farmers. This proved to be a rich source for speculation; I was kept busy at the board noting "the right seeds," "preparation of the soil," "watering," "weather," and, suddenly from Randy, "time!" Randy realized it takes different seeds different amounts of time to grow, and quite a long time between sowing and harvesting, no matter what the crop. Carrie suggested that communication would be necessary for the training and keeping of domestic animals—oxen, donkeys, horses. Malcolm exclaimed, "Clothes! They'd have to have words about how to skin animals and make the leather or fur soft and so it would last." "Shelter" and how to build or prepare it was Peter's suggestion.

At this point, the third graders were due at the library, so we had to break up. I would like to continue, either tomorrow or Monday, with some group work on *making* a credible language for the early humans, both hunters and farmers.

★   ★   ★

I spent the rest of our time in the afternoon exploring onomatopoeic sources for words. This related well to our work with word origins, but my primary reason was to get language ideas for a play about the English language that I wanted to write with them. First I worked with the third graders. I told them about the initial scene I had in mind, in which an exuberant group of children decides that language comes directly from the sounds things make. I told them I had planned that one little group of players should act out, "Splash! Ripple, ripple, ripple. Lap . . . lap . . . lap." I said I thought another bunch would act out animals. The students were full of suggestions: lions would "r-r-oar," dogs "bark! bark! bark!," kittens "mew! mew!," frogs "c-r-oak, c-r-oak," ducks "quack! quack!," crickets "chirp, chirp," little birds "peep, peep." John got carried away with all the sound effects and started crowing like a cock, but Peter interrupted him firmly, saying, "No, she wants something that is a sound that got turned into a real *word!*" I was astounded at his perspicacity, and his statement got everything back on track. The children started carefully considering whether these noises had become actual *words* in our language, and we got out the big dictionaries so we could make sure. We went on to the "b-a-a" of sheep and to John's new contribution, the "cackle, cackle, cackle" of hens. Cows do indeed "moo," and snakes "hiss." Owls "hoo-oo-t"; bees "buz-z-z."

When I asked them to think about a storm, they were equally enthusiastic. Lightning "cracks," Nick said. Then "thunder, thunder, thunder" is the sound that follows. Trees and branches "cr-ash." The first great drops of rain "plop, plop, plop," then heavier rain "pitterpatters." High winds "ho-owl" and "roar."

I showed the fourth graders the lists of onomatopoeic words suggested by the third graders, and commented that we still introduce onomatopoeic words into our language as new phenomena appear—

this wasn't just happening in the prehistoric past, it's been happening and will continue to happen. "Think about *cars*," I prompted. They thought about this, and decided that cars "swoosh" and "whiz" by at high speeds; and that they "beep" and "honk" in heavy traffic, and "put-put" as they idle. Old cars and big trucks "chug-chug" as they go up a steep grade. The children noted that we borrow onomatopoeic words from animal and storm contexts, for two, to express other things about cars; cars "roar," "rumble," "screech," and "crash." They "purr" and "buzz" and "hum." Paul did a marvelous imitation of the noise made by a big truck passing, and John imitated the scream of brakes, but Peter reminded them that we were talking about "real words." We decided that cars do indeed "zoom," and a big sportscar does "v-room!" as it takes off.

October 12

As follow-up to the previous week's discussion of onomatopoeia as a basis for language—and to our speculations about the matters that might have prompted language in the first place—we divided the class into three "tribes" to see whether we could develop our own languages. We mixed third and fourth graders, taking care to divide the assertive, articulate leaders as equally as possible among the three groups; we also assigned a teacher to each group. (My aide and I have an extra teacher on Wednesdays, as our intern is in the classroom all of that day.)

Before we started, I read the whole group the narrative notes I had written up on the previous week's session. As these notes complimented all of the children on their intelligent participation and quoted many of their wise observations, we started our work in a glow of self-appreciation and a clearer memory of what we had done in the last session. They were excited and eager to start, and we spent an extraordinarily productive half-hour producing nouns, verbs, and adjectives for communicating about the everyday life of cave people as the children imagined it. The words they suggested were often based on sounds, but also on the feelings certain sounds elicited. For instance, for all three tribes, a lion was called by the noise it makes ("roar!") and the words of all three tribes for deer or antelope ("clik-a-tat" for Tribe #3; "pitter-pat" for Tribe #2; and "clip-clip" for Tribe #1) were based on the sounds of delicate hooves swiftly running. Tribes #2 and #3 made the sound word "s-s-s-s" for snake. The words for other animals were also based on sounds: for Tribe #1, a mammoth was a "bum-bum," and for Tribe #3, a buffalo was a "boom-bah, boom-bah." For Tribe #2, there was a distinction between small birds ("eep-eep") and large ones ("eek"), whereas Tribe #3 decided that all birds were called "Ca! Ca!" All three tribes had words for danger or for warning: Tribe #1 called it "a-ru!"; Tribe #2 had three words, "AH!," "eya!," and "ooh-ooh!"; and Tribe #3 called it "Wa!" All three tribes chose open, shouting sounds that would carry long distances. Because the children were vividly imagining the cave people's experience, such sounds were instinctive for them. Tribe #3, on thoughtful consideration, decided that their warning sound would also mean "bad" in their language.

Tribe #3 made a number of interesting connections of sounds and meaning. They decided that their greeting should be a warm open sound: "Sha!" After their decision to name "bad" things ("wa," also their warning sound), they agreed that "good" should be expressed by the greeting sound, "sha." To express "many" and "few," Tribe #3 felt that "many" should have a luxurious, open sound ("mymah"). "Few," by contrast, should be sharp and thin ("nin"). Having decided that there should be a word for "man" or "mankind," they made the word "immalah," and this led them to "immalini" for "child." They coined words appropriate for a cry of help ("Woonah!"), for cave or shelter ("shonteet"), and for "yonder" or "over there" ("yim").

All three tribes decided on graphic sounds of disgust or nausea for "poisonous." Tribes #1 and #2 expressed it with "ugg!," while Tribe #3 agreed on a gagging sound "n-yah." The words the tribes picked for weapons were interesting, and graphic in different ways. Tribe #1's "thush" expressed both the sound of flight and impact, while Tribe #2's "fing" seemed to express "launch" as well as the sound of flight. Tribe #3 chose "oisch!" to express the impact and penetration of the weapon. As soon as they had chosen "oisch!" for spear, Tribe #3 saw a need for a word for "take" to go with it; "winsch" seemed to them to have the right gathering-in kind of sound.

Some similarities between words made by Tribes #2 and #3 are worth noting; conferring entirely separately, they came up with similar sounds for several concepts. For example, compare Tribe #2's "min" (for "few") and Tribe #3's "nin." Tribe #2 also saw the need for words for "man" and "child," but they went further than Tribe #3, choosing "ums" for "man," "umm" for "woman," "ummie" for "boy," and "ummette" for "girl." It was interesting that Tribe #2, however, developed more terms for general concepts and emotions than the other two tribes. They made a word for "day" or "light," "simph," and "night" or "dark," "dar"; for "cold," "tach," and for "hot," "garbanza." Tribe #2 also made a word for "busy," "do-no," and for "chopping, pulling, and hard labor," "uugh." Tribe #2's literary bent came naturally; their leaders are avid readers, with large vocabularies they use fluently in speaking and writing.

October 19

Today we announced the class' next project—a dialogue to be written by each student, using the language of his or her tribe. I gave each of them a copy of the tribe's language from last week. Each vocabulary had fewer than twenty words, and the children immediately saw the need for more words if they were to write a conversation. They returned to their groups and worked eagerly and ingeniously at adding more words so that they could write their dialogues as homework that night. They added more verbs: words for "find," "kill," "go," "run," "come," "get," "cut," and "see." Pronouns were necessary, positives and negatives, and names for more animals and other foods, like berries and nuts. Again the tribes, although working separately, came up with many words for things that were significantly similar. For instance, "berries" in Tribe #3's language was "lish"; for Tribe #2, it was "ush-ush." For Tribe #1, interestingly, it was "mm-da." Tribe #1, which last week had developed the smallest vocabulary, produced words for essential ideas they had not touched on before—shelter, man and woman, spear, yes and no—which had already been developed by the other two tribes.

Tribe #3 began to produce compound words to express more complex ideas. They decided that they needed a term for "agreed" or "understood." They chose "goolam," and then created its negative form, "ingoolam." They also felt there should be words for "good spirits" and "evil spirits." Going back to their terms for "good" and "bad," they produced "waggah" for "evil," "shageh" for "good." They used their word for "yonder" ("yim") to make a word for "where" ("akyim"). Words for "mine" and "yours" were "hoi" and "yo." Returning to sound-like and feel-like words for the verbs, they developed "chak" for "kill," "kleek" for "cut," "aha" for "find," "gway" for "go."

All of this was particularly exciting for me because the process mirrored so uncannily what language historians have imagined about the development of our Indo-European antecedent language. The similarities and differences among the three separate languages were exactly as visualized by historians—some words identical among three different locales, some words quite different. At the end of this session, the students in all three tribes made sentences in their own languages; the others tried to guess what they meant. Tribe #3's "many" word, unique to them, puzzled the others. They heard "mymah" and interpreted it as "mother." Abstract terms tended to mislead the "foreigners"; the more concrete, generally onomatopoeic words were instantly understood.

The students were all excited about making dialogues in their languages. They had noted down their new vocabulary, and we promised to make up index-card "dictionaries" for them. We discussed the best ways to compose the dialogues. Some felt it would be best to write the dialogue first in English and then translate it; others argued that a more natural conversation would come from using the language directly, composing thoughts and sentences within the framework of the new words.

November 2

Although the dialogues started appearing in my in-box the day after the assignment was made, ERB testing the following week prevented us from devoting class time to them. By today, testing and Halloween and UNICEF were behind us, and we could take a look at the dialogues.

The most successful ones were those written directly in the language; the words fitted together more fluently and articulately, and because the authors had worked within the limits of the existing vocabulary, there was no problem with missing words. Many, however, were bothered by the lack of prepositions and conjunctions; none of the languages had more than one or two. Efforts to write in English and then translate were bedeviled by the lack of complete vocabularies to express ideas and meanings. These could not be performed, for the most part, because they were full of untranslatable English words in parentheses. We tried performing a few, but the single scripts in childish handwritings made it difficult. I promised to xerox several for our next session. The need for a new vocabulary session for each tribe was evident, and the children got to work again. The index-card dictionaries proved unwieldy and inconvenient, and I resolved to ditto each new vocabulary in enough copies so that each student could have one.

Our intern, Kathy Tolan, had planned a trip to the Smithsonian Natural History Museum for the next week, and she suggested that the students should write a script in their own languages for the Neanderthal burial scene that we would see at the end of our "walk through the ages." This idea beautifully integrated three of our classroom objectives: first, the creating of an imaginary Stone Age language; second, research about primitive peoples for our social studies curriculum; and third, Kathy's need for a project that would dovetail with the students' social studies this year.

Summary of Second-semester Work

Each child made a book every year of his or her collected writings for social studies throughout the year; these were revised, recopied, proof-read, and inked before being bound in cardboard covers with a title painted in fancy gilt lettering. Most of our social studies time (and even some math, spelling, and reading time) during the last four weeks has been taken up with frenzied recopying, and inking of all the work that must be included in *"the* book." The triumphant completion of this *magnum opus* was one of the high points of the year.

In March the children decided that they would like to include their stories and dialogues in their tribal languages about the "Burial of a Neanderthal Hunter." This required several more tribal meetings to expand the dictionaries so that the conversations and burial ceremonies they had written in English could be successfully translated into their languages. Conjunctions, prepositions, special nouns, verbs, and adjectives were still needed. This proved difficult and time-consuming, but it became easier as we thought about the sights, materials, and needs of cave people. It was harder to find words for connecting and enhancing the terminology; when they got into the translations, they found that some of their invented words didn't fit well into the flow of spoken sentences, and they had to convene in their tribes again.

Matters of tense and number concerned them: how should they indicate future or past, several or solitary? They decided to state all verbs in the present tense (even when referring to past or future) to save time. The need to communicate clearly—and not necessarily in exactly the ways that English does—made for a very useful and enlightening discussion about how a language could be constructed in order to cover all the possibilities that must be envisaged. The students gained a deeper understanding of English grammar from trying to work out the meaningful constructions of their own. They puzzled long over whether they should make auxiliary verbs, for instance, or whether they would need passive verb forms to express certain meanings properly. They argued over whether they would need object as well as subject pronouns, and decided they should definitely have distinctive possessive pronouns. They realized why prepositions are generally short words, easy to say, and why articles can be important to a language.

When the dictionaries were complete enough to allow full translations, the children had to plan the form of their pieces. They decided that the story of how the hunter died would be a narrative, but that the dialogue at the graveside should be in play form, with the translations given in the tribal language. Writing in play form was difficult for some of the third graders. I typed the dialogues of those who really struggled; they were very pleased with how professional their work looked.

One great effect of creating language was that it made us feel a personal relationship to early man. Imagining landscapes and the activities of primitive peoples, sympathetically envisioning their tragedies and pleasures, their concerns and beliefs, all gave the children insights they would not otherwise have experienced so vividly. In a way, the students *were* the people they studied. They were all prompted to draw pictures of what it must have been like; their dialogues and chants for the graveside ceremony were full of the fears and emotions of the people they were imagining.

During our work, I read to the students from Jean Auel's *Clan of the Cave Bear* and William Golding's *The Inheritors*. These books helped them realize that much early communication was probably in the form of gestures and signs and sometimes possibly took the form (as Golding surmises) of mental telepathy. We discussed this, but we did not devise any gestural language. This might be a fruitful area for theater games and mime studies the next time I work with a group on early man. It would be interesting to see what kind of gesture and sign conventions they might invent to accompany the spoken languages they formulate.

Some Final Thoughts

In retrospect, many of the ways we spontaneously organized our work on this project turned out to be very sound. The division of the class of twenty-two into three small tribes made the work both faster and more interesting. Having an adult assigned to each group—to prompt the children for new ideas, to supervise, and, most importantly, to record the vocabulary as it was formed—also turned out to be valuable. The children needed our knowledgeable observations, side-coaching, enthusiasm, and critical judgments.

The background provided by our social studies work with evolution, primates, and early man was essential. Without clear ideas of what life was probably like for nomad hunters, the children would not have developed such a large vocabulary of appropriate and vivid words. I have always felt (following Gesell's hypotheses) that eight- and nine-year-olds are closer, emotionally and intellectually, to the people of the stone age than they can be at any other age. Their sense of intimate relationship to the hopes and fears of early man, and to the inventions and resourceful adaptations of cave people to their environment, seems to give them an almost telepathic connection with the thoughts and feelings of those peoples. During the times that we were working with our languages, in addition to Golding's and Auel's work, we referred to Richard Leakey's *The Dawn of Mankind* and Richard Attenborough's *Life on Earth,* as well as the Time-Life books on primates, the missing link, and early man. The huge mammals they saw at the Smithsonian, the movies they saw, the replicas of skulls they held in their hands, the arrowheads and hammers they examined, all added to the students' imagination and enthusiasm. If you know, as Robert Claiborne says in *Our Marvelous Native Tongue,* what people needed and how they lived, you know what terms had to be included in their language. Likewise, "If you know the things people talked about, you are bound to know a lot about the things they saw and did, which in turn will reflect where they lived and how they got a living."

The children were imaginative, resourceful, and tremendously interested throughout the whole process. The challenge for the teacher is to maintain their natural spontaneous creativity while making appropriate and prescient modifications and criticisms. With almost no encouragement from me (although I wanted it to happen), my tribe started producing compounds of words they had already created in order to express new ideas. But because I responded enthusiastically or lukewarmly to their suggestions for words, I had a strong influence on their ways of forming their language. When I felt they were exploring directions that might prove unprofitable, or I felt they were not really *thinking* about a new term, I would encourage them to try a new tack or think harder. At the same time, my enthusiasm about their good ideas and my faith in their abilities inspired them to better and greater efforts. The children went about the business of envisioning their languages with high seriousness; this was not just a game. Periodically they looked inside themselves for inspiration: "What would it *really* have been like?"

Questions about tense, gender, and syntax arose naturally during the children's efforts to compose sentences in their languages. By the end of the year all the tribes had established some common rules about how their words were to be used in narratives. (For instance, rather than struggle with creating conjugations for verbs, we decided that—like strangers with only a slight knowledge of the language of a foreign country—we would establish tense by speaking always in the present tense or infinitive including some kind of time reference: "I go tomorrow" or "I go last week." Our pronouns, generally, were single forms: "I" being used for "me" as well, "we" for "us." Our criterion was *meaning*. However, I can imagine, with more work on a language project like this, that the proprietary feeling about their creation might make very careful grammarians out of the students, giving them invaluable insights about their own language and why it is used the way it is.

The most important result of this project was, for me, the uncanny sense of community the students came to feel with their forebears. To make languages for them was like meeting them and talking to them. They became personally involved with the lives of these "friends"; naturally and eagerly they sought to know as much as they could about them. I had never been able to generate this empathy before, although I have been teaching (and deeply interested in) the subject of early man for many years. As Robert Claiborne says, "Language . . . is what makes us human." It is the sense of warmth and humanity that distinguished our studies of early man this year.

★　　★　　★

Burial of a Neanderthal Hunter

As imagined by Paul Delaney, fourth grade

This took place in Japan 70,000 years ago. A Neanderthal family lived there, and the father had just died from being attacked by a vicious saber-tooth cat. The father's name was Heyb, and his wife's name was Herk; his son was called Baba.

At Heyb's burial ceremony, the priest Baryy led the chanting and the singing. They sang a tune that went something like this: "Ashymalletama! Ashymalletama!"

They laid Heyb on a bearskin in a hole they had dug for him in the floor of the burial cave. Then they put food in beside the body. They set up a pyramid of cave bear skulls beside the grave. They put the bearskin and bear skulls there because they hoped the cave bear god would protect Heyb from ferocious animals and enemies in the afterlife. Then the ceremony began:

BARYY: O Wofa Shontee Grawn! Shama yoabwinschin for imma ab coomablooh!
(O Great Cave Bear! Give your protection to this man in the afterlife!)

HERK: O, Shontee Grawn! Abwinsch li naflah woonah-hoya, abwinsch li naflah immawag-gahs. Abwinscha li shanash wallid yo wurra-wurra!
(O Cave Bear! Protect him from danger, protect him from enemies. Keep him warm with your hide!)

BABA *brought* HEYB's *spear and laid it in the grave beside him.*

HERK: Abwinsch yo oisch! Chak r-roars, boombah-boombah, hu-hu-hu-hu-hu, clik-a-tat! O, Grawn, shama li mymahwurra-wurras!
(Keep your spear! Kill lions, buffalo, hyena, and antelope! O, Bear, give him many animal skins!)

Then HERK *brought meat and laid it beside* HEYB.

HERK: Chimchok ab coomablooh.
    (Eat in afterlife.)

Then HERK *brought flowers and laid them in the grave.*

HERK: Winsch lahshah flah hoya.
    (Take flowers for me.)

Then BABA *brought a jug of water for* HEYB.

BABA: Winsch tinga fa coomablooh.
    (Take water to afterlife.)

Then they all said things about him in life.

HERK: Li wofa. Li chak boombah-boombah flah hoya.
    (He was great. He killed buffalo for me.)

BABA: Li woonah hoyo ab farnah, fa oisch boombah-boombah.
    (He helped me on journey, to spear buffalo.)

BARYY: Li woonah immalah dava abshablooh.
    (He helped mankind love life.)

Then they covered his grave and left.

★　　★　　★

Dictionary for the Language of Tribe #3

A
almost, nearly: *umps*
animal skins: *wurra-wurra*
antelope, deer: *clik-a-tat*
arrow: *foom*
afterlife: *coomablooh*
again: *anoo-anoo*

B

bad: *wa*
bear: *grawn*
berries, fruit: *lish*
bird: *Ca! Ca!*
bow: *strek*
buffalo: *boom-bah, boom-bah*
bury: *abshonte*
brother: *beemah*
bone: *calti*

C

cave, shelter: *shontee*
child: *immalini*
come: *coom*
cut: *kleek*
carry: *coomwah*
chief: *immawolfa*

D

dead: *ost*
disagreement: *ingoolam*
drink: *glum*
danger: *woonah-hoya*
dad: *fyma*

E

eat: *chimchok*
evil, evil spirits: *waggah*
enemy: *immawaggah*

F

few: *nin*
find: *ah-ha*
fire: *crik-shoosh*
food: *gahm*
fruit, berries: *lish*
fight: *waggahdaga*
flower: *lahshah*
for: *flah*
from: *naflah*

G

go: *gway*
good: *sha*
ground, dirt: *glunt*
give: *shama*
grow: *shablooh*

H

he: *li*
help!: *woonah!*
hunt: *gritch*
hurt: *eesh*
hyena: *hu-hu-hu-hu-hu*
healthy: *mymasha*

I

in, on: *ab*

J

journey: *farnah*

K

kill: *cha*
knife: *shlit*
keep: *abwinschah*

L

leave behind, abandon: *ha-wah*
lion: *r-roar*
life: *abshablooh*
let: *ama*

M

man: *imma*
mankind: *immalah*
many: *mymah*
me: *hoyo*
mine: *hoi*
meat: *vean*

N

nut: *nang*
no: *nunna*

P
poisonous, poison: *n-yah*
protect: *abwinsch*
protection: *abwinschin*
peace: *shagama*

Q
quick: *tic*
quickly: *tic-tac*

R
run: *padda-padda*

S
spirits: *gah*
see: *cahn*
safe: *abwinschla*
she: *lo*
sister: *shemah*
skull: *kallak*
sky: *skimla*
sleep: *slen*
sick: *ishko*
spear: *oisch*
stop!: *stek!*
storm: *onnya*
steal: *waggah-waggah*
sorrow: *schlimma*
sigh: *speena*

T
take: *winsch*
to: *fa*

U
understood, agreed: *goolam*

W
water: *tinga*
where?: *akyim?*
with: *wallid*
warm: *shanash*
wife: *weemah*
warrior: *imawaggahdaga*
when: *akyi*
we: *lila*

X, Y, Z
yours: *yo*
over there, yonder: *yim*

Ellen Lupton

PERIOD STYLES: A Punctuated History

GREEKANDLATINMANUSCRIPTSWEREUSUALLYWRITTENWITHNOSPACEBETWEENWORDS
UNTIL AROUND THE NINTH CENTURY AD ALTHOUGH·ROMAN·INSCRIPTIONS·LIKE·
THE·FAMOUS·TRAJAN·COLUMN·SOMETIMES·SEPARATED·WORDS·WITH·A·CENTERED·DOT·
EVEN AFTER SPACING BECAME COMMON IT REMAINED HAPHAZARD FOREXAMPLE OFTEN A
PREPOSITION WAS LINKEDTO ANOTHER WORD   EARLY GREEK WRITING RAN IN LINES
ALTERNATING FROM LEFT TO RIGHT AND RIGHT TO LEFT   THIS CONVENTION WAS CALLED
BOUSTREPHEDON MEANING AS THE OX PLOWS   IT WAS CONVENIENT FOR LARGE CARVED
MONUMENTS BUT IT POSED DIFFICULTIES FOR READING AND WRITING HANDWRITTEN TEXTS
AND SO THE LEFT TO RIGHT DIRECTION BECAME DOMINANT   A CENTERED DOT DIVID·
ED WORDS WHICH FELL AT THE END OF A LINE IN EARLY GREEK AND LATIN MANUSCRIPTS AND
THE MORE VISUALLY·DISTINCT HYPHEN WAS INTRODUCED IN THE ELEVENTH CENTURY
MEDIEVAL SCRIBES OFTEN PUT MARKS AT THE END OF SHORT LINES TO MAKE A SOLID TEXT ‡§°∷⁊]
THE PERFECTLY JUSTIFIED LINE BECAME THE STANDARD AFTER THE INVENTION OF PRINTING
THE EARLIEST GREEK LITERARY TEXTS WERE DIVIDED INTO UNITS WITH A SHORT HORIZONTAL
LINE CALLED A PARAGRAPHOS   PARAGRAPHING REMAINS OUR CENTRAL FORM OF ORGANIZING
PROSE AND YET ALTHOUGH PARAGRAPHS ARE ANCIENT THEY ARE NOT GRAMMATICALLY
NECESSARY   THE CORRECTNESS OF A PARAGRAPH IS AN ISSUE OF STYLE WITHOUT STRICT RULES
LATER GREEK DOCUMENTS SOMETIMES MARKED PARAGRAPHS BY PLACING THE FIRST LETTER OF
THE NEW LINE IN THE MARGIN   THIS LETTER WAS OFTEN ENGLARGED COLORED OR ORNATE
TODAY THE OUTDENT IS OFTEN USED IN LISTS WHOSE ITEMS ARE IDENTIFIED ALPHABETICALLY AS
IN DICTIONARIES OR BIBLIOGRAPHIES ¶ A MARK CALLED CAPITULUM WAS INTRODUCED IN EAR-
LY LATIN MANUSCRIPTS ¶ IT IS RELATED TO THE PARAGRAPH SIGN USED TODAY ¶ IT USUALLY OC-
CURRED INSIDE A RUNNING BLOCK OF TEXT WITHOUT BREAKING ONTO A NEW LINE ¶ THIS
TECHNIQUE SAVED SPACE ¶ IT ALSO PRESERVED THE VISUAL UNITY OF THE TEXT BY MAKING THE
PAGE INTO A CONTINUOUS LINEAR STREAM SIMILAR TO THE UNBROKEN FLOW OF SPEECH
    BY THE SEVENTEENTH CENTURY THE INDENT HAD BECOME THE MOST COMMON PARAGRAPH
BREAK IN WESTERN PROSE   THE INDENT DIVIDES THE TEXT INTO VISUALLY APPARENT UNITS
THUS ALLOWING THE READER TO PERCEIVE ITS BASIC STRUCTURE IN A GLANCE   AN INDENT IS
MORE ABSTRACT THAN A CAPITULUM BECAUSE IT IS A BLANK SPACE NOT A PHYSICAL MARK

| propter diuerfas rationes nuptias cor.trahere probi bentur quas i libeis dige florum feu pandectarum ex neteri iure collectarū enumerari permiffimus Sci aduerfus ea que di | bũc cafũ pofuit õ nu. p'.tti.õ pfia pê-tate. bſ⌐x.ulgo.f.q pfrm ŏrmõftrare fi pofſũt f illicitũ ut.ff.õ fta. bo.uulgo. cſ⌐Bec bũ.f.uulgo ɔcepti f vic bũ õqbˀ løgf.f.illicite cõcep. dſ⌐Jncert' ē cnt | s.que calul õecreto₂₂/vel lumarij crebro uan q̃ plura eifde paleis õecreta fcripta ₂₃ loco õcbite locatif.cumq₃ glofa oedina ria.atq₃ addicõib₃ õni Bartholomei bri: :ónu lrĩs capitalib₃/et caufarũ imicijs.ad b)õepingedo,cafu/fpada õmutmmur fa: lro õcrotales cũ clofa oedmari 1 õni bri: |

---

† Early printed book containing the "capitulum," origin of the modern paragraph symbol. Here this mark is used to key marginal notes (1478).

‡ Early German printed book in which the light linear punctuation contrasts with the heavy gothic text. The diagonal slash, called a virgule, later became shorter and developed a curve, like the modern comma (1472).

EVEN AFTER THE ASCENDENCE OF THE INDENT THE CAPITULUM REMAINED IN USE FOR IDENTIFYING SECTIONS AND CHAPTERS ALONG WITH OTHER MARKS LIKE THE SECTION § THE
† DAGGER † THE DOUBLE DAGGER ‡ THE ASTERISK * AND NUMEROUS LESS CONVENTIONAL OR-NAMENTS SUCH MARKS HAVE BEEN USED SINCE THE MIDDLE AGES FOR CITING PASSAGES AND KEYING MARGINAL REFERENCES PRINTING MADE MORE COMPLEX NUMERICAL NOTES POSSIBLE BECAUSE THE PAGES OF THE TEXT WERE CONSISTENT FROM ONE COPY TO THE NEXT

PUNCTUATION SERVES TO GOVERN THE INTERIOR OF A TEXT AS WELL AS ITS FORMAT THE LIBRARIAN AT ALEXANDRIA WHO WAS NAMED ARISTOPHANES DESIGNED A GREEK PUNCTUA-TION SYSTEM CIRCA 260 BC HIS SYSTEM MARKED THE SHORTEST SEGMENTS OF DISCOURSE WITH A CENTERED DOT·CALLED A COMMA·AND MARKED THE LONGER SECTIONS WITH A LOW DOT CALLED A COLON. A HIGH DOT SET OFF THE LONGEST UNIT·HE CALLED IT PERIODOS·THE THREE DOTS WERE EASILY DISTINGUISHED BECAUSE ALL THE LETTERS WERE THE SAME HEIGHT·PROVIDING A CONSISTENT FRAME OF REFERENCE FOR THE DOTS.

THE SYSTEM OF ARISTOPHANES IS THE BASIS FOR THE MODERN COMMA·COLON. AND PERIOD·WHOSE FORMS WERE ESTABLISHED BY THE SEVENTEENTH CENTURY·IN THE LATE MID-
‡ DLE AGES THE VIRGULE/A THIN/DIAGONAL SLASH STILL USED AS A FRACTION BAR AND AN EITHER/OR SIGN/WAS OFTEN USED TO INDICATE SHORT PAUSES/AND IT EVENTUALLY SANK AND DEVELOPED A CURVE, LIKE THE MODERN COMMA, WHILE A VERTICAL PAIR OF DOTS CAME TO MARK THE COLON: THE PERIOD BECAME A POINT RESTING ON THE LINE.
* § THE SEMICOLON WAS INTRODUCED IN THE SEVENTH CENTURY; THE INVERTED SEMICOLON APPEARED IN THE EIGHTH CENTURY: CONTEMPORARY WITH THE QUESTION MARK. IT IN-DICATED A PAUSE·; HALFWAY BETWEEN THE COMMA AND THE SEMICOLON; THE INVERTED SEMICOLON HAD FALLEN OUT OF USE BY THE MID FIFTEENTH CENTURY. THE EXCLAMATION POINT, WHICH HAS A SIMILAR DOTTED FORM, WAS RARE BEFORE THE RENAISSANCE!

ARISTOPHANES TOOK HIS TERMS FROM THE THEORY OF RHETORIC, IN WHICH COMMA, COL-ON, AND PERIODOS REFER TO RHYTHMICAL UNITS OF SPEECH. THUS EARLY PUNCTUATION WAS LINKED TO ORAL DELIVERY. IT WAS CONSIDERED RHETORICAL, RATHER THAN GRAMMATICAL, AND IT REGULATED PACE AND GAVE EMPHASIS TO PARTICULAR PHRASES, RATHER THAN MARK-ING THE FUNDAMENTAL LOGICAL STRUCTURE OF A PASSAGE. MANY OF THE PAUSES IN RHETOR-

)ISI RESERATÁ QUAL,ITER A
INE FINE EXUL,TERIS;ĆTI
OCO QENTURA CI PREDIX
JUIANEPASTUUS ÇODOSE
URUSERITTEDI;HAEC AL

)er habuiſſe, quo alerétur: quid eſt enin
nagnum ipſi magiſtrae rerum omniū
t parenti naturae? quid arduum ; quic
lla tandem non poteſt? qui ſtellas; qu
olem; qui coeli coniuexa; qui terras o·
nnes, ac maria; qui mundum deniq; iſ

* Text which includes the semicolon, colon, and period, as well as the inverted semicolon, which marked a pause halfway between the comma and semicolon (8th century AD). Note that this text is written entirely in capital letters and has minimal word spacing.

* In this printed text of 1495, the question mark, semicolon, and inverted semicolon are similar in size and shape; today the scale of the question mark is like that of a letterform, while other marks are very small.

ICAL DELIVERY, HOWEVER, NATURALLY CORRESPOND WITH GRAMMATICAL STRUCTURE: FOR EX-AMPLE, WHEN A PAUSE FALLS BETWEEN TWO CLAUSES OR SENTENCES.

ALTHOUGH IT WAS RARELY USED BY THE GREEKS, THE SYSTEM OF ARISTOPHANES WAS REVIV-ED BY THE LATIN GRAMMARIAN DONATUS IN THE FOURTH CENTURY A.D. ACCORDING TO DONATUS PUNCTUATION SHOULD FALL WHEREVER THE SPEAKER WOULD NEED A REST, PRO-VIDING BREATHING CUES FOR READING ALOUD. OFTEN THE MARKS WOULD FALL AT SOME STRUCTURAL POINT, LIKE THE END OF A CLAUSE OR SENTENCE, WHERE A BREATH WOULD NOT BE DISTRACTING. THIS STRUCTURAL ASPECT, HOWEVER, WAS NOT ESSENTIAL TO THE SYSTEM.

THE THEORIES OF DONATUS WERE GRADUALLY MODIFIED BY LATER WRITERS, WHO AD-VOCATED AN INCREASINGLY RHETORICAL USE OF PUNCTUATION, TO CONTROL THE RHYTHM OF READING AND TO EMPHASIZE PARTICULAR WORDS AND PHRASES. AFTER THE INVENTION OF PRINTING, GRAMMARIANS BEGAN BASING PUNCTUATION ON SYNTAX RATHER THAN ON SPOKEN SOUND: IT MARKED THE GRAMMATICAL STRUCTURE OF A SENTENCE. PUNCTUATION CAME TO BE DEFINED ARCHITECTURALLY RATHER THAN ORALLY. THE COMMA BECAME A MARK OF SEPARA-TION, THE SEMICOLON FUNCTIONED AS A JOINT BETWEEN TWO INDEPENDENT CLAUSES, AND THE COLON BECAME A MARK OF GRAMMATICAL DISCONTINUITY. SLOWLY WRITING WAS BECOM-ING DISTANCED FROM SPEECH.

RHETORIC, STRUCTURE, AND BREATHING ARE ALL AT WORK IN MODERN ENGLISH PUNCTUA-TION, WHOSE RULES WERE MORE OR LESS ESTABLISHED BY THE END OF THE EIGHTEENTH CEN-TURY. ALTHOUGH STRUCTURE IS THE STRONGEST RATIONALE, PUNCTUATION REMAINS A LARGE-LY INTUITIVE ENTERPRISE. A WRITER CAN OFTEN CHOOSE AMONG SEVERAL CORRECT WAYS TO PUNCTUATE A PASSAGE, EACH WITH A SLIGHTLY DIFFERENT RHYTHM AND MEANING.

THERE WAS NO CONSISTENT MARK FOR QUOTATIONS BEFORE THE SEVENTEENTH CENTURY. ANCIENT GREEK TEXTS USED THE PARAGRAPHOS TO SHOW CHANGES IN DIALOGUE. DIRECT SPEECH WAS USUALLY CONSIDERED TO BE ANNOUNCED SUFFICIENTLY BY PHRASES LIKE HE SAID. „THE DOUBLE COMMA WAS INITIALLY USED TO POINT OUT IMPORTANT SENTENCES AND WAS " LATER USED TO ENCLOSE QUOTATIONS. ELIZABETHAN PRINTERS OFTEN EDGED BOTH MARGINS " " OF A QUOTED TEXT WITH DOUBLE COMMAS. THIS CONVENTION TREATED TEXT AS A SPATIAL " " PLANE RATHER THAN A TEMPORAL LINE, FRAMING THE QUOTED PASSAGE LIKE A PICTURE. "

A a B b C c D d E e F f G g H h I i J j K k L l M m N n O o P p Q q

1 nuſpitꝰquáꝛꝯ parꝯú inpꝏꝺi · Al ꝯꝛꝼaꞡꝛꝯꝰꝛ maꞇuꞃa ꝯuꝼ·quani ꝼ oꝛꝯunam uirꝯuꝯꝯꝰdomaſ cuꞇc 1 m ꝑꝯꝛꝼ· quiſꝯꝯſoꝉꝯ ꝼꝼꞇꝯoniſ ꝫ	cum etiam Cęſar rebus maximis geſtis ſinȷ ac iudiciis Senatus ad auctoritatem eius o ciui locus ad rem publicam molandam eſ ſint conſecuta. Primum illa furta muliebr fecerat bonam deam ꝗ tris foroꝛes impuni Qui cum Tribunus plebis pęnas aſediti perſequi uellet: exemplum pręclariſſimur

† In this text, written in the classical script called Carolingian, the majuscule is paired with the miniscule to make a formal beginning for each line (circa 10th century AD).

‡ The design of this roman typeface is based on Carolingian handwriting; classical roman capitals are paired here with the miniscule letters (1469).

† BOTH THE GREEK AND ROMAN ALPHABETS WERE ORIGINALLY MAJUSCULE: ALL LETTERS WERE THE SAME HEIGHT. greek and roman minuscule letters developed out of rapidly written scripts called cursive, which were used for business. minuscule characters have limbs extending above and below a uniform body height. alcuin, advisor to charlemagne, introduced the carolingian minuscule, which spread rapidly through europe during the flowering of scholarship which began in the 8th century a.d. and culminated around the twelfth century. during the spread of the carolingian script, condensed, black minuscule scripts, now called "gothic," were also developing; they eventually replaced the classical carolingian.

a carolingian manuscript sometimes marked the beginning of a sentence with an enlarged letter. This character was often a majuscule, presaging the modern use of minuscule and majuscule as double features of the same alphabet. Both scripts were still fundamentally separate modes of handwriting, however.

‡ In the fifteenth century, the Carolingian script was revived by Italian intellectuals known as "humanists." The new script, called "lettera antica," was paired with classical roman capitals. It became the basis of the roman typefaces, which were established as a European norm by the mid-sixteenth century. The terms "uppercase" and "lowercase" refer to the drawers in a printing shop that hold the two fonts. Until recently, Printers liberally Capitalized the initials of any word They deemed worthy of Distinction, as well as Proper Names. In modern German Writing the First Letter of every Noun is marked with a Capital.

§ The roman typefaces were based on a formal script, used for books. *The cursive, rapidly written version of the Carolingian minuscule was employed for business and also for books in the less expensive writing shops. Called "antica corsiva" or "cancelleresca," this kind of handwriting was the model for the italic fonts cut for Aldus Manutius in Venice in 1500. Aldus was a scholar, a printer, and a very successful businessman. Italic script conserved space, and Aldus developed it for his internationally distributed series of small, inexpensive books. Following its handwritten model, the Aldine italic used roman capitals. Tagliente advocated the use of italicized capitals in the early sixteenth century.*

§ The space-saving Aldine italic above is paired with roman capitals, as in the earlier Carolingian handwritten text at left (late 15th/early 16th c.).

* *Fat Face*, designed in 1810, is an early display type. Later boldface fonts would be integrated into unified type "families" which include roman, italic, and bold variations of a single letter style.

In modern American grammar schools, students are taught two styles of handwriting manuscript, reserved for official or artistic purposes, and *cursive, for everyday rapid* *writing. The distinction between* manuscript *and cursive handwriting is an ancient con* *vention based on practical needs.* The typewriter, invented in the late nineteenth cen tury, has replaced cursive writing for all but the most casual or intimate func tions. Most standard fonts are based on manuscript: *a few are based on cursive.*

Aldus set entire books in italic; it was an autonomous type style, unrelated to roman In France, however, roman faces were becoming a standard, and *italic wa* gradually subordinated to the roman. Roman was the neutral, generic norm with *italic* played against it for contrast. The pairs UPPERCASE/lowercase and roman/*italic* each add an inaudible, non-phonetic dimension to the alphabet

Before italic became the official auxiliary of roman, scribes and printer had other techniques of emphasis, including enlarged, **heavy,** colored, o gothic letters. Underlining was common in medieval manuscripts, and it remain the conventional substitute for italics in handwritten and typewritten texts. Th insertion of s p a c e between important letters is used for e m p h a s i s i

* German and Eastern European book t y p o g r a p h y. **Boldface** fonts were no common until the nineteenth century, when display advertising created a de mand for big, black types. Most book faces cut since the early twentieth centur belong to families of four: roman, *italic,* **bold roman,** and ***bold italic.*** These are u ed for systematically marking different kinds of copy, like headings, caption body text, notes, quotations, and references. For modernist book designers lik Jan Tschichold, Carl Gerstener, and Massimo Vignelli, changes in typographi size, style, color, and spacing should construct a consistent, meaningful pattern These parameters build a secondary system of "punctuation" on top of the basi conventions of writing. What effects might the computer have on writing in th future? Although conventions like the left-to-right line are unlikely to change, th spatial organization of texts could become more elaborate as variations i typeface, color, size, and column arrangement become trivially available.

John Oliver Simon

Poetry across Frontiers

In February of 1986, John Oliver Simon and Roberto Bedoya, two poets from Oakland, California, spent a week in Mexico City teaching poetry writing, with local poets, to elementary school children. In April, three colleagues from the Mexican residency (poets Jorge Lujan, Juvenal Acosta, and Roberto García Moreno) returned the visit, working with children in Oakland. The program was sponsored by California Poets in the Schools and the National Museum of Anthropology in Mexico City. This is the first such international exchange we know of, and is documented in Un techo del tamaño del mundo/A Roof the Size of the World *(see the bibliography at the end of this essay). In the excerpts below, Simon translated the children's poetry, most of which was written in Spanish.*—Editor

In most cases, we began talking about the concept of Flower and Song, "flor y canto," the *xochitl in cuicatl* of the Aztecs. We pointed out that the Aztec codices show an unadorned word coming out of the mouth of a king or a god to indicate ordinary speech; but when the word that emerges from the mouth is decorated with flowers, that is poetry. "The flowered word" mediated between man and the universe, between the community and the gods. In order to create this "palabra florida," we must employ the imagination: that faculty within us that makes images, makes pictures, fantasizes, and travels beyond the confines of logic and the classroom. In poetry, we play with words, as if words were as light as petals and feathers, as if what we say had as much meaning as the songs of birds.

Acrostics (Roberto Bedoya)

This introductory exercise uses a name of a person or a thing as a skeleton on which to hang a poem. The trick is to integrate a little narrative or play of ideas without creating a choppy phrase for each letter.

Roberto tiene el pelo
Oscuro como un conejo negro
Brincando sobre las montañas
Enloquiéndose al encontrar su comida como unos
Rábanos
Tirados sobre la
Oscuridad.

—*German Herrera Suárez*

Roberto has dark
hair like a black rabbit
leaping on the mountains
going crazy to find his food like some
radishes
thrown into
darkness.

—*German Herrera Suárez*

Questions (John Oliver Simon)

This exercise takes off from Pablo Neruda's posthumous collection *El libro de las preguntas (The Book of Questions)*. "What distance in round numbers / is there between the sun and the oranges?" "Why couldn't Christopher Columbus / discover Spain?" "How many weeks in a day / and how many years in a month?" The assignment is to write a poem composed completely of questions. Few of these succeeded as a whole poem, but some of the individual questions are arresting.

How long does it take a burro to climb a building?

—*Carlos Enrique Jiménez Hernández*

What size clothes does the sun wear?

—*Jorge Enrique Mejia Rosas*

Lies to Quetzalcoatl (John Oliver Simon)

In the gallery devoted to the sacred city of Teotihuacan in the Museo Nacional, there is an impressive reconstruction of the Pyramid of Quetzalcoatl, adorned with seashells representing water; the goggle-eyed masks of Tlaloc, god of the rain; and the fierce plumed heads of the Feathered Serpent. These are so huge that you can stick your arm up to the shoulder in the mouth of the god. Legend has it that if you

do so and then tell a lie, CHOMP! Quetzalcoatl will bite off your arm.
The assignment, then, was to tell lies to Quetzalcoatl—with the ultimate paradox in mind that a good lie can be more true than the truth.

Quetzalcoatl, god of water,
of song and fire.
His pyramid has a thousand
heads of birds and water
issues from those heads,
at night the moon comes by
and dances with the sun and
fifty rabbits play
a jazz song,
while some burros
fire rockets.

—*Gabriel Gutiérrez García*

★ ★ ★

Quetzalcoatl God of water
lion full of dove's feathers.
Soul of steel God of the universe
passionate for love but
if anyone does something to him
he is fierce with warrior's blood
his pyramid full of hearts
with shells and fish.

—*Esmerelda Hernández Mendoza*

★ ★ ★

I am the god
of dance and my fangs
sing, I have tiny fangs
like hands
with my yellow mouth
I say colored words
and when I fall
to earth I change
the words to music
I look upon music
and dance everywhere
and inside of me
there is dance and music
and men surrender
themselves to me

my secret saying is:
rhythm and horror
give rhythm to the horror.

—*Israel Bautista*

Haiku (Jorge Lujan)

In Mexico, the first and third lines of haiku usually rhyme. Juan José Tablada, whose home in Coyoacan is preserved as a national shrine, was the best known *haikuista* of Mexico. He writes:

Tierno saúz
casi oro, casi ambar,
casi luz . . .

Tender willow,
almost gold, almost amber
almost light . . .

Jorge Lujan's haiku recipe with fourth graders neither rhymed nor counted syllables:
1. First line: something usual
2. Second line: something that happens quickly, at once
3. Tie them together, wrap it up, what does it all mean, what happens next?

My desk is always messy.
I shut my desk and left.
Then my desk is clean and I'm messy.

—*Lorena García*

★　　★　　★

The street is dark
people go along the street
and people scare the darkness.

—*José Miranda*

Hymn to the Sun (John Oliver Simon)

On their first day in the National Museum, the children seated themselves in the outdoor auditorium and were greeted with the invitation to write a *bienvenida* (welcome) to the sun. Children contributed one line apiece, orally, while poet Alberto Blanco acted as the group scribe. After a while Otto-Raúl Gonzalez suggested we stop saying what the sun does and simply address it: "Hot mass! Giant orange! Balloon of fire covering us with light!" Then Alberto suggested we ask the sun questions (following up on the previous Neruda/Questions exercise). Finally I noted that we had covered three manuscript pages and it was time to begin seeking a way out of the poem. Subliminally, or rather through process, the idea of a poet's strategy within the poem was conveyed. What surprised us was how *pre-hispanic* the poem was, even in the absence of specific suggestions or stimuli to that effect.

Hymn to the Sun

Hi!
Hi, friend!
How are you?
You who shine
and give us light all morning
and illumine the Mexican earth
—our country—;
you who say goodbye to us
with rays at evening.
Your heat and brilliance
give us joy and enthusiasm
for work.

We can't look at you directly
but we see you in the mind
with the eyes closed.
You who illumine
all the corners of the world,
at evening
you seem to be covered with blood.
You who make us wait
for the fresh morning,
from some places
you let yourself be seen often.
You are really our friend.

And when someone is sick
you make him better the next morning.
You who give the plants light
and make the trees green again,
you who warm
the water of the pool
you truly give us life.
You who make shine
the water of the sea,

you also make the rainbow appear
which feeds us with happiness
every time we see it.

Hot mass!
Giant orange!
Balloon of fire covering us with light!
A giant ball!

Why do you never fall to earth?
Why can't we look at you directly?
Why do you hide every night?
Why can't we see you all day?

Did you ever catch cold
And where do you sleep at night?
Why can't we touch you?
Why don't you ever move?

You who dominate the whole city,
may you never cease to shine,
because for us you are everything;
there is no one like you.

Goodbye religious star!
So long friend of light!
You are a golden dragon
and your shining amazes us.
That is all we can think.
Never cease to be our friend.
Goodbye, comrade of the soul!

Emerge from the Animal (John Oliver Simon)

Every Mesoamerican culture shows a preoccupation with the motif of
the god or hero who emerges from the mouth of a beast. Tezcatlipoca,
the tempter, comes out of a tiger's mouth (or wears a tiger's skin, revealing only his face); Quetzalcoatl is born out of the jaws of a serpent.
A masterpiece of Toltec art shows a bearded warrior coming out of the
mouth of a coyote encrusted with abalone and mother-of-pearl. The
Aztec eagle knight wears the eagle mask, and the tiger knight is dis-
guised as a jaguar. Kukulcan, at Uxmal, comes out of a snake's jaws,
while the anonymous earth goddess of the Huastecas appears in the beak
of a parrot. Standing outdoors in the door of the Temple of Chac, outside the Mayan Hall—and thus in the mouth of a monster animal-god
of the rain—I gave the assignment: what animal is inside you, what

animal comes out of you, or out of what animal do you emerge? The heavens responded: it began to rain as the children wrote their poems.

The Tiger

The tiger is an animal
that only has two lives,
one inside me
and the other in the body of space.

   —*Soledad Funes*

★   ★   ★

What's inside Me

A while ago I discovered
that I had
a cat inside me
because when they
treat me well I'm
affectionate, understanding,
loving, but when
they mistreat me I
get mad and behave
differently than usual
I behave badly,
I'm dense, difficult,
just
like a rooster, that's why
I said what I had
inside me because
unfortunately today
I discovered that I don't have
anything inside me.

   —*Claudia Uribe García*

★   ★   ★

Chac

Chac is raining, Chac is crying
raining loosens his sadness, out of an animal,
discharging his fury weeping,
finally, we all came out of an animal

   —*Juan Sosa*

★   ★   ★

Coyote Knight

It's a man swallowed by the imagination of a Toltec.

—*Jamsré Torres*

Songs of the Animals (Roberto Bedoya)

Using a model poem written by a fourth grader in California, we asked the children to write about animals, using colors, seasons, and the five senses.

> In my heart lives a horse
> that horse says to me
> come and I'll take you to the country
> get up on me and you'll see
> how much fun we will have
> galloping and jumping.
>
> —*Azahel Estudillo*

★   ★   ★

My Hen

> My hen
> my hen
> is mine
> is mine
> on her little path
> on her little path
> goes into the night
> the hen is mine
> the hen is mine
> there are lots and lots
> there's no other like mine
>
> —*Francisco Morales Rosas*

The Singing Shoes (several poets)

The rhythms of the *lirica infantil* of Mexico are as alive to recent immigrant children in the U.S. as Mary-had-a-little-lamb is to standard-culture Americans. The accents of the *corrido* and *mariachi* are as alive in the inner ear as the latest rap from the ghetto blaster. And what about the other rhythms of life, the shoes slapping, the galaxies revolving, red and green and yellow lights, dusk and dawn, birth and death?

Bark

When the mailman
comes by I hear a
bark when the newspaper
boy comes by I hear
a bark I'm tired of
hearing sounds that go
bark bark bark I'm tired
of it because I'm trying
to sleep when the garbage
man comes the barks get
even louder so I have
to buy a gun and
waste my money and
on every Tuesday I have
to kill the garbage man so I
can sleep. But this goes
on and on. But one day
I might be in jail
for killing the garbage man
but the dogs will still
go bark, bark, bark
and bark.

    —*Gilbert Vega*

        ★   ★   ★

Little Coyote Coyote

Little coyote coyote
where are you going?
To the hacienda of Saint Nicholas
and there I will
eat a little hen
that you won't give me
and the one that you gave me
I already ate
and the one you will give me
I will eat
how do you like it
fried or roasted?
fried
so heat up the butter
so heat up the butter

    —*Guadalupe Jiménez*

★   ★   ★

Shoes Singing

I went to school
shoes singing rapidly
I went to open the door
shoes singing rapidly
I went to the dance
shoes singing rapidly
I couldn't stand it already and
shoes singing rapidly
I stood out on a mountain
and shoes singing rapidly
I threw them in the garbage
and they sang more rapidly
they said you're getting mad
you're getting mad
you're getting mad

    —Ricardo Ahumada

Letter to Mexico (Roberto García Moreno and others)

Within Chicano children, there is a complex magnetic image of
Mexico. They felt a special connection to the dramatic disaster of the
earthquake that shook Mexico City, September 19, 1985. They like
the idea of writing letter-poems that can actually be sent to Mexican
children.

For my friend far away,

The wind in Oakland is like
a blue bird with wings
a thousand meters long.
The wind in Oakland forms
the trees, some are like winged
crocodiles, others like
falling squirrels.
In my neighborhood the cats'
eyes explode at night like
rockets going up afire
into space.
The houses in my neighborhood
are like castles, at night
above the castles a flashlight

goes out to look
for lost princesses.
Here in Oakland
peoples' smiles are
flavor of mango,
some people smile because
they see dinosaurs in the street.
My smile is like
the city of Mexico.
Kindness has many colors here:
blue, green and yellow
and smells of strawberries
and is big as the moon.

—*Collaboration*

The Memory of Poetry (Roberto Bedoya)

After working with a poet, children report that their ways of looking have changed. "It took the real me out of my body." "It showed you how to get ideas from ordinary things." "Poetry is about a person that wonders around." At the end of the workshop, Roberto Bedoya asked his students at La Escuelita in Oakland to write about the power and meaning of poetry.

The Power of Poetry

I was listening to music.
It sounded like violins playing with trumpets.
I was in an angry mood.
All I had to do was pick up a pencil and start writing;
It sounded better than anything I heard.
I could hear the music echoing in my head.
All I did was pick up a pencil and start writing
what came to my head.
When I was done I would change the world a little bit.
And there was music waiting to be heard.
It's not like music where you turn it into a record
so people can play it.
It's like fun homework just by picking up a pencil
and start writing.
And there was my music.

—*Alma Martínez*

Annotated Bibliography for Teaching Poetry in Spanish

Un techo del tamaño del mundo: A Roof the Size of the World, ed. John Oliver Simon (Oakland, Calif.: Oakland Unified School District, 1987). Documentary of an international poetry-teaching exchange between California Poets in the Schools and the National Museum of Anthropology in Mexico City. Bilingual text with forty writing exercises and hundreds of student poems from Mexico and Oakland. To order, send $10 to John Oliver Simon, 2209 California, Berkeley, CA 94703.

Light from a Nearby Window: Contemporary Mexican Poetry, ed. Juvenal Acosta (San Francisco: City Lights, 1993). Important anthology of twenty Mexican poets born since 1945.

Diccionario de la imaginación, ed. Jorge Lujan (Mexico City: Taller Nacimiento, 1986). Jorge Lujan independently invented the idea of poetry teaching in a private workshop in Mexico. His students, ranging from seven to twelve years old, have produced superb poems. Spanish text. To order, send international money order for $10.00 to Jorge Lujan, Av. Arteaga y Salazar 446, Casa 5, Colonia Contadero Cuajimalpa, Mexico DF, 05500, Mexico.

La Luciérnaga: Antología para niños de la poesía mexicana contemporánea, ed. Francisco Serrano with illustrations by Alberto Blanco (Mexico City: Editorial Cidcli, 1983). A comprehensive and delightful collection of twentieth-century Mexican poetry chosen for children, with magnificent collages by Blanco. Spanish text. This anthology is generally available in better bookshops in Mexico City, and can probably be ordered through Spanish-language distributors such as Bookworks in San Francisco.

In Xochitl in Cuicatl: Flor y Canto: La poesía de los Aztecas by Birgitta Leander (Mexico City: Instituto Nacional Indigenista, SEP, 1972). The "flower and song" poetry of the Aztecs is fundamental to the deep culture of Mexican and Chicano children. Nahuatl texts are available in Spanish and English for the teacher who's willing to hunt through libraries and bookstores. Some pre-Columbian texts are translated (into English) in Jerome Rothenberg's anthologies *Technicians of the Sacred* and *Shaking the Pumpkin*.

Antología de la poesía hispanoamericana, ed. Juan Gustavo Cobo Borda (Mexico City: FCE, 1985); *Antología de la poesía hispanoamericana actual,* ed. Julio Ortega (Mexico City: siglo ventiuno, 1987); and *Poesía Mexicana II: 1915–1979,* ed. Carlos Monsiváis (Mexico City: Promexa Editores, 1979). There is no shortage of excellent anthologies in Spanish of modern Latin American poetry. The North American teacher who wants to use these books in a bilingual classroom must first find the books, and then sort through the poetry to find works that are appropriate and accessible to children. A daunting task.

Poets of Nicaragua 1918–1979: A Bilingual Anthology, translated by Steven F. White (Greensboro, N.C.: Unicorn Press, 1982), and *Poets of Chile 1960–1985: A Bilingual Anthology,* also translated by Steven F. White (Greensboro, N.C.: Unicorn Press, 1986). These excellent anthologies make available the important recent and contemporary poetry of Nicaragua and Chile in facing bilingual format. There are many gems here that can be used in the classroom. Highly recommended.

A Nation of Poets: Writings from the Poetry Workshops of Nicaragua, translated with an introduction by Kent Johnson (Los Angeles: West End Press, 1985); and *Nicaraguan Peasant Poetry from Solentiname,* translated by David Gullette (Los Angeles: West End Press, 1986). Naïve and moving poems by peasants, soldiers, and students, recounting experiences of love and revolution. Bilingual text.

Roots & Wings: Poetry from Spain 1900–75, ed. Hardie St. Martin (New York: Harper & Row, 1976). Bilingual anthology of the great poems from *la patria madre* in this century.

Destruction of the Jaguar: Poems from the Books of Chilam Balam, translated by Christopher Swayer-Laucanno (San Francisco: City Lights, 1987). New English edition of lyric passages from one of the great Mayan books.

Volcán: Poems from El Salvador, Guatemala, Nicaragua and Honduras, translated by Alejandro Murguia and Barbara Paschke (San Francisco: City Lights, 1983). Excellent bilingual anthology from Central America. Many poems with a political orientation.

Love Poems from Spain and Spanish America, translated by Perry Highman (San Francisco: City Lights, 1988). Bilingual anthology.

The Renewal of the Vision: Latin American Women Poets 1940–80 (San Francisco: Spectacular Diseases Press, 1987). The poetry establishment in Latin America is heavily male-dominated: a sampling, for instance, of anthologies of Peruvian poetry is ninety-seven percent male! But some good woman poets, such as Blanca Varela in Peru, Rosario Castellanos in Mexico, Claribel Alegria in El Salvador, and Gioconda Belli in Nicaragua, with a host of younger writers, challenge that assumption. Bilingual text.

El Libro de la Escritura by Pingüino Tinto (New York: Teachers & Writers, 1989). An expanded, revised translation of T&W's *The Writing Book,* a creative writing workbook for students in grades 3–6, students in elementary Spanish, etc. The only such workbook in Spanish. Includes many good examples.

Dale Davis

Sing in Me, Muse

Ancient Greek in the Elementary School Classroom

> *Take me all over.*
> *There is no place.*
> *I live all over.*
>
> —Teresa M.

Where are the classics in school today?" James Laughlin, the poet who founded New Directions Publishing Corporation, asked me a few years ago. "Why don't you take Homer in, and try *The Odyssey* in elementary school?" was the suggestion of this writer who continues to keep the work of writers such as H. D., Federico García Lorca, Ezra Pound, Kenneth Rexroth, and William Carlos Williams in print, along with the work of Robert Duncan, Nicanor Parra, and Octavio Paz.

A few months later, as a writer-in-residence with the New York State Literary Center, I found a home for *The Odyssey*. The Craig Hill Elementary School, in Greece, New York, enabled me to combine Ancient Greek literature in English translation (as the inspiration for student writing) with the school's prescribed social studies curriculum on Ancient Greece, in a two-day-a-week, two-month residency with three sixth grade classes. The usual language arts, reading, and social studies periods were set aside for my work.

The goal of the residency, named GREECE/GREECE/GREECE, was for the teachers and students to come to feel Ancient Greece through its poets. The culmination of the residency was to be the participation of Robert Fitzgerald, Professor of Rhetoric and Oratory at Harvard, and translator of *The Iliad* and *The Odyssey*.

I began my own preparation for the residency by reading Kenneth Rexroth's *Classics Revisited*. What I responded to, what excited me most in Rexroth's book, I typed, page after page, to share with the teachers.

After Rexroth I revisited Jane Ellen Harrison's *Mythology*, and again I selected passages for the teachers. I also spent time with C. Kerenyi's *The Gods of the Greeks* and *The Heroes of the Greeks*. A postcard from Robert Fitzgerald added C. M. Bowra's *Homer* to my reading list.

The residency unofficially began in November with three study sessions with the sixth grade teachers, who supportively and energetically attended after school. The first session consisted of the many pages of what I had typed from my background reading, presented for the sheer enjoyment of reading, as reading, not to categorize or to classify, but to provide a personal "map" of where I had been. I encouraged everyone to record their thoughts and questions in response to the material, and to begin to chart their own maps. I asked the teachers to begin discussing with their students all the cultures the students had studied since they had been in school and to ask how the cultures were alike and how they were different, and why cultures were studied in school. I also suggested that the discussion involve what the students had read from those cultures. We were without Ancient Greek. Robert Fitzgerald had suggested C. M. Bowra's *Homer* "for the Greekless." The second teacher study-session focused on how Ancient Greek literature was going to be presented in the residency. I handed out three translations of Meleager's "Heliodora" from *The Greek Anthology*, by Dudley Fitts, W. R. Paton, and H. D., along with two comments on translation:

> And finally. I have not really undertaken translation at all—translation, that is to say, as it is understood in the schools. I have simply tried to restate in my own idiom what the Greek verses have meant to me. The disadvantages of this method are obvious: it has involved cutting, altering, expansion, revision—in short, all the devices of free paraphrase.
>
> In general, my purpose has been to compose first of all, and as simply as possible, an English poem.
>
> —Dudley Fitts, *One Hundred Poems from the Palatine Anthology*

> Since these are "old Chinese poems," dating from the second to the twelfth century, should not this oldness be somehow suggested in the translation? My answer to this is an emphatic no! Their oldness is no more than historical accident; all were unquestionably new when they were written. *The Greek Anthology* is even older and embraces a longer time span, yet no reputable modern translator that I am aware of makes any attempt to suggest this fact in his translation. The good translator, it seems to me, no matter how he may project himself back into time in order to understand the ideas and sentiments of his author, must, when it comes to getting the words over into another language, proceed as though he himself were the author, writing the work afresh today.
>
> —Burton Watson, *Chinese Lyricism*

Our introduction to the literature of Ancient Greece would be, by necessity, through the critical rendering of an appreciation by a translator. During the third teacher study-session we went over the material gathered together by the teachers for the residency: books and maps of Ancient Greece borrowed from every known location in the school district, ready for whoever wished to go further than what was presented in class. Copies of Robert Fitzgerald's translation of *The Odyssey*, and of his *Spring Shade, Poems 1931–1970*, soon arrived. The classroom residency officially began in January, with eight poems by Sappho, translated by Mary Barnard, Willis Barnstone, Guy Davenport, H. D., Richmond Lattimore, Kenneth Rexroth, and J. Addington Symonds, typed, photocopied, and passed out to each student.

During these first sessions on Sappho I read aloud the English translations of the eight poems. I asked the students to think of questions, such as What is it like to want something, have it right in front of you, and not be able to touch it? What is it like when you want to do and not do something at the same time? and What is it like to lie awake alone at night? I asked the students either to describe the effect of Sappho's poems on them or to write directly to her.

Sappho Talks

Sappho's poems are lilies
that speak with their heart.

   —*Kelly H.*

Sappho lets me know who she is.
She is holy.

   —*Randy P.*

To Sappho

It is I who needs,
who grabs for what is not,
that feeling of feeling
that flows through my heart making holes,
the dream inside the dream.
I am so close I can touch
the wind of my dream,
the speech of nothing.

It chases me.
It knows. It knows
I need the place that is not there

the place that sleeps beneath my body
past the deep where I come from,
the land of the feeling which is not known.

Time passes itself,
sleep of the same world
that has no body.

    —*Denise Z.*

To Sappho

The gift of a translator is the poems
he uncovers.

    —*Renée K.*

I then asked the students to select their favorite translations of each of the eight poems. Class discussion, in each subsequent session, focused upon how the translations differed, and how, through the choice and arrangement of words, translators arrived at their English versions of the poem.

Class discussion on Sappho led Michele and Traci to place their own work beside Mary Barnard's, Willis Barnstone's, Guy Davenport's, and H. D.'s translations of the very same poem.

A TEST OF TRANSLATION: SAPPHO

69

This way, that way

I do not know what to do: I
am of two minds.

    —*Mary Barnard*

Shall I?

I do not know what to do:
I say yes—and then no.

    —*Willis Barnstone*

I don't know which way I'm running.
My mind is part this way, part that.

    —*Guy Davenport*

I know not what to do:
my mind is divided.
—*H. D.*

I rip myself in half:
my mind is another me.
—*Michele*

Running
Running away from myself
I am not quite sure which way
—*Traci*

Following the classroom sessions on Sappho, I introduced the students to *The Greek Anthology*. We read poems by Meleager, Nossis, and Plato in English translations by M. S. Buck, H. D., Dudley Fitts, I. W. Mackail, and W. R. Paton. (I also distributed copies of the poems in Greek so that the students could see the shape of the poems in Ancient Greek.)

I asked the students to think about questions that come out of the poems: What is it like to live where you live? How can you hold on to something you cannot place in your hand? What is the one "country" we are all alive in? As with Sappho, I also asked the students to focus upon how the translations differed, and to note how the individual translators arrived at their English versions of the poem. Our discussion focused on the choice of verbs and adjectives, how the tone of the poem is set by the translator, and the decisions a translator must make.

Before leaving *The Greek Anthology* I asked the students to write what it meant to them.

The Greek Anthology
for Dudley Fitts
Your gift is the life of the words.
The poems tug like shining stars
in my mind,
life while I grow.
—*Chris S.*

The Greek Anthology

There is a solemn rose
I share
with all who can see.

    —*Fran P.*

The Greek Anthology

Minds beyond the world
I hold you
reminding myself
I want more.

    —*Julie W.*

I hold on with my dreams
going down my spine
and back up.
That name is that name is that name.

    —*Benny S.*

The poet knows the world
by the clock that gives time by thought,
by the fish that dreams to walk.

    —*Fran P.*

Song

Look, the empty-hearted fall noplace.
Down nothing meets nothing
Connecting God to nowhere.
Words strung begin a Metaphor,
A place of a blank someone
Like mysteries of ground, hot burning
Ill of summer snow
Knowing a shapeless horse galloping noplace,
Thinking Muse.
Everywhere half feelings
Turn outside, the flower of nobody worlds.
Like the spring air H. D. is my body
Thinking a dream inside tomorrow.

    —*Gino V.*

In the beginning of the second month of the residency, I held another study-session with the teachers: time to catch our breath, to chart where we had been, and to lay the final groundwork for *The Odyssey*. The "Postscript" to Robert Fitzgerald's translation was to be our guide through *The Odyssey:*

> If the world was given to us to explore and master, here is a tale, a play, a song about that endeavor long ago, by no means neglecting self-mastery, which in a sense is the whole point.

I used the game of Gossip to introduce Homer's authorship of *The Odyssey*. Since neither Homer nor his audience were readers, Homer spoke *The Odyssey,* and his audience heard it. I wrote two lines on a piece of paper, and then whispered the same two lines into the ear of a student. That student whispered what he or she heard into the ear of the next student, and so on, student to student, up and down the rows. We compared the two lines said aloud by the last student with the two lines I had written down; the difference was tremendous.

Next, I wrote two lines in iambic pentameter on a piece of paper, and whispered the same two lines into the ear of one of the students. We followed the same procedure with the last student saying aloud the two lines which he or she heard. There was very little difference between the two lines said aloud by the last student and the two lines I had written down.

I used Gossip to show how, in Milman Parry's words, "Homeric lines were constructed out of metrical formulas." I mentioned Albert Lord's work calling attention to the "phonological context," the formulas available in the memory, such as the alliterative and voweling pattern, used by the storyteller or singer, and the extent to which a formula determines invention.

The students and the teachers were now aware that it was unlikely that Homer himself wrote *The Odyssey* down, and that our reading was due to "a sedentary labor, or joy, sustained at a work table" by Robert Fitzgerald, the poet, the translator, the reader who was giving us Homer. I introduced Homer with an anonymous poem from *The Greek Anthology* translated by W. R. Paton:

> Of what country shall we record Homer to be a citizen, the man to whom all cities reach out their hands? Is it not the truth that this is unknown, but the hero, like an immortal, left as a heritage to the Muses the secret of his country and race?

I focused my *Odyssey* classroom work on Book One ("A Goddess Intervenes"), Book Two ("A Hero's Son Awakens"), Book Five ("Sweet Nymph and Open Sea"), Book Six ("The Princess at the River"), Book Seven ("Gardens and Firelight"), Book Nine ("New Coasts and Poseidon's Son"), Book Ten ("The Grace of the Witch"), and Book Eleven ("A Gathering of Shades"). The librarian and the music teacher (who emphasized the role of a stringed instrument in the development of a story) also read the *Odyssey* aloud to the students, as did the classroom teachers during the Reading and Social Studies periods.

During my classroom sessions I questioned the students about listening, about looking, about the home of their own imaginations, what it looks like there. I discussed the Greek word *metaphor,* "to move from one place to another," and then questioned the students about a journey to the home of their imaginations, asking where they might stop en route for a rest, and who would ask them to stay there instead of continuing on their journey. We talked about metaphor as a way of seeing, a way in which everything becomes, and everything is, something else.

★   ★   ★

I introduced Robert Fitzgerald through his own poetry:

Phrase

Sorrowful love passes from transparencies
to transparencies of bitter starlight
between antiquities and antiquities so simply

as in evening a soft bird flies down
and rests on a white railing under leaves

Love things in this quietness of falling
leaves birds or rain from the hushes
of summer clouds through luminous centuries

Touch unconsolable love the hands of your ancestors

Robert Fitzgerald walked into the Craig Hill Elementary School carrying his green Harvard bookbag over his shoulder. His first words to the classes were, "A message from the heart is in all poetry. Poetry reproduces the speech of the heart, which, after all, must matter." We were the students of this poet who brought *sacred* to the meaning of the word *teacher.*

He began with Sappho, read her Pleiades poem to us in Greek, and wrote it in Greek on the board. Fitzgerald proceeded with the assumption that, Greekless or not, we were with him. He wrote the English equivalent directly underneath the Greek and then asked everyone to take out the eight poems by Sappho in the different translations. He then read aloud the English translations of the Pleiades poem:

> The moon has set, and the Pleiades.
> It is the middle of the night,
> Hour follows hour. I lie alone.
>
> —*Guy Davenport*

> Tonight I've watched
>
> The moon and then
> the Pleiades
> go down
>
> The night is now
> half-gone; youth
> goes. I am
>
> in bed alone.
>
> —*Mary Barnard*

> **Alone**
> The moon and the Pleiades
> are set. Midnight,
> and time spins away.
> I lie in bed, alone.
>
> —*Willis Barnstone*

> The moon has set,
> and the Pleiades.
> It is Midnight.
> Time passes.
> I sleep alone.
>
> —*Kenneth Rexroth*

He spoke of what was happening in the poem: "Night was going on, the stars, and the moon were going down, time passes, I lie alone," and added, "When even those companions, the moon and the Pleiades go down, I am all alone. The loneliness is intensified."

He read the poem in Greek again, slowly giving the rhythm, the beat. Then he went back to the board and wrote:

The westering moon has gone
With Pleiades down the sky.
Midnight. And time goes by.
And I lie here alone.

    —*Robert Fitzgerald*

I had mailed Robert Fitzgerald all the material I had prepared for the residency: my preparatory reading, the material on Sappho, *The Greek Anthology,* and *The Odyssey,* and copies of the students' writing. He used the material as points of reference with the three classes. At one point, he suddenly stopped the class and stated:

You've shone as the morning star among the living,
Now you are dead, you shine as the evening star among
the dead.

Then he added, "Some Plato in the air for you."

At another point he introduced the elegiac couplet of *The Greek Anthology,* using an original composition, the first line by himself, the second line by Vladimir Nabokov:

No one has ever seen Cynthia flustered or drunk or befuddled
Cynthia prim and polite, Cynthia hard to outwit.

Asked by a student how he became interested in Greek, he replied that it had been when his sixth grade teacher wrote two Greek words on the blackboard. The Greek words, in English, meant "horse river," or "river horse," the English equivalent of "hippopotamus":

ἵππος   ποτάμος
HIPPOS   POTAMOS
HORSE   RIVER

    —*Notes taken in class by Benny S.*

Fitzgerald spoke of the opening sounds of *The Odyssey* in Greek: "We can hear faintly underneath the sound of sea water slapping under the ship's hull, quite a splendid set of noises." He concluded each class by reading aloud from *The Odyssey,* Book One, in Greek.

    ★   ★   ★

When I came back for the last day of GREECE / GREECE / GREECE, one week after Robert Fitzgerald's visit, I did not have to give a writing assignment. When I walked into each classroom, the students began writing:

Homer
for Robert Fitzgerald

Homer's song is Ancient Greece
unraveled in a poem.
The color of the words
is life
piercing.

—*Chris S.*

★   ★   ★

Dreams of Homer
for Robert Fitzgerald

Pieces and bits of the *Odyssey*
spin into dreams.
I imagine Homer.
My dreams tell me
I know this tiny light
shining in,
Homer
breaking through
to see me.

—*Tracey M.*

★   ★   ★

Robert Fitzgerald

I throw my body up seeing what it is like
to be a bird,
soaring so high I can touch the sky.

Homer's song can only be sung by the birds,
but I can sing that special song
in my dreams.
I hear that song
tingling,
I hear Greek in my own words.

—*Jason R.*

★   ★   ★

Cynthia

Talking, his hand walking
back, forth, his eyes sparkle.
A perfect yellow tulip

takes the chalk, writes "flustered,"
politely.

No one ever thanked Cynthia.

    —*Gino V.*

★   ★   ★

How
    for Robert Fitzgerald

Cynthia is a word I remember, and the word Pleiades.

Greek is a land of air tunnels
that holds dreams.
To learn Greek is to learn
a poem is a word
that tells what it wants to tell,
that gives a taste of what can't be tasted.

    —*Mike D.*

★   ★   ★

Image
    for Robert Fitzgerald

I look at my paper.
You look at the blackboard,
empty, lonely, blank, alone.
Are you listening? Do you hear?
You, Robert Fitzgerald, drowning
in poetry,
Do you believe in love? Do you love?
You, teacher of teachers, poem of poems,
Stuck in a world that nobody else knows,
alone,
A melody of words, singing with your heart,
You, the only tree on that land,
Sailing on that lake alone, thinking,
"Will I live forever, do I want to?"

You are the circle of life,
You, dreamer.

    —*Michele M.*

    GREECE/GREECE/GREECE was the combination of a reading list, teachers who were willing to risk total immersion with their own interest and time, serious research for each classroom presentation, a visit from Robert Fitzgerald, and a poet who designed and carried out the program, and who agreed with Fitzgerald's answer when he was asked what the difference between a sixth grade classroom and a Harvard classroom was: "None. A classroom is a classroom."

The Reading List for GREECE/GREECE/GREECE

Barnard, Mary. *Sappho, A New Translation*. Berkeley, Los Angeles: University of California Press, 1958.

Barnstone, Willis. *Greek Lyric Poetry*. New York: Schocken, 1972.

Bowra, C. M. *Homer*. London: Duckworth, 1975.

Buck, M. S. *The Greek Anthology*. Philadelphia: Privately printed, 1916.

Davenport, Guy. *Archilochos, Sappho, Alkman*. Berkeley, Los Angeles: University of California Press, 1980.

Doolittle, Hilda (H. D.). *Heliodora and Other Poems*. Boston: Houghton Mifflin Company, 1924.

Fitts, Dudley. *One Hundred Poems from the Palatine Anthology*. Norfolk: New Directions, 1938.

Fitzgerald, Robert, translator. *The Odyssey*. Garden City, New York: Anchor Books, 1963.

Fitzgerald, Robert. *Spring Shade, Poems 1931–1970*. New York: New Directions Publishing Corporation, 1971.

Harrison, Jane Ellen. *Mythology*. New York: Cooper Square Publishers, 1963.

Kerenyi, C. *The Gods of the Greeks*. New York: Thames & Hudson, 1978.

———. *The Heroes of the Greeks*. New York: Thames & Hudson, 1978.

Lattimore, Richmond. *Greek Lyrics*. Chicago: University of Chicago Press, 1955.

Mackail, J. W. *Select Epigrams from the Greek Anthology*. London: Longmans, Green and Company, 1928.

Paton, W. R. *The Greek Anthology*. Cambridge, Mass.: Harvard University Press, 1969.

Rexroth, Kenneth. *Classics Revisited*. Chicago: Quadrangle Books, 1968.

———. *Poems from the Greek Anthology*. Ann Arbor: University of Michigan Press, 1962.

Watson, Burton. *Chinese Lyricism*. New York: Columbia University Press, 1971.

Wharton, Henry Thornton. *Sappho: Memoir, Text, Selected Renderings, and a Literal Translation*. London: John Lane, 1898.

Shelley Messing

Teaching Poetry en Dos Languages

During a residency at I.S. 206 in the Bronx, I began to develop a syllabus for teaching Spanish poetry to bilingual elementary school students. When I started the ten-session residency I was aware of two potential stumbling blocks. The first was that I was coming into a new school in late April, that less responsive time of year when teachers and students alike are smitten with warm weather, late-in-the-school-year inertia. I was no exception to this mood. I had already finished residencies in two other schools and was tired of most of the exercises I had been using. Recognizing my fatigue, I was able to turn the second potential stumbling block—my limited familiarity with a bilingual population—into a challenging teaching experience for me and my students. I decided to create a new bilingual poetry syllabus.

Although I had studied Spanish in high school and had recently refreshed my speaking abilities when I visited Spain, I had always been afraid of teaching those Spanish-speaking poets I liked because I was afraid they were too difficult for younger students. To really do justice to the poems, I thought, they needed to be heard in their native language. I didn't feel confident that my poor Spanish pronunciation would allow the children to hear the rhythms, sounds, and nuances of the language. Yet I have always tried to teach children that poetry comes out of our own lives and is a natural part of language. It seemed important to affirm the sounds that most of these children hear in their homes, by sharing with them the rich heritage of poetry in Spanish.

I thought the solution to this problem might be to involve the children and, if possible, their teacher, in my own learning process—to have them teach me Spanish as I taught them about poetry. With this thought in mind I immersed myself in poetry in Spanish, intending to find poems I hadn't taught before and that might inspire powerful writing. I tried these poems out on two of the three classes I worked with. Ms. Campos's bilingual 6–8 class provided the greater challenge because her students were more recent immigrants to this country and therefore closer to their native Spanish language than they were to English. Although most of Mr. Feinberg's 5-1 students spoke Spanish, they were all fluent in English. I used the same syllabus for both classes, but we focused on the bilingual aspects of the lessons more in Ms. Campos's than in Mr. Feinberg's class, where the children could already write easily in English.

Methodology

Right away I explained my hope that as I taught both classes something about poetry and helped the students develop as writers, the students would help me improve my Spanish pronunciation and comprehension. Over the ten sessions I brought in six poems, each in Spanish and English. We began by reading a poem twice in Spanish. Ms. Campos, whose first language was Spanish, often read the poem first. This satisfied my desire for the children to hear the poem read with proper inflections. In Mr. Feinberg's class, each time I selected a different student to read first. Then I read the poem in Spanish. The children would correct me whenever I made a mistake.

Next, we read the poem twice in English. In Ms. Campos's class particularly, I encouraged those students who did not feel comfortable reading English to volunteer. Sometimes we divided the English reading into stanzas so that the task would not seem so overwhelming. It also gave more people a chance to read each day. I worried that the children who were bilingual might focus on their deficiencies in English instead of recognizing how much potential they had for mastering two languages and understanding two cultures. Since they were already fluent in Spanish I wanted them to realize that they were in the middle of a process and that with practice and time they would soon speak their second language with as much ease as the first. That was one reason why I let them hear me struggle through the Spanish readings. It took away some of their own embarrassment over mispronunciations and allowed them to see another person (and a teacher) grappling with language. It was a way for all of us to learn that we could share our skills with one another. I encouraged Ms. Campos's students to correct each other. It was very moving to watch these children work together. There never seemed to be a sense of superiority or inferiority attached to criticism. These issues were not as important in Mr. Feinberg's class, where the main problem was overcrowding (there were thirty-nine or more students in this class).

After reading the poem in Spanish and English, we discussed it in detail. We began by listing words or lines that confused us, then broadened our discussion to the poem as a whole. Our focus would switch back and forth between structure and content of each poem. The weight I gave to either depended upon a particular poem and what I hoped to accomplish in each writing exercise.

I depended upon the bilingual students a great deal when we compared the Spanish poem to its English translation. We talked about what often gets lost in translation—sound, rhythm—and the students showed me examples of Spanish lines where the sounds were clearly richer and filled with greater meaning.

At this point I would introduce the writing exercise. In Mr. Feinberg's class, everyone wrote in English. I gave the children in Ms. Campos's class a choice. Initially they could write in whichever language they felt more comfortable. However, I also explained that if they chose to write in Spanish we would have to translate their poem into English afterwards, so that I could understand it. Ms. Campos proved to be invaluable throughout the class. She would sit down with each child writing in Spanish and with me, and the three of us would translate the poem together. I would also go around the room and try to work with those students who, despite their difficulties, were trying to write entirely in English. The students sat in groups of six or eight at rectangular tables and, invariably, one student was able to translate Spanish phrases into English, while another used the dictionary to look up correct spellings or to verify definitions. They worked as a team. This was less the case in Mr. Feinberg's class, where students tended to work individually. They were a useful group to try the same poems out on. Many of them had a facility with language, so I could see which poems inspired creative responses without the additional problems of language difficulties.

The Syllabus

Lesson 1: "Sueños" ("Dreams") by Nicanor Parra
I began with the poem "Sueños" by the Chilean poet Nicanor Parra because I thought it would be an easy poem to encourage reading out loud and a written response. "Sueños" is a list poem describing many bizarre, surreal dreams. The poem has elements of surprise and repetition (each line begins with, "I dream of"). We discussed the value of each of these elements as writing devices. Then each person in the class was able to read one line out loud. I asked the students to try to translate the poem before looking at the English version, to exemplify

our recent discussion about the difficulties of translation. After attempting to translate a line or two, most of the class began to glance at the English version. (This exercise would probably have worked better if I had posed it as a "mistranslation exercise" with a group of children unfamiliar with Spanish. Then they would have had more freedom to create their own meaning for the poem.) From there, I asked them to write about any strange dream they could remember. Everyone wrote, but the responses seemed to lack a certain depth that I try to encourage in writing. I would hesitate to use this lesson again unless I came up with a more structured exercise. I had chosen not to ask them to use the same repetition scheme that Parra used because it seemed too facile and limiting.

Lesson 2: "Nadie" ("Nobody") by Nicanor Parra

Nadie

No se puede dormir
Alguien anda moviendo las cortinas.
Me levanto. No hay nadie.
Probablemente rayos de la luna.

Mañana hay que levantarse temprano
Y no se puede conciliar el sueño:
Parece que alguien golpeara a la puerta.

Me levanto de nuevo.
Abro de par en par:
El aire me da de lleno en la cara
Pero la calle está completamente vacía.

Solo se ven las hileras de álamos
Que se mueven al ritmo del viento.

Ahora sí que hay que quedarse dormido.
Sorbo la última gota de vino
Que todavía reluce en la copa
Acomodo las sábanas
Y doy una última mirada al reloj
Pero oigo sollozos de mujer
Abandonada por delitos de amor
En el momento de cerrar los ojos.

Esta vez no me voy a levantar.
Estoy exhausto de tanto sollozo.
Ahora cesan todos los ruidos.

Sólo se oyen las olas del mar
Como si fueran los pasos de alguien
Que se acerca a nuestra choza desmantelada
Y no termina nunca de llegar.

Nobody

I can't get to sleep
Someone is making the curtains move.
I get up. There's nobody there
Probably the moonlight.

Tomorrow I have to get up early.
And I can't get to sleep:
I have the feeling someone's knocking at the door.

I get up again.
I throw it wide open:
The air hits me full in the face.
But the streets are completely empty.

All I can see are the rows of poplars
Swaying in the wind's rhythm.

This time I've got to stay asleep.
I gulp the last drop of wine
Still glittering in the glass.
I straighten the sheets.
I give a last glance at the clock
But I hear the sobs of a woman
Abandoned for cheating in love
Just as I close my eyes.

This time I'm not going to get up.
I'm exhausted from so much sobbing.
Now all the noise stops.
I hear only the waves of the sea
As if they were the steps of someone
Who comes toward our dilapidated cottage
And never stops coming.

In each class we talked about the night noises in the Bronx and
how they differ from those that Parra described hearing in Chile. I asked
the children to write their own poems detailing what causes them to be
sleepless at times. They wrote about the sounds of disco, rap, and Spanish music; about mice scratching; about partying in their buildings,
around their blocks, and in nearby parks; about arguments in the street

or at home. This lesson, with its concentration on sounds, allowed me
to stress the importance of details and of specificity in a new way.

What I Hear at Night

The radio playing Spanish music
My mother snoring
The dog barking
A lady screaming at her cat
The person next door crying
A person whistling
The wind going through the trees

—*Nicole Estemera, fifth grade*

★   ★   ★

I hear the sound
of the water
from the sink
and fights
outside
and bikes and cars
stopping after they go real fast
like a screech
and the steps
from people walking

Once
I was awake and
I heard the steps
of someone coming
into my room
it was my father
he scared me
he was checking to see
if I was asleep

—*Jacqueline Miranda, sixth grade*

Lesson 3: "Sorpresa" ("Surprise") by Federico García Lorca
Robin Messing (another poet-teacher and no relation to me) and I were
having a discussion about the prevalence of violence in our daily lives,
as well as in the larger context of our society. I said that I wanted to find
a way to discuss violence with my classes and that I wanted to find an
approach that would encourage students to write about violence from a
personal perspective. Robin loaned me a collection of Lorca's poems

that had been translated with great care and skill by the poet Paul Blackburn. She suggested I look at the poem "Sorpresa," which describes the strangeness the poet experiences after viewing the dead body of an anonymous man lying in the street with a knife through his chest.

Surprise

The dead man lay in the street
   with a knife in his chest.
No one knew who he was. How
the streetlamp trembled!
   Madre.
How the little streetlamp trembled!
Between the night and the morning. No one
could lean over his eyes open on raw air.
   How come
this dead man lies in the street, what?
with a knife in his chest, & that no
one should know who he was?

   —Translated by Paul Blackburn

Sorpresa

Muerlo se quedó en la calle
con un puñal en el pecho.
No lo conocía nadie.
¡Cómo temblaba el farol!
Madre.
¡Cómo temblaba el farolito
de la calle!
Era madrugada. Nadie
pudo asomarse a sus ojos
abiertos al duro aire.
Que muerto se quedó en la calle
que con un puñal en el pecho
y que no lo conocía nadie.

   —Federico García Lorca

I brought the poem into my classes and initiated a discussion about global violence. In both classes we talked about the events in Atlanta and about the recent death of Northern Ireland hunger striker/political prisoner Bobby Sands. The radically different responses of both classes to these topics paralleled the levels of the poems that the students wrote later. In Mr. Feinberg's class the children were largely apathetic about the topic. I was not completely surprised by this because I had already begun to see that having thirty-nine or more children in a classroom creates a situation in which a teacher spends a great deal of time simply trying to get the children to listen. It was obvious from their earlier writing that they were bright, energetic, and opinionated. However, when I asked them to describe incidents of violence that they had witnessed, only a few wrote empathetically about the topic.

Again, there was great contrast in Ms. Campos's class. We had a highly sophisticated discussion about racism, prejudice, and poverty. Their poems were vivid and full of emotion.

> One day in my building
> this old man was going down the stairs
> and this guy took all his money
> and threw him down the stairs.
> A lady seen him.
> She called the cops.
> They were checking the roof
> when my mother heard people running.
> She came downstairs and
> the ABC News was there.
>
> —*José Sanchez, sixth grade*

* * *

> Muerto se quedó en la cama
> porque murio de un ataque al corazón
> Murio a la madrugada.
> La policia se lo llevó
> y lo enterraron.
> Mi tio se murio en Navidad.
>
> They found him dead in bed
> because he died of a heart attack
> He died at dawn.
> The police came and took him
> and he was buried.
> My uncle died on Christmas.
>
> —*Rubin Rodriguez, sixth grade*

* * *

The Person on the Street

> When I see you walk the street
> I just have to look away.
> Just watching you I can see

you really need a home
with heat, food, and love,
and can't keep on going this way,
just a woman on the street.

—*Tanya Brown, fifth grade*

Rose Maria Ortega's poem about El Salvador managed to discuss political violence through a strong personal image:

Ayer murio
Un pobre hombre que no sabía
Donde vivia.
La vida era tan agría que
No sabia donde ir.
Yo oido que en El Salvador
Ha muerto mucha gente,
Personas inocentes
Que no tienen culpa.
Así es la vida.
Yo espero que no contínue.

Yesterday, a poor man died
Who didn't know where to go.
Life had treated him bitterly
So he didn't know what to do.
I have heard
That many people have been killed
In El Salvador,
Innocent people
Who were not to blame.
Such is life!
I hope it does not continue.

Lesson 4: "Canción de Jinete" ("Song of the Horseback Rider") by Federico García Lorca

Canción de Jinete

Córdoba.
Lejana y sola.

Jaca negra, luna grande,
y aceitunas en mi alforja.
Aunque sepa los caminos
yo nunca llegaré a Córdoba.

Por el llano, por el viento,
jaca negra, luna roja.
La muerte me está mirando
desde las torres de Córdoba.

¡Ay qué camino tan largo!
¡Ay mi jaca valerosa!
¡Ay que la muerte me espera,
antes de llegar a Córdoba!

Córdoba.
Lejana y sola.

Song of the Horseback Rider

Córdoba. Remote
and alone.

Black pony, big moon,
olives in my saddlebag.
Altho I know all the roads,
I will never arrive at Córdoba.

Over the plain, over the wind,
black pony, moon red.
Death is looking at me
down from the towers of Córdoba.

Ai! this road is long!
Ai! my valorous pony!
Ai! that Death awaits me
before I come to Córdoba!

Córdoba. Remote
and alone.

—Translated by Paul Blackburn

Both classes agreed that this lyrical poem sounded better in Spanish than in English. I used the poem to teach repetition as a structural device. ("Córdoba. Remote/and alone" is repeated at the end of the poem.) I asked each class to think of the first time they were traveling to a place and what they imagined that place to be like. Then I asked them to think about how that compared to their first impression of that place. I told them to start their poems with the name of the place they were writing about, and to add two details immediately following the name that described their feelings about that place. The center of the poem would describe the place in more detail, and the ending would mirror the poem's beginning.

The use of repetition here seemed more open-ended than that of "Sueños." Even though I had given a fairly restrictive assignment, it hadn't stifled the students' desire to write, and their poems did not seem like "formula" poems.

Empire State Building. Big Windows.
You can see everything.
Waiting for the elevator,
going up for a short time,
I saw through the window
small things, like the Twin Towers.
I saw people from the window.
They looked like ants and mice walking.
Empire State Building. Big windows.
You can see everything.

—*Diana Travieso, sixth grade*

★ ★ ★

America

New York. Industrialized
And polluted.

The plane is traveling
And I start thinking:
What is it going to look like?
How are the people going to speak?

I imagine, in a thinking sort of way,
That the streets are spotless
And the garbage is in a neatly kept can.
The people are speaking with an English accent.

Although I speak the same language
I thought they'd speak differently.

And yet, I held all these questions.
I started joking away.
But in my mind
I felt sad
Because some of my family was behind.

New York. Industrialized
And polluted.

—*Kim Tranquada, fifth grade*

Lessons 5 and 6: "Oda a la Tormenta" ("Ode to the Storm") and "Oda al Traje" ("Ode to the Clothes") by Pablo Neruda
Encouraged by the students' positive response to structure, I decided to teach two odes by Neruda. After discussing the definition of an ode, we read each poem. Ms. Campos warned me that the "Ode to the Storm" might be too long and difficult for her class, but I gambled and asked her to read the whole poem out loud for them. They loved the poem's rich imagery, as did Mr. Feinberg's class. "Ode to the Clothes" is shorter and simpler to understand. I asked each class to suggest possible subjects for odes and I wrote a list of them on the board.

I decided that it would be fun to write a collaborative ode in each class before encouraging individual responses. We selected one object from the list, went around the room, and came up with group odes:

Ode to Food

Food, you taste nasty, especially liver
You make me fat
Sometimes you give me a stomachache
But when I'm weary, you give me energy
Sometimes you don't fill me up
Sometimes I get mad at you
because you make my teeth fall out
when you're too hard
You taste good too—
like barbecue spare ribs, candied yams,
sweet potato pie, chicken, pizza,
corn, and Chinese food
Food, you keep me alive

   —*Class collaboration, fifth grade*

                    ★   ★   ★

Ode to a Bed

I love you bed
I sleep comfortably in you
You feel soft
I want to squeeze you to death
You never stay naked
You always look so pretty wearing sheets
You help me fall asleep
You let me be with my pillow
Sometimes you're too soft
Sometimes you're too weak
And I feel uncomfortable

When I leave you I feel sorry
My terrific bed I love you

—*Class collaboration, sixth grade*

After we applauded our collaborative efforts I asked the students to choose an object from the list and write their own odes to it. There were odes to smelly socks, odes to pillows, odes to litter, and odes to nature. One of the funniest odes was Beatrice Moore's "Ode to Panties":

Ode to Panties

Panties, you keep me nice and comfortable.
Sometimes you stink, so I change you.
You make my butt feel good.
Panties, you are better
than men's underwear.
They are white
and have no designs.
Panties have daisies and flowers.
I like new panties. They are cold
and make both your sides feel good.

Teaching, if it is to be successful as well as sustaining, must be about reciprocity. My work at I.S. 206 was satisfying for a number of reasons. It allowed me to build speaking skills in Spanish and to become a student at the same time that I was growing as a teacher. It allowed the students to be successful in writing and understanding poetry because the textures of the Spanish-language poems we used were more resonant with their familiar culture. Our discussions of translation forced all of us to concentrate on sound, rhythm, and precision in language in a very immediate way. It pleased me that Ms. Campos became fully involved in the project; she played an enthusiastic role as translator, reader, and poetry lover. But it seems to me that the most important thing that happened was the unusual way in which some children were able to move back and forth between the two languages and to work together in small non-hierarchical, non-competitive groups with the common goals of overcoming deficiencies and learning to become better writers and speakers of English.

Bibliography

Lorca, Federico García. *Poems of Federico García Lorca*. Chosen and translated by Paul Blackburn. San Francisco: Momo's Press, 1979.

Neruda, Pablo. *Nueva Odas Elementales (Further Elementary Odes)*. New York: G. Massa, 1956.

Parra, Nicanor. *Poems and Antipoems*. Edited by Miller Williams. New York: New Directions, 1967.

Bill Bernhardt

Individual Writing in a Collective Country

Visitors to China (and the Chinese themselves) are fond of contrasting the individualism of the West and collective consciousness of the East. The westerner, so this argument runs, thinks of himself or herself only as an isolate, whereas a Chinese person perceives himself or herself primarily as the member of a group such as a family, clan, work unit, or the Chinese people as a whole. Like most clichés, this formulation contains some truth. Still, however the Chinese think of themselves or we of them, the fact remains that there are a billion discrete individuals living in the People's Republic of China and each one is his or her own person, with personal likes and dislikes, a unique face, and a distinct voice.

When I think back to the teachers and students with whom I worked during my seventeen months in China, what comes to mind are images of those individual faces and echoes of those voices. And what formed those faces and voices was each person's inner life and experience, no less individual than my own.

Of course, people in both countries—the United States and the People's Republic—are often taught in school to write as if one's inner life and voice didn't exist. Assigned "public" topics, such as gun control in the U.S. or modernization in the P.R.C., generally elicit the same sort of characterless mush. Invited to write from their own experience, however, students in both countries produce writing that is full of images, unexpected turns and phrases that stick in the mind long after the writer's name is forgotten. In both countries, although the students' personal writing is their best writing, the educational authorities tend to tolerate it as a "step" on the way to a more formal, impersonal mode of expression.

When the Chinese students and teachers write about themselves they don't necessarily write about the things foreigners want to know about them. Like American students, they write about whatever they are thinking about. So we may be disappointed if we expect their work to answer our questions about life in China. For the most part, they give us perceptions and feelings rather than judgments and opinions. Reading what they have written reminds us: these are people just like us, in that they speak most often of matters outside the public sphere.

English is, of course, a foreign language for all of these writers. For years, it could be studied only through books, without access to the sounds of an English-speaking voice. Only recently have tapes, radio broadcasts, and teachers from Britain and America brought the living language to Chinese ears. So it is not surprising that there are traces of "chinglish" in the examples below—English words fitted to Chinese phrasing and intonation. I could have, by the use of my red pencil, forced the writers to revise their work so that it would satisfy standard conventions of written English. In fact, they would have preferred me to do so. Perfectionism is a dominant value in Chinese academic life.

I have to admit that while reading these pieces I find a number of expressions that would probably grate on my ear if I encountered them in the students' speech. I couldn't allow any student of mine to say "arm-by-arm" instead of "arm-in-arm," or substitute "not long" for "after a while," without calling it to his or her attention. But as written, literary usage, such departures from standard English seem not only valid but charming. They give the work a greater sense of particularity and liveliness. This response surprises me a little. I'm used to thinking that spoken English is the freer form of our language. I had forgotten the old and useful notion of "poetic license." Perhaps we can discover certain potentialities of our own language only when it is used by sensitive foreigners forced to make deliberate choices where we need only select a ready-made phrase.

For the most part, my Chinese students hadn't had much experience of writing as self-expression—in English or Chinese. Writing had always been an exercise in which expressiveness was subordinated to correctness. The notion that one writes to unlock the store of personal images and feelings was new to these students, yet was eagerly accepted when I encouraged them to transcribe the first thoughts that came, without conscious regard for the rules they knew so well. Here are some examples:

> The snow flakes were falling down, down, quietly and softly . . . all was white . . . a small child peering out the door was so fascinated by the beauty that she ventured to stagger out into the deep snow until taken by some adults, crying desperately for what she was not allowed to enjoy.

*   *   *

I like Saturday. If there is a dance in our school I go there to dance, or share a walk outside with my girlfriend who is studying in another department of our school. She has a golden voice. I often enjoy some famous arias sung by her. We always sing as we stroll arm-by-arm. We walk on and on; at last we find a quiet place, sit down shoulder-to-shoulder talking about our life, feeling, affection, and ideals. It seems as if the words came endless. From this we feel our life is valuable and worth appreciating. Sometimes we also keep silent in the dark.

*   *   *

One night in the fall of 1973 . . . my friend and I came in secret to an empty house. The former owner had been thrown in jail for his Soviet espionage activities. "They have a study full of books," he assured me. He let me stay outside the window sill and lurked into the darkness inside like a monkey. Not long, he poked out his head beaming happily. "Now lend me a hand please." Because he committed the excusable burglary in a hurry in my portion of the property there were several copies in English—I knew this by the words "the" and "rose." They were poetry books. How did an English poem sound? I wanted to read them and thus learned English. The poems were my only texts for quite some time. But, in fact, I could hardly understand them. They kept my English grammar confused until I came to college.

*   *   *

the leaves are lisping
down on the ground
a little girl of five
big for her age
was wandering alone
along a country road
which had many a curve and bent
she held in her bare hand
a brown bottle without lid
inside was a cricket
it got out and hopped away
while a running car ran it over
but no not over
for it leapt toward a safe spot
though pulling a wounded leg

★   ★   ★

I was planting sweet potatoes. The men's job was to carry water here from a hundred meters away. When we had nearly finished, I noticed an old man cutting down the wild trees beside the road. He put a branch into the cut and then banded it. I was curious to know what he was doing so I went there. "Why are you doing this?" I asked. "To make these trees produce pears," he answered, while wrapping a piece of cloth on the joint. I was very attracted. Immediately I fell in love with it. I carefully watched him operating. Suddenly an idea came into my mind, "Why not do this with young cotton plants? So we can have cotton trees, then people could do less work to grow cotton." I told this to the old man and asked for his advice. He smiled and said, "You may have a try. I have no experience of that."

I saw a tall tree before me. So many cotton flowers were hanging on the branches. They were as white as clouds, as big as bowls. Near it, there stood a wheat tree. The shape of the grains was like dates with a pale pink color. It was so magical that I could not believe my eyes. I opened my eyes widely to make sure that I was not in a dream. The scene was so clear, how could it be a dream? I wanted all the villagers to see this wonder. I went to call them . . . they laughed at me; they didn't believe it. I persuaded them to follow me. But to my great surprise, when I came back there was nothing left on the cotton tree. The wheat trees had all gone. There were two deep pits where the trees formerly were. "Who has stolen the treasure trees?" I cried. Then I woke up.

★   ★   ★

I had a small black suitcase given by my mother, in which I put all my favorite playthings. I could sit by it for hours, counting my sweets, papers I had collected, putting the cobblestones in a bowl of water and watching their beautiful decorative patterns. Sometimes I told my toy baby many stories. There was a broken clinical thermometer lying at the corner of my small suitcase. Each time I looked at it, I could not help laughing at myself.

One day my little sister Ping-ping was ill. After taking her temperature, my mother asked me to put the clinical thermometer back in the drawer, warning me, "Hold it tight! Don't drop it! It's easy to break." I didn't pay any attention to it before my mother's words, but now it interested me so much. I looked at it, thinking, "Why? What if I drop it?" I loosed my hand and let it fall on the ground. It broke in two pieces. My mother was very angry. . . . I was beaten for the first time. But strange to say, after punishment I still felt a bit of satisfaction.

★   ★   ★

Outside my window
Stands a poplar tree,
Grand and straight
With bald branches stroked by the early spring wind.

Weeks ago on its twigs
Appeared small buds.
Oh, not leaves they were,
But flowers of the poplar.
Gently a breeze passed by
Like upside-down millets they swing and swayed.
Yet the flowers began falling down,
Springling about under the big tree.

Again on the twigs
There spring out small buds.
Well, tender young leaves they were,
Light green sheeted in soft downs.

Through them penetrated gleams of the setting sun,
And what a light these little pieces shining!
Not orange, nor golden, nor green,
Only a mixed color of these three.

Outside my window
Stands the poplar tree
Murmuring and whispering,
Quietly it is talking with the night wind.

What is happening in these passages is that the writers are discovering what it means to write for oneself, the stage of writing that is most neglected—and also most crucial—in schools everywhere.

Kenneth Koch

I'll Carry You Off to Sing with the Train, Maria

Teaching Poetry to Children in Other Countries

After my experience of teaching children to write poetry here in the United States, I did the same kind of teaching in other countries and in other languages—in Haiti, France, Italy, and China. I did the foreign teaching, I think, mostly out of curiosity: to see if the teaching would work, and to see what kinds of poems the children would write. I didn't think that the ease, excitement, and spontaneity, the quick and poetic responsiveness of my students at P.S. 61 in New York were exclusively American phenomena. I wasn't sure, though, that the kind of teaching I had done at P.S. 61 could inspire children to write poetry in other countries, with other languages, and with their own highly developed literary and artistic traditions. I found that it could. Taught in much the same way as the children in New York, my students in Port-au-Prince, Paris, Rome, Shanghai, and Beijing responded enthusiastically, understood poems, and wrote well themselves.

The differences in how these different children wrote were less obvious than the similarities. The French children were a little more sophisticated, ironic, and literary—but not much more—than the others; the Italian children somewhat more open, unembarrassed by strong feelings. The Haitian students, once they got going, were vivacious, playful, and a little wild. My American students were perhaps the best at being "crazy," at following fantastic ideas out to the end. The Chinese children had a way of their own of mixing the fantastic with the plain and practical: cars on a road looked like a dragon; wishing to go to the moon (a characteristic wish of my American students) became a wish for the moon to come to one's house.

Such differences depended partly on the particular children of a country I happened to be able to teach: for example, the École Alsacienne students in Paris were literarily sophisticated in a way that the students at the Genzano school outside Rome were not, quite apart

from their being French or Italian. My relative knowledge or ignorance of the children's language was also a factor. My French is pretty
good, my Italian is shaky, and, knowing no Chinese, I taught with an
interpreter there. Each diminution of my knowledge of the language
brought with it a lessening of nuance and perhaps even of imagina-
tiveness in what I was able to help inspire the children to write.
Another factor was the length of time I taught: in France, as in Italy,
for about two months; in Haiti for only a week; in China for two
weeks. In France and Italy, I had time to try out an idea in one class,
then use it more effectively in another. Or what children wrote in one
class could give me an idea for another poem, another lesson, to give
to another class. In Haiti and in China, whatever results I got I had to
get quickly; there wasn't much time to try things out. Despite these
differences, the remarkable similarity is that all these children liked
writing poetry and wrote it well. The ease, excitement, spontaneity,
and responsiveness I had been immersed in at P.S. 61 were all around
me, also, in the classrooms of Beijing, Paris, Rome, Port-au-Prince,
and Shanghai.

The idea of writing poetry in school, expressing feelings and sensations, and having fun doing it, is at least a familiar and respectable
one in America, even if it is not often put into effect. Not so in the
other countries I taught in, and this unfamiliarity was an obstacle of
sorts. The problems it caused were not with the children but with
teachers, who were skeptical of what I could accomplish, and of administrators who didn't want to let me try. As soon as I did manage to
get into a school, the children were won over; and, in every case,
teachers and administrators were themselves won over by what the
children wrote. Teachers at the École Bilingue were very skeptical:
Cela ne marchera jamais. Two of them ended up teaching poetry classes
themselves. This was characteristic of what happened. In China and in
Italy, teachers I worked with taught poetry while I was there and afterwards. They all did it well, strange as it was in the schools where
they taught. I wasn't surprised that the teaching worked, but I was
surprised by how well it worked. Despite apparent difficulties, poetry
seemed to reach the children, to move their imaginations, as directly
as bright colors or a spring breeze.

I sometimes began with easy *Wishes, Lies, and Dreams* kinds of lessons, such as a Wish Poem or a Lie Poem, but mostly I used lessons like
those in *Rose, Where Did You Get That Red?*: I read aloud and talked
about a great poem, then asked children to write poems of their own in

some way like it. Most often, I used poems in the children's own language as models: poems by Baudelaire, Rimbaud, Breton, for example, in France; by Dante and Petrarch in Italy; by Li Bai (Li Po) in China. As at P.S. 61, I paid no attention to whether or not the poems I used were considered suitable for children of this or that age. If something strong and simple in the poem appealed to me, I assumed I could teach it. Here is a brief account of what happened in each country.

My overseas teaching began in 1975 in Haiti, where, at the invitation of the American ambassador, I taught poetry writing for one week at the Lycée Toussaint-L'Ouverture in Port-au-Prince. Though my stay there was short, the vigor, energy, and talent with which the Haitian students responded was impressive. Also impressive was the swiftness with which this lively response came, after a beginning that seemed full of problems. In the first place, not only was I teaching (for the first time) in a language not my own, but also it was not really the language of the students. At home and on the street they spoke Creole; French was a language they learned at school. Thus, when I asked if I could teach ten-year-old students, the Minister of Education said, "No, they wouldn't be able to write well enough." I was given, instead, students aged fourteen to sixteen. These older children had had time to learn more French. Furthermore, no one had written poems in school. The French system of education was, if anything, even stricter in Port-au-Prince than it was in France. You were in school to learn and to do this and this and this—not that. In the halls of the *lycée* a man walked back and forth holding a whip. An education official told me, "Oh, he never uses it," but all the same. My Haitian students, at the start, were fearful, puzzled, and hesitant to speak. By the second or third class, though, poetry found them and they found poetry, and difficulties disappeared. By the fifth and last class I had been given an assistant who had the children writing poetry in Creole; they recited, and some even sang, these poems in front of the class. Among the poems I taught were Blake's "Tyger" and Rimbaud's "Vowels." Here is a Blake-inspired poem, with what seem to me some characteristic Haitian surprises, such as the calm mélange of the domestic and the magical and the inclusion of one line in Creole (I've translated the French lines but left the Creole line in the original):

> Little cat what's going on that you're drinking the dog's milk
> My eyes why aren't you looking at me
> My hands why don't you have twenty-five fingers
> Quardrumane why are you so good-looking

> Monsieur Moulongue pou ka ça ou vole conca tout—e tan oua-p
>   vole poul moun-yo
> Tomtom why do you like to beat like that "I am poor I need help"

These are some lines from a lesson on Rimbaud:

> B is black because I am in love with a black girl named Babeth and
>   every time I write the letter B I see it black . . .
> A is white because it looks like a house not painted

I taught in France after Haiti, during the winter and spring of
1975–76. I had classes in two prestigious private schools in Paris—the
École Bilingue and the École Alsacienne—and in two public schools
in the primarily working-class Paris suburb of Petit Clamart. My eighth
grade students at the École Bilingue had sophisticated responses to
Rimbaud's "Vowels":

> I green like the stems of pale flowers
> O yellow like a lemon on a plate
> U white like the Pastilles Vichy in the subway . . .
> E blue as the city on a starry night . . .
> The number One is white like an old teapot
> Two is violet like a very big drawing
> Three is black like the moon hidden by the sun
> Four is brown like blond hair. . . .

To my sixth grade students at the École du Pavé Blanc in Petit
Clamart I taught Baudelaire's "L'Invitation au Voyage," an invitation
to the poet's beloved to travel with him to a country that is as beautiful, warm, and sensuous as she is: "My child, my sister / Think of
how sweet it will be / To go out there and live together / In the country that is like you . . . / There, everything is beauty / Luxury, calm,
and voluptuousness. . . ." My younger French students had shown an
interest in such voyages in writing Wish Poems—

> I'd like to live on the sun with Nathalie . . .

> I'd like to live in the comic-strip world . . .

The example of Baudelaire inspired strange, dreamy, sensuous, detailed
versions of such wishes:

> Mother I want you to come with me to that country where all is so
>   mysterious and so magnificent

And there are those exotic fruits that grow on the hill, hiding the
setting sun that is red as a ruby reflecting in the big wall mirror
that you put up to keep death from coming to take us away . . .

You'll have flowers in your hair, dresses with long trains, long as the
wind that blows from the north
You'll see volcanoes talking to you about their mysterious adventure . . .

I taught an "I Never Told Anybody" lesson (a poem of secrets) to
the sixth grade students at the École Bilingue and to the seventh grade
students at the École du Pavé Blanc. The idea is to put in each line
something you've done or thought or felt but never said. I used two
different poems in teaching it—Rimbaud's "Dawn" (about a magical
morning walk) at the École Bilingue and Mallarmé's "Apparition"
(about a mysterious nighttime dream-like vision) at the École du Pavé
Blanc. "Dawn" inspired confessions of feelings about nature; "Apparition," of feelings about the night and dreams—

I never told anyone that I discovered the language of my fishes
I never told anyone that a flower gave me one of its petals . . .

I've never said that I talked to the wind . . .
And I've never said I have a talking flower . . .
I've never said that I was the ocean
I've never said that I have a secret in the ocean.

    (École Bilingue)

I never told anyone that I believed that in the evening a horseman
    dressed all in black put up the night
I never told anyone I believed that in the morning a horseman
    dressed all in white put up the day. . . .
I never told anyone I dreamed that an angel came to rock me to sleep. . . .

    (École du Pavé Blanc)

I used Rimbaud's "Cities" ("Houses of crystal and wood that move
on invisible rails and pulleys . . . The hunting of bells cries out in the
gorges . . .") to inspire poems about an Ideal City. The children wrote:
"I live in a city where everything is yellow in the morning / Orange at
noon, and red in the evening. / There are no cars in that city. / Everybody walks around in a bathing suit"; " my house [is] filled with wild
animals and trees." I used André Breton's poem "The Egret" as a model
for an "If only" poem. Breton's poem is full of wishes for the impossible—it begins "If only the sun were shining tonight." My students,
like Breton, put an impossible wish in every line:

If only the radiators were as cold as a photograph
If only I wrote as well as a lamp that lights up a red leaf like saliva

Another poem by Breton, "Free Union," has some fantastic praise
of a woman in every line ("My wife with shoulders of champagne . . .
With fingers of new-cut hay . . ."). I asked my seventh grade students to
praise someone or something that way:

My dog of snow, of fire and of air,
My dog of foam, of sparks and of rock,
My dog of diamond, my dog of ruby,
My dog green with hope and pink with affection.

One remarkable poem was about a door:

My door of glass which is made of sand and of dust
My door of vegetable glass which is transparent . . .
My brilliant door of glass where the moon and the stars are reflected
My door of glass which encloses the wall of the past
My door of glass which saw the world born . . .
My door of glass which will see the world die
My door of glass which was dead before it was born.

Encouraged by what happened in France, I managed to find a way,
two years later, to teach in Italy. I taught in three schools on the out-
skirts of Rome for several months. In France I had used nineteenth-
and twentieth-century poems, those being the ones I knew best; in
Italy, for similar reasons, I used mostly Renaissance and earlier poems
(Petrarch, Dante, Angiolieri, Cavalcanti) but not entirely (also Leopardi
and Marinetti). I used Petrarch's sestina "To Every Animal That Lives
on Earth" to inspire sestinas. Dante's "Guido vorrei" (which begins
"Guido, I wish that you and Lapo and I / Were carried off by magic /
And put in a boat, which, every time there was wind, / Would sail on
the ocean exactly where we wanted . . . ") seemed a wonderful poem
to teach to ten-year-old Italian children. Though it has mysteries for
scholars, its main idea is engagingly simple: "Friend, I wish we had a
magic vehicle that would take us anywhere we wanted and where we
could do as we wish." I asked the children to use names in their poems, as Dante uses the names of his friends Guido and Lapo, in making
their wishful invitations. Some of these had the sweetness and restraint
of the original:

Cynthia, Luigi, Rosalba
I would like you to come with me
To travel around the earth on a white and blue ship

Others had mostly its intensity:

I'd like to take you on a train, Maria
I'd like to take you to Rome on a train, Maria
I'd like to sleep on the train, Maria
I'd like to take you with the train to Venice, Maria
I'll carry you off to sing with the train, Maria
I'll give you a kiss on the train, Maria
I'd like to shoot you with a pistol on the train, Maria
I'll kill you on the train, Maria
I'll marry you on the train, Maria

I taught a poem by the thirteenth-century poet, Cecco Angiolieri, an extremely aggressive sonnet in which most of the lines begin "Se fossi" (If I were): "If I were fire, I'd burn up the world / If I were the wind, I'd blow it away. . . ." My Genzano students were happy to join in the destruction:

If I were a window I'd throw my teachers out of me
If I were a crane, I'd demolish the school
If I were a panther, I'd bite President Leone

I taught Cavalcanti's poem "Perch'i' no spero," which begins "Because I do not hope ever to return / Little song of mine, to Tuscany / Go you, lightly and softly / Straight to my lady. . . ." Once it is there, Cavalcanti wants his poem to talk to his lady about him. I asked my students to write a poem addressed to their poem itself, asking it to do something for them, anything at all. The results were, sometimes, like Cavalcanti's poem, full of strong feeling:

Oh my poem
Go and speak of me
To my ancestors and to everyone I know
Speak of my kind teacher
Good like a father
Oh my beautiful poem say to all
That the world is more beautiful, if the
People are kind
Go, I pray you
I, it is obvious, can't visit the world
Go, you are my only hope.

There was something in Leopardi's poetry I thought I could teach to children, but it took me a while to find it. There seemed to be no helpfully imitatable form in poems like "La Luna" and "L'Infinito" but there was the strong presence of a feeling I thought the children would respond to: loneliness, solitude. For the Leopardi class, I read "La Luna" and "L'Infinito" aloud, explained what was difficult in them, and talked about their atmosphere of loneliness. I asked for poems about times of being or feeling alone. For form I suggested beginning every line with the word *alone (solo* or *sola)*.

> Alone the bird flies in the month of September
> Alone with a girl in a car in the dark
> Alone in my room thinking of my little dog who died
> Alone I was studying one summer morning . . .
>
> . . . I was alone in the country
> I was alone in the mountains
> I was alone in a boat
> I was alone in class

I taught Marinetti's "To a Racing Car" (it begins "Vehement god of a race of steel, / Automobile drunk on space") somewhat as I had taught Breton's "Free Union," to inspire a poem of exaggerated praise or boasting:

> My piano, when I want it to, turns into the ocean, the universe, the mountains . . .
>
> My car runs not on gas but on gold
> My car moves faster than light
> My car cries because I go to school
> My car has a blue fiancé . . .

My Italian students openly expressed their enthusiasm for their new subject:

> Don't worry, Poetry,
> I'll never abandon you
> Even if when I grow up
> I forget about you
> I beg you, make me remember
> Of you, the beautiful thoughts that I had
> When I knew you . . .
>
> Poetry you seem a person dressed in white in the middle of many people dressed in blue I know you right away . . .

Teaching in China was my most ambitious endeavor, since I didn't know the language and I had very little idea of what Chinese education, or Chinese schoolchildren, were like. (I was invited to China to read and lecture in 1984 by the Writers Union. Teaching in schools was something that was worked out after I got there.) I taught six lessons in Beijing and four in Shanghai. In Beijing I taught with Zhu Ciliu, a professor and poet, who was perfectly bilingual. Facing the two hundred children the Chinese authorities had given me as students, I would speak for a minute or two—explaining the poetry ideas, giving suggestions—then turn to Zhu Ciliu who would translate for the children what I had said. Timidity and unsureness led me to use simple poetry ideas like Wishes and I-used-to-but-now for my first six lessons. In China I really didn't know if the teaching was going to work at all. The children, however, sitting there, being told through an interpreter to write poems, which I don't believe they had ever done in school (certainly not this way), were at first puzzled, then quickly excited. They wrote, covering their notebook pages with Chinese characters, at what seemed to me an incredible pace:

I wish I had a box in which there was everything . . .

I wish Newton had not been born yet so the law of gravity would be
   my discovery
I wish summer would last forever so I wouldn't have to say good-bye
   to my beautiful skirt with flowers on it . . .

I was very very fat, too fat to walk
Now I am very very thin, like a bamboo.

These first lessons having gone well, I felt bold enough—with a great deal of help from Zhu Ciliu—to use some classic Chinese poems as models. Zhu Ciliu suggested this quatrain by the eighteenth-century poet Liu Zongyuan, which describes a scene partly by saying what is not there:

No birds flying over the hills
No one on the mountain trails
Only a fisherman in palm cape and straw hat
Fishing alone on a river in falling snow.

In the original, the first two lines begin with the word *meiyo*, "there is not." Zhu Ciliu read the poem aloud and wrote it on the blackboard. I asked the children to begin their first two or three lines with *meiyo* and then conclude with a word like *only* to say what *was* there. Each line of

Liu Zongyuan's poem has seven Chinese characters. I told the children they could if they liked make their lines of seven characters, too:

> There is no green grass
> There are no sweet-smelling flowers
> Over the blurry barren hill
> There is only flying snow
>
> No one walking on the path
> No bird flying in the trees
> Only one person on a bench
> Reading out loud in a foreign language

Another class was based on some lines by Li Bai about the Yellow River:

> The Yellow River with its water from the sky
> Flows on and on into the sea . . .
> Bursting through the Kunlun Mountain in the West
> The Yellow River roars across ten thousand li and leaps over the
>   Dragon Gate

I told the children to imagine they were looking at something that was very long and that came from far away—like a river, a mountain range, the sky—and to write a poem about where it began, where it went, and where it ended:

> A gust of hard wind from the Yangtse River
> Raising up flying sand blowing moving stones
> Ranging as if in a land with no people
> Roaring roaring until it stops at the Huang Po
>
> Shan Yin Street comes from the sky
> Deep and long it leads to the earth
> The stream of cars runs without end
> Like a huge dragon it rolls to a distant place.

The best poetry, it turned out, was as inspiring to children in China, Haiti, Italy, and France as it has been to my students in New York. French children were moved by Baudelaire to create landscapes that mirrored their feelings; Italian children, following Dante and Cecco, to propose ideal voyages and to create vigorous invective; Chinese ten-year-olds found mysterious solitudes in present-day Shanghai as Liu Zongyuan had found them in the eighteenth-century countryside. No matter how much I had expected, these results were surprising, suggesting, as they did, the probable universality of the power—still, sadly, by so many, unrecognized—of children's imagination and intelligence.

Jack Collom

What I See in Children's Writing

I have never worked a day in school without getting excited about some of the things the kids wrote. Generally speaking, though, their poetry shows little sustained versification skill, precision of thought, conscious subtlety, or breadth of metaphoric reference. Lacking these possibilities for involvement (or distraction), the mind turns to and focuses on the tiny "moves" from word to word, musical, imagistic, ideational. The effect is a back-to-basics concentration that seems refreshingly simple and aesthetically solid.

Children tend to write works that contain wonderful flashes of poetry. They show little appetite for revision and their writings are often conventional or generalized. But they, being youthful, are "naturals." The descriptive word most often applied to children's art is "fresh." What does this mean? I think it chiefly means that, in lacking a sophisticated adult context of moral or other philosophical acceptability into which impressions must fit, the child is likely to get simple, direct, sensory takes on phenomena, and find words to match. The verbal juxtapositions may thereby be full of surprises. However significant the elaborate adult skills are in poetry—and this is not to deny that significance—the spirit, the vivifying spark, remains surprise, which is proof of accuracy to the moment, of originality.

The first day's writing in my workshops is usually in the form of "I Remember" poems. Each "line" of the poem begins with the words "I remember." I encourage students to write in the terms of ordinary talk and relate personal memories, using details. The matter of details needs a lot of pushing: kids, though having the fresh eye and beginning to order their world, often lack faith in the personal fact. This tends to produce unedifying essences like "I remember going to the movies with my friend" (end of memory). Lively examples are best for urging detail.

I remember when I was in third grade and my best friend liked the same guy until we found out he was making love letters to Nancy Grand. I remember when my best friend and I gave the biggest Halloween party ever and he left Nancy so he could get some soda. My friend was dressed as a man so she asked Nancy for a dance. Nancy was so romanced dancing she did not know she was on the edge of the swimming pool. As she fell she cried out, saying, "Oh you rude gentle man!"

—*Eyerilis Femandez, fifth grade*

In "making" love letters, the oddity forces a fresh look at the word *making* and at what is done to produce a love letter. "Making" love letters seems a solider venture than "sending" or even "writing" them, thus a greater challenge to the frustrated girl duo. The speed and economy of statement make the introduction of the third girl, Nancy, coming right after the second girl, a socko expansion. "Biggest . . . ever" by its exaggeration casts the event into the archetype-familiarity of myth or fairy tale. "Romanced dancing" is both odd and concise and adds the musical focus of rhyme. "As she fell" skips over the push, but we know it more quickly than if we had been told. There is a formal, poker-faced tone (effective by contrast with the content)—as in "As she fell she cried out, saying, 'Oh you rude gentle man!'"—that charms by its oddness, intensifies the slight fairy-tale flavor, and illuminates the paradox in the "man's" both dancing and dousing. (I recommend that you read the student examples a second time after reading my comments.)

I remember going to the store with my uncle and I got shot.
I remember going to school and they mugged me.
I remember going to the movies and a monster tried to eat me.
I remember going home and my mother was not there.
I remember going to my friend's house and he would not let me play.
I remember going to the park with my friends and one of them hit me in the head with a ball.
I remember making new friends and one of them hit me with a spitball.
I remember watching TV and it broke on me because I kicked it.

—*Danny Santiago, fifth grade*

Memory coughs up, typically, catastrophe, more easily believable and interesting, even to oneself, than blessedness. There's a shift of reality level from "shot" and "mugged" to the monster line, and that shift retroactively changes the light in which we take the first two lines, introduces playfulness. Also, the abruptness, the lack of transitional devices, lets the change simply be there. Adults often lose poetry via attempts at palatability of shift. The understatement, then, of "my mother was not there," the lack of ornament, shows that mere absence can be as disastrous as violent attacks are. Then the piece goes off into a humorous accumulation of futility, with a mea culpa bow at the end. A shapely, funny (but not whimsical) confession.

> I remember when there was a fire in my building. I went to
> school. Everyone asked me what happened. I was so happy.
>
> —*Gilma Alvarez, fifth grade*

An adult would not, generally, admit so clearly that the happiness of getting attention could supplant the fear proper to a fire. And simplicity makes it stand out.

> I remember the day I had to go away down to the lake.
> I remember the water was light like the sunlight. In the early morning.
>
> —*Oyelino Genao, fifth grade*

"In the early morning." If this sentence fragment were written by an adult, I would think it a derivative attempt at poetic tone. But because I trust a kid—this kid—not to have mixed that much in literary style, I'm brought back to the thing expressed, a key slant on the identity of water and light, in lake dawn. This child's "ignorance" is a transparency for pure observation.

> I remember when it was snowing, all of that snow comes from the
> blue sky and ends up on the street.
>
> —*Cynthia Gomez, sixth grade*

The child's touch, syntactically, is the use of the term "blue sky" (not just "sky"). The presence of "blue" makes the color (white) of the snow implicit, which in turn brings out the complicated color and all of the street. Which in turn, by contrast, opens thoughts of what whiteness "means." All because of "blue."

> I remember when I locked myself in the bathroom in the dark. The
> darkness came over me like a monster and swept my feet with fear.
>
> —*David Kalicharan, sixth grade*

"Swept my feet." A perfect kid's-observation. That he chooses feet makes the monstrousness more inclusive (head to foot), but the verb "swept" is the crux, one of those applications never seen before but instantly recognizable (language thereby extended).

I remember when a car hit me and I jumped up into the hot air.

—*James Gausp, sixth grade*

"Hot" makes the car-reality emerge. With the presence of temperature, the car is no longer merely a hitting thing. The air heat, being sensory, reminds us of the car's heat, motor, smells, dirt, metal, gas.

★　　★　　★

Writing about common things (hand, egg, hair, street, floor, rock, etc.) helps express and maintain the sense that in overlooked daily minutiae reside endless energies for us.

NYC Street

Cars honking people talking all the
stores open big crowds in the stores
drop your twenty-dollar package does anybody care no nobody they all just
step on it they don't look where
they're going just want to get home!

—*Juan Martinez, seventh grade*

Lack of punctuation (common with kids) in this case creates an unbroken rush appropriate to the New York street, and in many cases promotes the everything-flows sense much poetry seeks to uncover.

By the way hair comes out in the morning, it describes the
experience you could have had during the night.

—*Priscilla Leon, eighth grade*

"Comes out" is the perfect verb form, with its dual meanings of emerge and result, and "could have had" seems to hint at dream, without denying the chance of "real" adventure.

New York can be colorful when thunder and lightning are splashing
through the dark skies . . .

—*Maria Villacis, eighth grade*

Most adults would not be loose enough to apply "splashing" to thunder too, but it gives the dimension—sound *and* light—that raises images, even questions, rather than wrapping them up.

The egg amazes me,
its oval shape is so soothing . . .

—*Jorge Gezao, sixth grade*

That soothing is amazing amazes me, and that oval shape is soothing soothes me.

> A nose is like a hole in the wall. But that's not all. It falls between your mouth and your eyes, but when it falls it snores.

> *—José Rodriguez, seventh grade*

Children love rhyme. Adults love rhyme. Many in the poetry workshop business have scorned rhyme because we know more subtly expressive alternatives (and because we've been following our own historic rebellion), and because we know kids do abuse rhyme. Often they do let it take over and thus blot out everything else. But rhyme is great; it does give a simple power, often funny by the nature of sound (extreme emphases). It makes solid connections. Also, kids often use rhyme in scattered ways. In this poem, the double use of "falls" is very quick.

★   ★   ★

The acrostic is an admirable form for student use. There's only one letter of requirement per line, which gives kids enough to go on (they are often at sea without a form to work from) but doesn't over-dictate. The acrostic's lightness tends to stimulate surreal juxtapositions and other originalities. Also, the requirement comes at the beginning of the line (not at the end as with rhyme), so after the initial letter the rhythm is free. Acrostics encourage interesting linebreaks, show the kids that lines are not just sentences or thoughts, but also sound units and fragmentation devices. The form abets the development of subtle, surprising, "off" connections between the spine-word and the text, as well as the economy of the list and near-list (elimination of connectives).

> Again
> Left alone,
> Offended by others.
> No one cares when my love
> Escapes and comes to an end.

> *—Martha Perez, eighth grade*

"Escapes" is an "off" usage hinting that even benevolent love may be a prison of sorts. That to be left alone "offends" is similarly interesting.

> Running in circles
> Of love and passion,
> Brainless.
> Everything is

Really happening because I am
Thinking of you.

—*Robert Marte, eighth grade*

A spirited love solipsism.

Under the artificial me which
No one really knows, I try to
Deliver the message that I hope
Everyone will see. What is
Right or wrong, I am
Starting to find out.
Trying to know which one I should do.
Although I am confused and
No one is listening and I am almost near
Death,
I'm trying to
Nervously tell
God to fill me with understanding.

—*Jane Martinez, eighth grade*

This elaborate, sincere poem has, perhaps by luck, an appropriate confusion that balances the nervous rhythm (mostly via linebreaks) to express a mental process shaking along towards the goal of understanding.

Closed is
Like blocking
Off
Something that might be
Excellent, or maybe it's just a plain
Door.

—*José Garcia, sixth grade*

Line-length here delineates a shapely double shutting—the slow "off" prefiguring the final "door."

Period

Pacing every sentence,
Erasing every meaning,
Riding always at end,
In and out of things;
Outstanding point never
Dies.

—*Richard Suarez, sixth grade*

"Pacing," "erasing," "in and out" and "never / Dies" bring up a matrix of complex questions about the effects and nature of a period it would take books of philosophy to close again.

Climbing a mountain and
Reaching the top seems to
Open the gates of the
Sun rising and
Shining over me.

    —Joyce Walters, fifth grade

The relationship of "Cross" to the lines is original but immediately clear—the religious spirit calling out the light.

Every
Day is like a
Dream from
Yesterday.

    —Eddy Almonte, seventh grade

Complete daily prophetic fulfillment in one's given name. Also the musical resonance of "everyday/yesterday," "day/dream" and the name "Eddy."

Crying
Roses
Every moment
Every day
Pretending I like it.

    —Maribel Cairo, seventh grade

A fresh and perfect rendition of the Ugly Duckling situation.

Pisces
Is my
Sign
Cool
Every time. Can't
Stop thinking why I'm so fine.

    —Ana Grullon, seventh grade

A charming boast. Interesting vowel progression, with an "I" in every line but one.

Bouncing
Along
Like the ground was just there to
Let it spring back into the air.

 —*Juan Martinez, seventh grade*

Neat. Check the rhythm, which is ball-like (as the bounces get shorter).

Fire is an
Incredible friend
Ready to turn into an incredible
Enemy.

 —*Santiago Negrón*

Rhythmically shows the turn.

Math is
An interesting subject.
To me it is a
Hymn of numbers.

 —*Carmen Alvarez, sixth grade*

The last line a beautiful epiphany.

Open your mind to the
Universe and
Run back home and get your lunch.

 —*Juan Lugo, seventh grade*

A perfect deflation of overexpansion.

★ ★ ★

I've found collaborative poems to be extremely rich, especially as training. Due to the compositional trade-off, the burden of intentionality is lifted. Instead of a point to make, the work's main thrust is toward a common language. The resulting "gap" tends to be filled with association and response. Focus on syntax as play (a big attitudinal step toward mastery) is encouraged by fragmentation of story and sense.

I have seen
the tree on the corner
in a spring bud
and summer green
yesterday

it was yellow gold
then a cold wind began to blow
now I know you really don't see a tree
until you don't see its bones.

 —Tamara D. and Yvonne Luna, seventh grade

Here the "moves" resemble those of a contemporary poem, adult. "Seen" is echoed in "tree . . . corner"; "corner" expresses a fitting vulnerability of position. "In a spring bud"—a natural prophecy. "Summer green"—sound of "seen" again, also seasonal progression. "Yesterday" is sensible and rhythmic. "Yellow gold" among the spare lines is a striking extravagance, appropriate redundancy. The next line rings the *o* and blows out the tight rhythm. The last two lines leaf out even more and serve as a perfect summing up thought, with sound unsullied.

flea
flea fly flow
vista
commala commala commala vista
na, na, na, na, na, na a vista
she's eni meine epo meine who wa
awa who meine
shana meine epo meine oh wa awa
he's bip billy epo an tope sho
wa awa
awa ani shhhh.

 —Sandy Arthurton and Jodi White, ninth grade

Original experimentation with sound. The burden of sole authorship removed, the authors had the nerve to play with the poem.

The Moon—It's a Busy Place

Stars walking all over,
Working hard to shine,
Who still after years get very little
pay. But they get a day off to watch
their favorite program "The Jetsons"
and afterwards go out to light and
play with their pals, but all of a
sudden bang boom pop poop a little
star with her star-pox who got sick
and wants to find out from what, so
she goes to the doctor and finds out
she's allergic to the moon.

 —Estella Pando & Maritza Rodrigues, seventh grade

Astral anthropomorphism, a little goofy charm.

★   ★   ★

The "lune" (adapted from the form invented by poet Robert Kelly) is a simplification of formal haiku. Instead of counting syllables, in which act many kids become overly concerned with the mere mechanics, one counts words: 3/5/3. With lots of good examples, students will demonstrate a fine apprehension of the power of tiny, non-exposi-tional, word-by-word effects, plus the necessity of balanced rhythm, which looms large in a short piece. Thus there's a push toward the knowledge that ideas do not exist without their expressive articula-tions; and the importance of language "per se" is brought home.

> When the sun's
> rays hit the shades, it
> lights up lines.

This piece (dashed off by a Nebraska fifth grader) excellently illus-trates that poetry can be plain talk of the immediate environment (sun striking venetian blinds on classroom window). It is also a deceptively complex maze of sound correspondences and play: simple rhythms in lines 1 and 3 contrasting with syncopation of line 2 (differing syllable lengths, comma pause, consonantal percussion), *n*'s around soft "the" in line 1 forming a soundswing, "ray-shades" assonance and "hit-it" rhyme, soft central "the" repeated; five terminal *s*'s, "lights-lines," "sun's-up," *n* again in "lines," *t* in "lights"—until "lights up lines" car-ries more import than the physical window pattern alone. I advise students that the author probably didn't calculate all this, but that through a careful, though nonspecific, concentration these musical phrases just came.

> In trains people
> are like crazy because they
> push to fit.
>
> —*Richard Gard, fifth grade*

Idea—concisely crushed. And that it is crazy to "push to fit" is an idea with benevolent social repercussions.

> Sky is light.
> Sun will fill the air.
> You will see.
>
> —*Monica Grief, fifth grade*

Double meaning (see and understand) of last line covers the matter, eye to brain. Plenty of scope in a tiny poem.

Peo, Peo, Peo.
The bird in the window
is very hungry.

—*Naomi Rodriguez, sixth grade*

To me, "peo" makes hunger immediate and religious.

In every snowflake
there is a beautiful village
waiting for you.

—*Anelsa Lugo, sixth grade*

A lovely thought, though not too original (perhaps influenced by children's literature).

Black is dark,
red and yellow very bright.
Purple is both.

—*Brenda Tavarez, sixth grade*

Perfect economy in an original classification of colors.

★　　★　　★

To give students an unknown word to define playfully allows them obvious free imaginative rein and a chance to imitate a style (the dictionary). Nothing else to do, so play will out. Asked to make poems this way, the students are likely to expand the sense of pure image play.

Mosaic:

a brass instrument or a two-legged animal or a Chinese calendar or a
　　French word or a drop of blood.
a pair of moccasins, a new traffic sign, children from another planet.
a married boy, a crazy cloud.
something made of horses' legs. a person's name that comes from the
　　sky and glows in the dark.

The person is a cloud that glows in the dark. It comes from the sky and sings through the night. Every night I hear the tone, it sounds so beautiful that I sing with that person. Then that person comes out from the sky and starts singing the song once more. Then I knew who the person was, but she's beautiful. She told me her name and it was Mosaic. Then she sang a song about her name.

—*Sandra Santiago, fifth grade*

Praline:

a duck with a burned leg.
a bag of dirty tricks.
a line of peas.
a beautiful flower with the scent of Death.
a mouse that sucks blood.
a soft road with cushions to sleep on, or maybe a tent.
a pair of blue pants.
the planet of the peas came on TV,
the green takeover.

　　—Daniel Constant, sixth grade

I don't want to dwell on haiku here, but one of the chief effects in such compression may be a stunning time-warp, as in:

Snow on a bare tree,
suddenly sunshine comes through.
Pop! The leaves come out.

　　—Maribelle Suarez, seventh grade

You don't have to make
your bed, because sooner or
later you'll be dead.

　　—Marc Santiago, seventh grade

★　　★　　★

One of the great areas of possible expression, which are at least as poignantly available to children's sensibilities as to adults', is that of place. Kids are, by nature of their special need to define themselves, especially keen in getting takes on their surroundings, and are also likely to be open, without prejudice, to the local facts. Generally, kids need only be pushed in the direction of details to uncover a vivid, individuated articulation about the places they know.

Feeling low and
Feeling down,
I go to the special place.
I quietly sit, forcing myself to stay.
I was out, now I'm back.
Now I want to play.
But my fingers won't bring forth a melody.
I try to imagine myself far away from what is reality.
I'm sitting in a little corner of the room.
It's small and it's ordinary.

But it's my special place.
Because it's the only place that I can
Run away with my mind.
Sitting very still,
Only my fingers doing the moving.
I concentrate very hard.
And suddenly I'm not there any more.
I'm in my imaginary world, completely gone.
The only trace of me that's left in
My little corner of the room
Is the melody that my hands bring
Forth, from the magic box in front of me.

—*Jane Martinez, eighth grade*

This place in the Dominican Republic is in the country. There is no electricity but there is a feeling of necessity to talk in the dark. We make jokes and riddles but then there's sleepiness and people start to leave. We are all in what you might call a shack but there's no doors, just logs, which hold the shack up, and the roof is all of tree palms. Now it's very dark, we put one candle in the middle of the shack and then the candle goes off because of the breeze. So then we wait and then moonlight comes from the sky of the night. And the moonlight gives light to the outside of the shack, which is good; when we go we can see where we are going. It sometimes gets spooky and I get nervous but the stories, jokes, and riddles calm me down. After that I sleep on the rocking chair.

—*Rafael Torres, eighth grade*

★ ★ ★

Innocence—of literary conventions, of a matured scheme of thought, of regular English usage—in children allows certain brightnesses to come through that tend to pass less freely into the poems of adults. Relative innocence of grammar and syntax leaves room for oddities of expression to emerge, and force the reader to take a fresh look at the words or combinations used. Innocence of philosophy (except the most obvious generalities) allows original and concrete juxtapositions of ideas. The concreteness, the dominance of sense data, leads to speed, concision, sudden leaps and shifts, and playfulness of association, qualities that seem to resemble the momentary workings of the mind. Innocence of literariness encourages unembellished, "natural" speech patterns, with their own history-honed rhythms, economy, and fitness of emphasis. Innocence makes possible an ease of communication with the moment. Children's works sometimes have a clear documentary authenticity of the author's immediate awareness.

These qualities, resulting from lack of sophistication as I take it, are valuable. In adults' poetry, violations of English standards are commonly allowed, even encouraged, as artistic experimentation, and then judged on how they seem to work. Children may be similarly abetted in their originalities. (I often wonder how many striking images or phrasings are thought of only to be crossed out or deemed "stupid" or "too risky," and lost to us all.) We understand the necessity of "the child in the poet," so why not create similar room for the poet in the child, without discrediting educational discipline? In fact, the child who takes to poetry experimentally will certainly develop a love of language, leading to increased mastery of standards as well as to an artistic sense. If the initiation into making poems comes with an appreciation for untrammelled, even jarring, verbal energies, the poetic impetus may then exist, in the first place, and then can move toward exactitude as work goes on. It's important not only to praise the students' poems but also to point out just how they seem to succeed, because technical details, especially when put in physical terms, can be both absorbing and reassuring to children. In any case, the seeing and judging of children's poetry should proceed case by case as, on whatever level, the best of it is made.

Peter Sears

What Do You Say about a Terrible Poem?

How sad it is
   how suddenly
It wakes you up
   reality

Just drifting off
   without a care
Then suddenly
   it's always there

Dragging you back
   no reason why
Ending your dreams
   not letting you fly

Taking your freedom
   of sailing in air
Leaving you wounded
   not wishing to dare

Clipping your wings
   making you low
Bringing you down
   not letting you go

It wakes you up
   it makes you see
Sad isn't it
   reality

To the student who wrote this poem is the teacher to say, "This poem is vague and corny"? No. Is the teacher to say, "The repeated use of 'it' is weak writing"? No. Besides, the student would take the comment as grammatical fanaticism and insensitivity to the clever ploy of revealing the subject in the last line. Is the teacher to say, "I prefer reality some-times to the dreams I have?" No. Yet all these criticisms are valid. The poem is terrible.

So what? The intent is not valid criticism, the intent is teaching. Not theoretical teaching. That's easy. This is hard teaching. This is more fun. The challenge is clear: if you cannot be honest and sensible with-out alienating the student, what are you to do? Nothing is more ticklish in English teaching than teaching poetry writing. One line of thinking begs off: "Just encourage them. Kids are so imaginative, you know." But encouragement of a poem like this one only leads to more of the same. English teachers are buried in such slop every year. As far as I can tell, poetry writing exercises produce the worst writing an English teacher sees. (Fiction writing exercises, on the other hand, don't seem to cause the same problem.)

Why? There is something about poetry that youngsters detest, or say they do, probably because they are afraid, which is part of the prob-lem. And when they write a poem, they usually drop every principle of good writing, from precision to punctuation. The common view of poetry is that it is elitist and obscure, translatable only by teachers. The students believe, therefore, that they are trying to create something unclear. But this common misconception about poetry is less crucial to teaching poetry writing than what students think about their own writing.

Take the poem at the beginning of this article. The student prob-ably likes it, likes the idea of how sad it is that reality "wakes you up" from your dreaming, and likes the rhyme. So is the teacher supposed to make the student see the poem as tripe so he or she will go on to write a decent poem? No, absolutely not. To encourage this student to write in any fashion other than this maudlin generalizing requires going into his or her thoughts about poetry. And this effort requires not only patience but respect for the ideas.

Why students write poetry is, I think, the most important point to teaching poetry writing. High school students write to express themselves, not to learn something about the genre. They want to hear themselves think, see themselves feel. They like this opportunity even though they may still contend that they hate poetry. If what they have written is unclear to others, they don't care. They know what they are saying. As for reworking a poem, why bother? "You write when you feel like it, and the way it comes out is the way it is. Once you have written it, it's done."

There is nothing wrong with one-shot self-expression if the teacher wants each student just to get something on paper. But teaching poetry writing is another enterprise altogether, one that requires taking on more formidable obstacles than "But I hate poetry" or "Do we really have to?" This is not to say that there aren't wonderful student poems blooming each year and that there aren't wonderful exercises that propel students into visiting their imaginations on paper. However, these are the exceptions. High school students are more conventional and cautious about their expression than they were when they were younger and will be when they are college age. Peer pressure is powerful to the point of being oppressive. Most high school poetry is terrible, and the students aren't interested in making it any better. Students don't want to write poems; they want to philosophize. They want to use poetry to pontificate about life, to carry on about what they like, to spout abstractions, to complain, and to wallow in tragic sadness.

That's what comes naturally to them. Using poetry to indulge themselves is the way they are going to come to a poetry writing exercise. Not all students all the time, but enough to depress teachers to the point where they want to say, "You are not writing poetry, you are writing philosophy." "Huh?" may be the response, yet the statement is not necessarily going to put students off. They might even like it. Philosophy sounds good, probably better than poetry. So go for it: "Philosophy is general and declarative; poetry is specific and evocative."

If the student asks what "evocative" means, you have yourself an opening. If the student contends, "But it rhymes, it's a poem," you needn't backtrack: "Rhyme is a possibility of poetry, a property of sound. You write rhyming philosophy." At which point the student may become dismayed and wander off. Yet your point may stick: "Poetry and philosophy are two ways of writing, of expressing yourself." And if you get a chance, ask, "Which do you prefer?" You can respond to "I don't know" with "You appear to prefer philosophy," which may provoke a question about the difference.

If the student lingers or comes back, you might suggest, rather than going into an abstract explanation, "What about writing the same idea in two different forms: philosophy and poetry?" A quizzical look allows you to pick up on one detail in the supposed poem and say with gusto, "Like this, see this detail—clear, concise—I really can see what you mean. And the words are good, very exact." If the student brightens up a bit, add, "Try fooling around with the other words to get ones you really like. Take some chances if you feel like it." If this encouragement falls as flat as a stack of essays on Sunday evening, and the student replies, "I don't know what you mean. I tried to do what you told us. You don't like mine, do you?" Then go for subject matter. Ask questions: "What were you thinking of when you wrote the poem? Did the writing set off other ideas? Did you end up going where you had planned to?" Talk process and subject. Get the student talking.

If the student becomes willing to go back to the original inspiration and to write again, then emphasize conveying an idea or feeling through real things, specific examples. And suggest that he write it as *prose*. Really. This way he won't be thinking about writing a poem. "I am now writing a poem" is the worst thing to be thinking when writing a poem. Not only does it distract you, but it also makes you careful. Even people who write long, hard, and well succumb to this danger at times. Prose lines, on the other hand, roll out easily and tend to clutter themselves nicely with all sorts of real items, details you can see; and these specifics you, the teacher, can bring out more by fooling around with line endings, making deletions, combining lines.

Fooling around? Yes. Writing poetry is serious fooling around. Like tinkering with a car. You tinker for fun and with purpose, to make the car run better. Like experimenting with a recipe: maybe add this and take this out. You are not sure what it's going to taste like, but you're curious. You will taste it, you invented it. You tinker with a poem for the fun of it and for the possibility of making it better.

If a student does a prose rendition of the grand philosophical statement and calls it a poem, make a copy and, right in front of him, tinker with it. You needn't change much; just stare at it and hold your pencil over a particular part. Then cross something out and ask the student, "Do you like the line better this way?" If he does, keep it. If he doesn't, restore what you crossed out. The key words here are "like" and "better." Your tinkering will come across as suggestions, as possibilities. The student will see that it interests you, that you are doing it first for the fun of it, and, most importantly, that the choices are *his*. *You* are not correcting, you are exploring. You are fooling around.

If the student isn't there with you, write all over it. Not in red pen. Mark the good stuff first. "KEEP!" capitalized. "YES" capitalized. Underline, circle. "DON'T CHANGE" is a comment students really like. Then put less emphatic marks by the weaker parts. Perhaps a question mark or a wiggly line in the margin or the word "fuzzy" or "I'm not sure what you mean" or "I can't see this clearly." Or maybe draw an arrow to indicate a possible jump to create more interesting connections by obliterating explanatory connectives. Perhaps suggest removing all modifiers, especially articles, and then replacing the ones he really needs and wants. Take the first three or four lines of prose and try them in a couple of different ways, not changing a word, and ask the student which he or she prefers. Or ask the student to do it. And if you get a chance to talk with the student, don't explain or theorize. Just say, "You've got something good here. I liked working with it. Now decide for yourself. Forget everything I've said and have some fun with it. If you want to show it to me again, fine. If you don't, fine too. Oh, and, if you feel like it, write some more."

Any interest on the student's part is a success, because what you have managed—by magic and force of character, of course—is a deft circumventing of the stubborn, common, student defense for one-shot writing. Just entertaining the possibility of changing one word to make the poem *better* undermines the prevalent teenage theory of what I call "spontaneous expression," the idea that the best way to say it is how it comes out first. (Other students may be hesitant about actually saying what they mean or feel they don't really have anything to say; for them, poetry is a good guise because it's obscure.) If this "spontaneous expression" theory comes up, take it seriously, show respect for it, and dismantle it. There is a vast difference between the impression of spontaneity and literal spontaneity. The appearance of effortless writing takes work. If your students don't buy this idea, use sports or dancing as an analogy. Don't let go of this point, it's critical.

The idea of spontaneous expression is important not only because many students entertain it—they want all things to be simple, to have answers—but it is also important, more important, because it raises a fundamental issue of writing: Whom are you writing for? The issue is audience. Poetry may appear to be a public art and students certainly know it that way—they read poems in books, on greeting cards, as graffiti—but they are interested in it more as a private art. Poetry allows them to express themselves, and it offers a wonderful advantage over other forms. You can hide in a poem behind fancy words, fragmented syntax, and obscure allusions. Writing poetry may be a lot more fun than reading poetry, but why hide? "I am not hiding. I write for myself. If I show it to some people and they like it, that's nice, but that isn't what matters." This is writing as personal expression. The audience is one. Maybe a few others, "if I feel like it."

The audience of one, of the self, is fundamental to high school students. It is an assertion of their independence. The importance of this is not to be underestimated. No wonder they are ill at ease with "analyzing poetry," morally ill at ease. They have even less sympathy with the idea of revising a poem. Showing them a famous poet's draft or your own isn't necessarily going to change their minds. Logic has no place here. To be willing to change one's poem is to sacrifice personal integrity for public approval, and adult approval at that. Reworking a poem must be presented as only a *personal* possibility, a way to make what you like better to you, not to the collective "they." Rewriting is a personal *choice*. Even the adamant student can be reached if he or she has more than one poem. "Which poem do you like better? Why?" Tell the student which your favorite is. Be specific. Point. Say what it is you can't understand or see clearly. If the poem is about an incident, ask about it. Maybe jot some notes and give them to the student, saying, "Here, these notes are interesting. I didn't realize how much was involved in the incident. This poem could be better, I think, if this important personal experience were made clearer. But that's up to you."

Maybe, just maybe, the student goes off grazed by the writing muse. That is, the rewriting muse. Not the sweet, generous, well-known one that drops a nice line in your ear, but the prodder, the picador, the provoker of "Let's-see-if-I can-get-this-just-right." The one called work. But the harder the work, the more fun. And if the student gets smitten by the strange places his fooling around with words takes him, then tell him straight: "Look out, this apparently harmless activity called writing isn't harmless at all. It can be addictive. You can lose time, sleep, money, and the patience of your friends . . . and what are you left with? Words—words and your screwball, screwloose curiosity!" This idea can penetrate the hardest of teenage craniums. For them, fair warning acts as a prod, not a deterrent.

Ron Padgett

Creative Reading

By the age of five or six, most of us know that reading can be done aloud or silently. We have been read to and we have seen other people reading silently. In school, oral and silent reading are confirmed as the two modes.

I remember my elementary school classmates reading aloud, stumbling over hard words and skipping small ones, their voices toneless or constricted, as the rest of us followed the text with our eyes. I remember their reading the words differently than I would have, and how uncomfortable their ineptitude made me feel. This procedure of having one student read aloud as the others follow silently is now considered pedagogically defective: it induces a herky-jerky, regressive pattern in the eye movements, the opposite of what the reading teacher is trying to inculcate. Likewise, choral reading is not so popular as it was; it causes students to read in a lumbering singsong mass whose drone causes the text to lose its meaning. Individual students still read aloud, but their classmates simply listen and do not follow the text silently with their eyes.

Oral reading has several benefits: it relates the students' speaking vocabulary to their reading vocabulary; it develops their ability to differentiate between the varying tones of text and to project those modulations; and it lends color and body—a physical presence—to the text. Oral reading also makes it possible for students to begin to listen to themselves. These are a few of the many good reasons for reading aloud.

Silent reading is trickier: it isn't always silent. Some people "move their lips," even going so far as to whisper the words. When I was a child, lip moving was associated with the way old people read; perhaps they read that way because they had never been told not to. My grandfather used to sit in his easy chair, reading the newspaper, unaware that a steady stream of subtle hissing was issuing from his lips (in whispering, the *s*'s always carry best). Just as we are forbidden to count on our fingers, we are forbidden to move our lips in reading, because the physical motion limits our speed. We can't *say* words as quickly as we *see* them, and there's the added possibility that we might stumble over words simply because we don't know how to pronounce them. Pure sight readers are often able to read and understand many words they've never said or heard, including words that can't be "sounded out" phonetically.

But silent reading has a more subtle and interesting aspect: when readers keep their lips still, but "hear" in their heads the words on the page. This silent hearing is called "subvocalization."

Reading specialists now urge teachers to discourage both lip moving and subvocalization. (My teachers never mentioned subvocalization.) Like lip moving, subvocalization is frowned upon because it reduces reading speed: you can't hear words as quickly as you can see them.

But what's the hurry? I *like* subvocalization. I enjoy books that have a definite "voice," a voice provided by the author. What this means is that the style is so distinct that we're able to communicate with what seems to be a specific person.

The author does this by writing either in the first or third person. Some types of books lend themselves readily to either first- or third-person treatment. Autobiographies and travel books call for the first person.[1] These are two of the simplest, most direct uses of the first person. But the first person is not always so cut and dried. In fiction, for instance, the "I" may not be the author; it may be a character created by the author to tell a story—the *narrator*. Although we usually assume a bond of trust between the author and us, we cannot assume a similar bond between the narrator and us. Sometimes the narrator tells the story in a self-serving way, or simply lies. And what if the narrator turns out to be a lunatic? We cannot blame the author for the mental or moral condition of the narrator, any more than we can blame any other character for such conditions. Third-person writing is somewhat less thorny. Here, the voice may be assumed to be that of the author, with no tricky intermediary.

However, the voice can have great range, from the impersonal statistical report to the novel whose author is so engaged in the story that he or she cannot resist interrupting it to comment, praise, or blame.

Although most books are cast in essentially either the first or third person, some have internal variations. Nonfiction in the third person is often interspersed with quotations in the first person. Some first-person novels might be more aptly called *first-people* novels: different chapters are narrated by different characters. Such novels often use those characters' names as the chapter titles ("Chapter 1: Bill. Chapter 2: Frederika"). In both these variations, though, the reader knows at all times who is speaking.

This does not hold true for certain modern works. In Joyce's *Finnegans Wake* we are hard pressed to say who is speaking. Is it the author? A character? Or characters? The same goes for Eliot's "The Wasteland" and Ted Berrigan's *Sonnets*. In a novel called *Antlers in the Treetops,* which I wrote in collaboration with Tom Veitch, the voice shifts every few paragraphs, from author(s), to one character, then another, then to an entirely different author or set of authors, requiring the reader to invent a new voice every few paragraphs.

For, if we become involved with a text, we tend to invent a voice to hear it in. We invent what we assume is an appropriate tone of voice, such as the laconic, manly voice of Hemingway in the Nick Adams stories, the sophisticated, subtly modulated voice of Henry James in *The Golden Bowl,* the robust voice of Whitman in *Leaves of Grass,* the angular, deceptively quiet voice of Emily Dickinson in her poems. Sometimes when I read these authors, I "hear" these voices quite clearly. This subvocalization has a bonding effect on me and the words. That it causes me to read slower is anything but a drawback, it is exactly what I want! I love the feeling that the author is speaking to me, as if we were in the same room. This is particularly exciting if the author lived far away and long ago.

Inventing these voices can be tricky, of course. If you misinterpret the material, you intensify the error by inventing a voice based on the misinterpretation. Inventing the voices of writers from other cultures can be particularly risky. For some, the temptation, when reading Chinese poetry, might be to "hear" it as if its authors were essentially one big lyrical Charlie Chan; that is, our cultural stereotypes can force widely different works into a single mold. In so doing, we take the work one more step away from the original, just as the translation into English did, and the further away we get from the original, the less of its character remains.

Work that has no character in the first place is immune to such misinterpretation. Dry, official, toneless writing is dry, official, and toneless in translation, and it has the same "voice" as that which issues from the mouths of so many public and private officials. Their vocabulary is hazed over with latinisms and riddled with jargon; their verbs are passive; their diction is wooden; their clothing is uniform; their manner is what passes for adult. These people—men, mostly— speak unnaturally because their speech attempts to imitate formal, written language, and rather poorly, at that. When our education does not succeed in teaching us to think in complex structures, we cannot speak in complex structures either. We cannot utter long, grammatically complex (and correct) sentences; we cannot arrange our thoughts into logical groups; and we cannot order such groups into a cohesive whole. To compensate, these public figures use technical jargon, fashionable "buzz" words, and important-sounding abstractions. Alas, such language precipitates into the culture, like acid rain. Inventing accurate voices for the texts written by such people can hardly be called invention; it is, rather, an exercise in memory. In public the speaker talks like bad writing, begins to think like bad writing, and in private often creates more bad writing. The whole chain of thinking, writing, and reading not only has no originality, but also has no connection with the natural voice. If only some of these people who make speeches and give news conferences would talk to us the way they talk (we assume) at home! If we cannot have a clear public speech of intellectual character, let us at least have a little down-home authenticity.

But we have little of that. So what's to do with such hopelessly dull material? Well, we can simply not read it.

Or we can try *voice substitution*. It's an old technique used by comedians, but never, so far as I know, applied to reading. All you have to do is substitute a voice different from that of the text. For example, when reading the text of a presidential press secretary, imagine it being delivered by Donald Duck. If the text of a "tobacco industry spokesperson" bores you, imagine it in the voice of a professional wrestler. If you are about to be glazed over by the platitudes of a school commencement address, imagine it being delivered in the voice of Marlene Dietrich or Hattie McDaniel. This is similar to a method used by comic musician Spike Jones. The typical Spike Jones song begins with soothing, romantic material, as in "Cocktails for Two":

> Oh what delight to
> Be given the right to
> Be carefree and gay once again,
> No longer slinking
> Respectably drinking
> Like civilized ladies and men.
> No longer need we miss
> A charming scene like this:
> In some secluded rendezvous. . . .

Suddenly, a maniacal voice shrieks "Whoopee!," a police whistle sounds, a gun fires, and the music goes completely wild. The vocalist maintains his suavity, but is constantly undercut with burlesque sound effects (his crooning of "And we'll enjoy a cigarette" is followed by an emphysemic cough). This undercutting radically transforms the original material. It's a shame more young people don't know about Spike Jones; he is a delightful way to learn about broad parody and burlesque.

Jones was the master of his style, but his range was narrow. You might want to try more subtle transformations. In any case, combine whatever voice with whatever material you wish, keeping in mind that the greater the difference in voice and text, the more bizarre (and sometimes comic) the effect.

A similar set of techniques can be applied also to reading good writing. Let's say you are hooked on the crime novels of Elmore Leonard. Let's also say you have a favorite uncle who used to run numbers. Why not imagine his voice reading Elmore Leonard to you? That's what the companies that produce spoken arts records do: they try to match up the voice with the material. They pair off Irish actress Siobhan McKenna and James Joyce's writing; they hire Jay Silverheels (who played Tonto in the "Lone Ranger" radio programs and movies) to read Native American poems and tales; they get spooky Vincent Price to read the horror tales of Edgar Allan Poe. You can use anyone's voice—a famous person's or a friend's—as the "voice" of the book.

When, after many attempts, I finally broke the Proust barrier and got so far into *Remembrance of Things Past* that I never wanted to get out, I found that the book provided its own voice for me to hear, the voice of Marcel, the narrator. It was a cultured, sensitive voice. One afternoon a friend came by for a nice, long chat. That night, when I resumed my reading, I heard *his* voice instead of Marcel's, but, given my friend's nature, the substitution worked fine. My friend became Marcel for that night. The next day I went back to using the original Marcel voice, refreshed by the respite from it.

The experience of hearing a friend's voice in my head was more frequent when I was in my early twenties. In those days I would often spend ten or twelve hours with Ted Berrigan, who was a Rabelaisian conversationalist with a highly distinct way of talking. Each time we parted, his voice continued to reverberate in my head. Everything I read I heard in his voice. Everything I said sounded as if he were saying it. Of course, the remembered voice "decayed" over the next few days and I returned to a more various way of hearing. (Every time I see the word "various," though, I hear a little of Frank O'Hara, who used the word "variously" so beautifully in one of his poems, and of Lionel Trilling, who used it frequently in his lectures.) People who are young enough to be impressionable but old enough to do good imitations are prime candidates for learning how to assimilate voices, store them, and use them in their reading. It also helps, of course, to live in a culturally diverse society, although I suppose that anyone with a television set has access to a wide variety of voices.

We should not overlook the possibility of applying *incongruous* voices to good writing. When the poetry of Wallace Stevens starts to sound a bit too solemn, I sometimes "hear" it in the voice of a Southern redneck. T. S. Eliot's poetry is particularly delightful when heard in an old-time hillbilly accent ("Aprul e-is thuh croolist munth"). I like to imagine how William Carlos Williams's poems—so American— would sound in an Italian accent. I would like to be able to "hear" an Eskimo cast perform *A Midsummer Night's Dream*, a Jamaican read *Paradise Lost*. Such unusual pairings result in what amounts to burlesque, but frequently in the burlesque you see clearly an aspect of the writer's work that was previously too familiar to be noticed. The forest and the trees are separated.

Our own voices are the most familiar of all. That is to say, when we speak we are so accustomed to hearing ourselves that we don't notice how we sound, unless the circumstances are unusual (a "frog in the throat," a tape recording, etc.). Most people, hearing themselves on tape for the first time, ask, "Is *that* me? Do I really sound like that?" The reason the voice on the tape sounds different is that we are receiving the sound waves solely from outside our heads, whereas when we speak, we hear the sound from both inside and outside our heads. The new experience of hearing ourselves only from the outside gives us quite a different view of how we "really" sound. Most of us immediately conclude that we sound horrible, partly because we are distressed to find that we aren't what we had always thought we were, partly because we become self-conscious when attention is directed— like a camera—on us.

In learning to read better and more creatively, however, attention to self is exactly what is called for. You need to ask yourself:

• Do I subvocalize?

• Do I subvocalize sometimes or always? Does the subvocalized voice flicker in and out?

• Do I subvocalize when it isn't necessary (as in reading the contents listing on a food can)?

• Do I subvocalize in different voices? If so, how do I arrive at those voices?

• Do I subvocalize in only one voice? What or whose voice is it?

Many people use a combination of the above. They don't subvocalize single words (like STOP on a street sign) or brief phrases;

nor do they subvocalize certain types of material, such as scientific and mathematical data, lists of facts, flat nonfiction, and the like. They do subvocalize some poetry (where the sound can be crucial to the whole experience of the work) and fiction (for instance, they might "hear" English novels in an English accent). But, by and large, the single most common voice used in subvocalization seems to be a ghost version of one's own speaking voice. This voice is the old reliable of voices, the one that arises naturally when needed, when no other voices suggest themselves. (It is also the one we hear when we think in words.) So in a sense, when we use our own voice for subvocalization, we are not simply reading to ourselves, we are appropriating the text, modeling it to our own tone, reshaping its emotional contours. Without changing the words, we are "rewriting" the text.

This discussion of voice in reading would be incomplete without mention of a relatively recent phenomenon: the availability of the author's actual voice. In the past thirty years, there has been a tremendous increase in the number of live performances and recordings by authors reading their own work.

In the past, relatively few American authors read their work to large groups in public. Coffeehouse poetry readings were not uncommon in Greenwich Village and the Lower East Side of New York in the 1920s and 1930s, but their audiences were small and localized. Most of the poetry readings in the 1940s and early 1950s were by "distinguished" older poets—mostly men, although Gertrude Stein was an exception—who were invited to read their poetry or perhaps deliver a talk at a university. The big breakthrough occurred when Dylan Thomas toured America. Thomas's musical and dramatic intonations swept listeners off their feet; you can get some idea of the distinctive power of his voice by listening to any of the recordings still available. I remember hearing his recording of "Fern Hill" when I was in high school. I had read the poem before, but I wasn't prepared for the great lyrical blast of his voice. It sent me back to the printed page, and when I got there and silently read the poem again, I could hear his voice "singing" it to me. To this day I subvocalize Dylan Thomas's voice when reading his work.

His voice is congruent with his work, as is Wallace Stevens's, Edna St. Vincent Millay's, Allen Ginsberg's, and many others. Other voices come as surprises. Whitman's voice—or what is assumed to be his voice, on a recently discovered recording—is more "Yankee" than I had expected. I read John Ashbery's early work for several years before hearing him read, and I subvocalized a voice for it, a voice something like John

Wayne's. Ashbery's real voice brought me up short. It seemed—partly as a result of my expectations—rather nasal. Later I adjusted to his voice, which blended perfectly with his new work, "perfectly" because in fact I was unable to read it without hearing his actual voice.

Did I understand his work any better, then? Some might argue that my original fantasy (the John Wayne voice) was in fact a more accurate representation of what has been called Ashbery's status as an "executive poet." Is there always an advantage—or ever an advantage—in being acquainted with the author's speaking voice?

After listening to hundreds of writers read their work, I've come to the conclusion that in some cases it helps, and in some cases it doesn't. Some good writers read their own work poorly, making you wish you had stayed home with your own fantasy of the voice. Some writers who seem good read their work in such a way that you realize, hearing them, that their work isn't that good after all; its faults are revealed by the glare of public presentation. Other writers, whose work sometimes may seem elusive on the page, come through with perfect clarity when they read it aloud. Here I'm thinking particularly of poets Kenneth Koch and Edwin Denby. Koch's gentle irony is perfectly clear and appropriate, as are Denby's shifting tones of everyday speech. When one goes back to their work on the page, it remains forever clarified. When hearing an author read, though, it's important to keep in mind that reading styles change, just as literary styles do. We shouldn't be disconcerted, for example, by the "old-fashioned" voice of "modernist" Ezra Pound.

The great opportunity we as readers have—with so many public readings, tapes, and records now available—is to be able to invite not only an author's work into our minds, but his or her voice as well. We have the opportunity of measuring the author's voice against whatever voice we had created for that author, and from there of pondering the relative qualities of both. From this we move toward a greater understanding of what the work is (or isn't).

To push it a step further, we can combine authors in any number of ways; we can, for instance, imagine T. S. Eliot in the unforgettable voice of Truman Capote, or vice versa.

★   ★   ★

Here are some other ways to experiment with reading aloud:

1. *Duets:* one person reads silently while another person reads a different text aloud. What effect does this have on the silent reader?

How does the selection of material change the effect? Alternative: have both read different texts aloud.

2. *Choral readings:* a large group of people—a classroom-full, for instance—simultaneously read different texts, creating a sort of sound environment. This can be orchestrated, to make it resemble the general hum of conversation in a restaurant, theater, or sports arena; to make it harmonious (as in a round such as "Row, Row, Row Your Boat"); to make it euphonious (perhaps creating an abstraction using a text with similar vowel or consonant sounds, or both); or to make it chaotic, with everyone reading completely different texts, either whispered or shouted. Another variation is to have a group read in unison a text that is identical except for, say, its nouns. (Such a text can easily be prepared by having each person do a fill-in-the-blanks.) What effect does such a reading have on the feel of the text? This exercise is not unlike the singing of "Happy Birthday to You," when everyone is in unison except when it comes to the name of the birthday person who is called by several different names. When the group momentarily divides at that point, the song always gets a little shaky.

Another option is to create word scenes. Have the group simultaneously read aloud words that suggest the following scenes:

- the ocean *(water, waves, whitecaps, splash, glug, crash, shhh, whoosh,* etc.)
- the desert *(sand, palm tree, hot, dry, lizard, thirsty, sun, gasp,* etc.)
- night *(cool, dark, quiet, crickets, moon, stars, sleep,* etc.)
- the woods *(trees, green, wind, leaves, crunch, quiet, buzz, calm, alone,* etc.).

A variation of these word scenes is to combine words and sounds, as in:

- an orchestra, in which the *sounds* of the instruments are supported by a basso continuo of sentences or words *about* music
- a barnyard or zoo, in which animal sounds are mixed with words about animals
- a factory, with whistles, chugs, booms, and clicks mixed with words about manufacturing.

These exercises are fun in themselves, but they also set us to thinking about how to read aloud material that might be considered unreadable. How, for instance, would you read aloud what the man is saying in figure 1?

Figure 1

The picture of the cussing man is a clue that makes the typographical symbols (in the speech balloon) into international symbols. Readers in Martinique or the Philippines or Israel would be able to "read" what he is saying.

SEMICOLON; for Philip Whalen

Semicolon   ;   like the head & forearm of a man swimming, the arm in foreshortened perspective, his head looking away ; his mouth's open in exaggerated O inhaling on the other side, his wrist's bent just about to re-enter the surf   ;   water dripping from the fingertips   ;   semicolon

Or a whole row of them

; ; ; ; ; ; ; ; ; ; ; ; ; ; ; ; ; ; ; ;

swimming off to Catalina

How would you read the semicolons in this poem?[2] Obviously, the poet has created this poem more for the eye than for the ear, which is partly why it's challenging to try to figure out a good way to read it aloud. Take a look at the poem below, by Paul de Vree. At first it looks like a bunch of random letters and parentheses thrown up into the air, but if you look at it for a moment you'll notice that the letters are those of the title of a famous song (with something else thrown in).

Now, how would you read it aloud? (I think I'd get a small group of friends to read it with me. I'd have everyone read or sing the words, out of sync, and perhaps with fluttery voices, since the parentheses remind me of birds fluttering around in the airy springtime Paris sky.)

Another exercise is called Megaphone. As you read any text aloud, get louder and louder, then softer and softer, then louder again, then softer again, and so on. The change in volume should have nothing to do with the text's content.

There are several variations on Megaphone, based on pitch. As you read aloud, start with your voice pitched low and have it gradually go up as high as you can; then back down, and so on. Or have a pitch "twist" on each word, so that the voice rises on each word:

♪♪ ♪♪ ♪

I want to go home

or falls on each:

╲ ╲ ╲╲ ╲

I want to go home

or alternates, one word with a rising twist, the next with a falling:

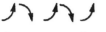

I want to go home

or with no change at all—a monotone:

⸻⸻⸻⸻⸻➤

I want to go home.

It's easier to read in a monotone if you imagine you're a robot or if you simulate a computer-generated voice. Intentionally reading in a monotone is particularly helpful for children whose oral reading tends to be toneless; the exaggerated monotone makes them realize that there is such a thing as tone and that reading aloud sounds so much better when it has tone, the way talking does.

Another skill valuable for reading is totally silent: listening. Listening is a form of reading, insofar as we "listen" to the words of what we read. Try the following listening exercise. Close your eyes and open your ears; that is, focus your attention on what you hear. Keep listening until you think you've heard everything there is to hear at the moment, sounds in the far distance and sounds up close (such as that of your own breathing). If there are voices around you, so much the better. Notice how you immediately became more aware of all these sounds.

Here's another listening exercise. Ask a friend to talk with you while your eyes are closed. Pay close attention to each word your friend says, not just to the gist of it. Notice the tone, volume, and pace, and check to see if the words are in complete sentences or in little fragments. Then have your friend close his or her eyes too and continue the conversation. After a while, do you notice that you feel closer to your friend? We feel closer whenever we really listen to the other person, undistracted by other sounds, including those of our own thoughts. We interlock with our friend's words, and, in that sense, we show respect. We show that we feel that our friend's words are worthy of close attention. Reading teachers, especially those who follow what is now called the whole language approach, are becoming more aware of the importance of listening. Discussing the reading abilities of the deaf and the blind, reading specialist Jeanne Chall says:

> Common sense tells us that the deaf would be the better readers because they can see the print. Yet the blind are the better readers. This happens because reading is closer to hearing than to seeing.[3]

Good teachers consider listening an active skill that must be practiced and developed, especially in light of the passive hearing most children grow up with, sitting in front of the television, which, after all, is primarily a visual medium, one whose words (and music) are often uninteresting anyway. But even those who grow up without television need to maintain their listening power, to overcome their natural tendency toward aural numbness. And if you want to read more creatively, the ability to listen carefully and continuously is even more crucial. Finally, here are two exercises, for one person.

1. Pick any book and alternate reading silently and orally from it, alternating words, phrases, or sentences (the larger the syntactical unit, the easier the exercise).

2. How slowly can you read aloud and still retain the meaning of a sentence? Try reading any text aloud, slower and slower, until you're saying it word by word. After you say a word, keep your eyes on it; don't peek ahead to the next one. When you've really slowed down to, say, one word per ten seconds, notice what your mind does in the silent intervals. After doing any of the exercises above, you'll find that your normal reading has become smoother, easier, and clearer.

New Reading

The twentieth century has changed the way we read, and the change has been relatively abrupt. The proliferation of advertising, the media "explosion," and the influence of modernism in literature have caused us to perceive words in new ways foreign to our ancestors.

Imagine that you are driving down a highway and you see, over on the right, the word "GAS," *six hundred miles* tall. The letters rest lightly on the ground, from where they sweep up through the clouds, their tops disappearing beyond the stratosphere. You would be astonished, like a hillbilly in the 1930s seeing a billboard for the first time. Until then the only words he might have ever seen—perhaps in the Bible—were tiny.

But you are sophisticated. You have seen faces fifty feet tall, moving and talking, as real as life. You are not like ninety-two-year-old Harold Clough who, at his first movie as a boy in rural Vermont around 1912, saw a train heading toward him and got up and ran for his life. You have seen words written in vapor across the sky, you have seen them dance around and around the tops of buildings, like a revolving halo, you have seen them fly toward you in different colors and explode (on television and in computer games). You've seen them flash on and off, buck like a horse, and spell themselves out in neon script.

You've seen them in a hundred different typefaces, big, fat, skinny, curly, leaning, antique, shadowed. Most of us have experienced these new presentations of words so often that we take them for granted.

Less common are the new ways of reading necessitated by modern literature. In 1897, when Stéphane Mallarmé's poem *A Throw of the Dice* was published, the literary page was given a new look: the lines, set in various sizes, were scattered around the page, so that the white space around the words suddenly took on an importance of its own. Christian Morgenstern's poem "Night Song" used symbols instead of alphabetical letters: it didn't need to be translated from the original "German." The shaped poetry of the past—in which a poem has the physical shape of its subject matter—experienced a rejuvenation in the hands of Guillaume Apollinaire (see his poem "It's Raining" in figure 4) and helped spawn what became known as "concrete poetry." The Italian Futurist poets espoused a kind of writing they called *parole in libertà,* or "words set loose" (see figure 5), and words, sometimes truncated or dislocated, appeared in Cubist collages and paintings.

In Switzerland, Germany, and France, the Dada poets experimented with chance poetry and sound poetry, as did Kurt Schwitters, the inventor of a one-man movement, Merz. Apollinaire and Blaise Cendrars brought "found" elements into their poetry, such as the overheard chit-chat in the former's conversation poem "Monday Rue Christine" and the latter's wonderful plagiarizations in his *Nineteen Elastic Poems* and *Kodak.* Both poets were also attracted to advertising: "You read the handbills the catalogs the posters that really sing / That's poetry and there are newspapers if you want prose this morning" (Apollinaire, "Zone"). Gertrude Stein's experimental repetitions made her prose pieces sound like delirious children's stories. Poets such as E. E. Cummings took words apart and put them back together in unusual configurations. James Joyce, in *Finnegans Wake,* let the words run on in a kind of cosmic babble.

Obviously, modern literature has caused us to read in new ways. But older literature does too. It all depends on what we mean by "new." For example, is reading E. E. Cummings for the first time really any more "new" than reading Chaucer (in Middle English) for the first time? The main difference between reading contemporary and classical literature is that the latter has accumulated a large body of commentary, from which we can learn how other people have read it. With contemporary literature, there are fewer such "support systems." In deciding how to read a piece of writing that is radically new, we have to rely on our own nerve, gut reaction, and sense of what is beautiful and valuable. The more flexible we are in our reading, the more

It's Raining

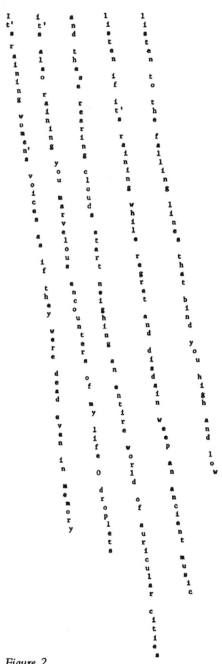

Figure 2

Figure 3

likely we are to be able to understand new work. If our literature is to be various and bold, flexibility in the way we read is crucial, because ultimately it is we who decide whether a work becomes part of our literature or just another forgotten book.

Finally, modern experimental literature has not only made us aware that there are many ways to read, but it has also intensified the traditional intimacy of simply reading a book, spending time alone with an author in some quiet corner.

Notes

1. Gertrude Stein, always exceptional, wrote someone else's autobiography: *The Autobiography of Alice B. Toklas.*

2. Ron Loewinsohn. *Meat Air* (New York: Harcourt Brace Jovanovich, 1970).

3. Jeanne Chall. *Stages of Reading Development* (New York: McGraw-Hill, 1983) p. 128.

Lorna Smedman

Collage

I glue a photograph of Kafka and Max Brod to a sheet of paper. They are sitting on a small couch, leaning towards each other, having an animated conversation. Max Brod is holding his infant son on his lap. Kafka is smiling, and almost touches Max's shoulder with a delicate hand. I want to enter their conversation, so I cut apart some words, and scatter the letters above the photo, hoping the men will use them to answer my questions. Focusing my mental concentration in a beam out of my forehead, I push it through the surface of the photo, into Kafka's mind. What are you saying? He doesn't respond. I try several times. The letters don't move. I form the question in the space between them, and increase its volume to scream level, but I can't break into their intimacy. Frustrated and angry, I go through the papers on the table and find a picture of two Mexican bandits, wearing big black hats and holding old-fashioned pistols. I cut them out and glue them down with their guns aimed at Kafka's and Brod's heads. This threat fails to startle them into talking. They don't even notice the bandits, and I don't have the heart to really get tough with them.

Stephen Vincent

The First Time I Heard the Word *Voluptuous*

I was sixteen. Though I was from California, an exchange student, I was up a tree in France—in Normandy. It was warm. It was July. The girl, the "sister," with whom I lived, she and I were up this big tree, about fifteen feet, a poplar, I think. It had white bark that shined a bit in the dark. It was after nine o'clock, not far from the village. We had finished the dishes. The family was so impressed that I would do the dishes, they had fired the maid.

But this word *voluptuous*, I had never heard it before.

I forget exactly at what point this was during the summer, whether I had actually kissed her yet or not, but I sure had already been *jealous*. I knew that word.

But up in this tree, in the high branches, with us almost leaning into each other, she was trying to say something, or suggest something, and her English was pretty fractured, and my French was consistently shoddy and forced, and this was a big word, with so many syllables for her to say in English, it was actually sounding more French to me, the tangibility about the way it came through her lips, as she repeated it to see if I could understand, if she could only pronounce it right, and, in reality, all I could imagine was something like an octopus, something smooth and slippery that you could feel move in several directions at once, because she was actually asking whether or not I was *voluptuous*, or if I ever felt *voluptuous*.

It might have been the other way around. She was saying it was something women felt, and men did not. Whatever it was, rocking on the limb of that tree, sometimes holding on with one hand, and pushing on her sweatered shoulder with the other, it felt, at sixteen, dangerously intimate, I mean the excitement going up and down my body in this tree, up there among the leaves, in the night with her whom I really liked, and I was actually relieved that there was something to take my attention off the situation, as I tried as hard as I could to imagine what this big fat word *voluptuous* might ever mean to me.

Peter Schjeldahl

The First Poem I Ever Wrote

It was the last day of fifth grade, 1953. In the afternoon we went with our teacher to the town athletic field for a picnic and games. At some point I lay on the grass and looked at the sky. There was a hawk soaring around up there. This wasn't unusual, but it gave me a strange feeling. I sat up and started writing.

It was a poem in stanzas, and I knew it was a poem because it looked like one. All I remember of it is a one-line chorus that repeated after every stanza:

Winged avenger from the skies!

When the poem was finished I felt dazed. I took it to the teacher. She read it and said something like: "That's nice, Peter, but what is this about a 'winged avenger from the skies'? That's very unpleasant. What does it mean? What does the avenger want to avenge?"

I should have answered, "It wants to rip your throat out." It was five or six years before I wrote my second poem.

Suzanne Zavrian

The First Poem I Ever Wrote

I spent most of my childhood vacations in Philadelphia with various aunts, and when I was eight I wrote home:

> I made up a poem: He has choclete in his wiskers and iceing in his beard and together his face is very smeared.

The letter even has literary references, punctiliously informing my parents that "I got two 25¢ books intitled 'The Hardy Boys: The Missing Chums' and 'Bunny Brown and His Sister Sue and Their Shetland Pony.'"

But the real poetry is in another Philadelphia letter dictated to an aunt before I could write and apparently written down verbatim:

> I went downtown today and do remember that you said to buy a bag so I did buy the most beautiful white pocketbook. It is almost exactly like a lady's, a bag that you carry under your arm and it has one of those little things that you can carry your money in.

> First we went to the magic restaurant and if you don't know about it I will tell you. You give some money to the lady there and she gives you nickels. You drop a nickel in the slot and the milk spits in the glass and you drink afterwards and it tastes very good and you put another nickel in the slot and you get a sandwich because when you put the nickel in the slot the case opens and you take the sandwich out. . . .

Oh, why did they close those magic restaurants!

Larry Zirlin

My First Metaphor

My mother tells this story, and she's told it several times. I was two years old, and while I'm surprised at how much I can recall from that age, I don't remember this particular incident.

I was running around in our kitchen. The furniture, the wallpaper, the appliances are all fairly clear to me, but what is sharpest in my memory is the juicer. It was a hand-operated model, all metal, painted white except for the black rubber sleeve on the handle and the chrome helmet which pushed down on the halved fruit. I loved to play with the juicer, moving the silver hemisphere through a three-quarter circle, back and forth. Thirty years later, E. T.'s head would rise and fall like my little man's shiny skull. But I understood the juicer was more than a toy—it was also the source of breakfast every morning.

To my mother this story is just another of the endless examples of how cute I was as a child. But I know it is my first metaphor. When, on maternal impulse, my mother picked me up and hugged me tightly, I said, "Why you squeeze me? I not an orange."

Madeline Tiger

The First Poem

When I think back to the beginning, Meryl's first poem rushes to my heart. I still know it by heart:

In Camp

In camp we have such fun
The happy children play and run
We go horseback riding and climb up mountains
And drink from beautiful, sparkling fountains.

—*Meryl Mann (1940)*

I was six, she was five. We were best friends, still are.

I thought it was so beautiful, especially the "sparkling," which reminded me of her voice and her laugh and her teeth and how much fun she had all the time. Her camp seemed like pure freedom, although I wouldn't have used that word, I'm sure; and all I really knew about her summer was that poem. I felt it—the poem, the life—as magical, beyond my own experience.

Poetry, I must have known right then, didn't just report on life, or represent its quality, but made it more *intense*. I wanted it.

I wanted to be one of the "happy children," running up to drink there. I envied her power: she had some kind of assurance, and access. I wanted to feel joy, and to write such poems. (If one didn't come first, maybe the other would.)

It took me about forty years to get poems from myself as delicious as that first one in the world—to come upon lines that made me feel as happy, beautiful, mysterious, full of good luck, like coming to sparkling fountains after a climb.

Francelia Butler

Meeting Louis Untermeyer

When I was about ten, my mother and father took me to Cleveland, Ohio, to see Louis Untermeyer, the anthologist and poet who was autographing books in Halle Brothers Department Store. Beaming, they brought me up to the celebrity, who was sitting at a small table with a stack of books beside him.

"My daughter writes poetry, too," my father announced proudly.

"Oh, she does!" Mr. Untermeyer exclaimed. "Then tell her to sit down and write me a poem."

I felt like the miller's daughter must have felt in "Rumpelstiltskin," when her father boasted that she could weave straw into gold. I panicked.

"Do as you're told," Father said.

"Just a short one," Mother added. "Do it right now."

I wrote down something and I knew it was dreadful. My brain, my hands, and my heart were frozen.

"Now take it to Mr. Untermeyer," Mother commanded. I even had cold feet. I could barely shuffle across to his table and push the paper before him.

He took a look at the piece of paper. His face was expressionless.

Just then, Father came up with the book he had purchased. Mother and Father waited expectantly while Mr. Untermeyer autographed it.

"Just look what Mr. Untermeyer wrote," Mother exclaimed. "Now aren't you glad we made you write that poem he wanted?" She read the inscription out loud:

To Francelia—
Sure that she will become the poet she deserves to be.
    Louis Untermeyer

My parents thought it was a good omen of my poetic future. It was the last poem I ever wrote.

Jeff Morley

Wishes, Lies, and Dreams Revisited

Jeff Morley wrote this essay in 1983, fourteen years after he and his classmastes were first taught by Kenneth Koch.—Editor.

Room 502 of P.S. 61 on Twelfth Street between Avenues B and C was already simmering with noise when Tommie Torres, whose desk was next to mine, whispered to me, "Mr. Coke is coming." I was a new kid in the winter of 1969; Tommie and much of the rest of the class had welcomed this teacher before. But like the time he tried to translate a dirty joke from Spanish, Tommie couldn't quite convey to me the hidden pleasure of what was involved. Then "Mr. Coke" himself strolled in, and the room bubbled over into a recess riot of desk thumping, foot stomping, laughing, squealing, saying hello, hand waving, and talking. His name—he wrote it on the blackboard—was Kenneth Koch. He was tall, upright, polite as a grown-up but sly as a kid, and the first thing he said was, "Let's take a walk."

More gleeful pandemonium. We all got up and paraded around the room, around the corner where the tall, wooden, brass-tipped window opener stood, past the blackboards at the front of the room, past the current events board with its pictures of President-elect Nixon and Mayor Lindsay, past the heavy sliding doors of the coat closet, across the back of the room where our reports on South American countries were pinned up, down alongside the tall windows and the clanking radiators, and back to our desks. This little tour, which would have been unthinkable in our regular day, put the fifth grade routine far behind us.

As the clatter subsided, Koch began talking about lies, how it wasn't good to lie but how we could lie in poems to tell about any crazy or untrue or funny thing we liked. We put our number-two pencils to our wide-lined paper, and the noise ebbed—this Koch was *serious* about writing poems—leaving a sudden absorbed silence. I started, trying to think up something that wasn't true, something completely untrue, as big a lie as I could come up with. It wasn't easy.

★   ★   ★

It is immodest but not inaccurate to say that the poems we wrote that year convinced many that young people could write poetry. In April 1970, *The New York Review of Books*—which not long before had featured a diagram of a Molotov cocktail—published a long article by Koch on our writings. Koch, a professor of English at Columbia whose own poetry is full of childlike colors and disasters, then turned the article into the introduction to *Wishes, Lies, and Dreams,* a book of poetry written by first through sixth graders at P.S. 61. When the book came out in the summer of 1970, the front-page review in *The New York Times Book Review* was ecstatic. *Newsweek* ran a complimentary if patronizing article about "slum children" who wrote poetry. David Frost interviewed several kids on his show. *Life* published a feature on us. So did *The New York Times Magazine.* Channel 13 taped some of the kids reading their poems, for station breaks. The auditorium at the 92nd Street Y was packed for a reading by the young poets.

As the idea that kids could write good poetry spread, the original P.S. 61 poets grew up and scattered. By the mid-1970s all of the more than 100 kids whose poems were published in *Wishes, Lies, and Dreams* had graduated from P.S. 61. Some went on to J.H.S. 60 on Twelfth Street, some to J.H.S. 104 on Twenty-first Street, some to private schools. Parents died, got divorced; families moved to Corona, Prospect Park, Staten Island, Long Island, upstate, out of state. Even the few who remained in the neighborhood moved away from grade school friends and toward high school, jobs, drugs, boyfriends, girlfriends, college, careers.

My own family fled the Lower East Side for the Midwest. In 1976 I came back east for college and work, but I had long since lost touch with everything about P.S. 61—everything including poetry. What Koch called "the great and terrible onslaught of self-consciousness" that inhibits poetry writing hit me at about age twelve, and its effects have never left. Dutiful swipes at freshman English and sophomore creative writing proved to be of little help in regaining the poetic delight of Room 502. I believed that poetry was like calculus—abstruse and impenetrable without advanced training—so it followed that we at P.S. 61 had never really written it, or had written it only in a childlike way, irrelevant to understanding "real" poetry.

Wishes, Lies, and Dreams had aimed to wipe out the presumption that kids could not write poetry like poets. Koch thought that most kids had the desire—and ability—to say something poetically, and all the reviews, articles, TV shows, and readings had proclaimed him right. But more than a decade after *Wishes, Lies, and Dreams,* I couldn't, in my gut, believe it. Something had squelched the poetic impulse in me after P.S. 61. I didn't like poetry because it, unlike the poems I wrote in fifth grade, had little connection to me.

Despite, or maybe because of, that realization, I wondered what had happened to everyone else at P.S. 61. Had our poems really meant anything to us in 1968 and 1969 besides a respite from our spelling tests and geography lessons? Were the poems just childish musings overblown by the period's enthusiasm for youth and self-expression? Would they still mean anything in the winter of 1983?

For the first time I read every single poem in *Wishes, Lies, and Dreams,* and I could understand why everybody from *The New York Times* newsroom to Room 502 had been thumping the desk. My premature jadedness as an undergraduate might have made me indifferent to Spenser and Yeats, but I couldn't help but laugh with pleasure at the poetry in Ana Gomes's little-girl romanticism: *Her tan looked like sand /. . . His hair was as wavy as the ocean.* And reel with Eddy Diaz's abandon: *The big bad baby bus came busy bussing down Avenue B.* And admire Fontessa Moore's cheer: *I have a hat / Full of laughs / A book of kisses.* And enjoy Michael Carlton's teasing: *When the sun goes down in my mind the sky is brown / In your mind maybe yellow, red or pink.*

But my new appreciation generated its own kind of skepticism. Added to my lingering estrangement from poetry was a pessimism that the world would have any use for poetry like this. As I began to track down the original P.S. 61 poets, I doubted that after fifteen years poetry could be anything more for us than a wish, a lie, or a dream.

★   ★   ★

For five minutes, maybe more, I was stumped by Mr. Koch's assignment. Lord knows I was one lying eleven-year-old, but how did I tell a lie to a piece of paper? And why should I? Finally I just decided to put down any old thing. Mr. Koch had said that was okay, so I began: *I was born nowhere / And I live in a tree / I never leave my tree.* These were definitely lies: I was born in New York, I lived in an apartment building on Avenue C, and I left it all the time. I had a picture of a treehouse in my mind, but otherwise I wasn't sure what this was going to lead to.

★   ★   ★

One of the first poets I catch up with is Ruben Marcilla. At ten in the morning he is relaxing in his tree-shaded, two-story brick house on West Jackson Street in Mountain Home, Idaho (pop. 7,522). He is watching the soaps and waiting for Andy the crop-duster to stop by. For fifty bucks cash, Ruben is going to paint "ANDY'S FLYING SER-VICE" on the doors of the man's pickup. As far as twenty-five-year-old Ruben is concerned, life forty miles south of Boise beats life south of Fourteenth Street hands down.

Ruben grew up with his mother and three brothers in Haven Plaza at Thirteenth and C. Unlike many other former P.S. 61 students, he doesn't have particularly exciting memories of writing poetry. Koch taught poetry at P.S. 61 only one year before Ruben moved on to J.H.S. 104. Hearing one of his old poems long distance, Ruben sounds a little embarrassed. It begins *My little green plant was like a big jungle / Her earrings were as green as jade / When I opened the box I saw all the colors of the rainbow.* Ruben says he doesn't write poetry anymore.

He learned sign painting at Art and Design High School, and while he loved it, hanging out was his top priority. His friends were mostly "criminals, real bad guys," he says. He wanted to own a gun.

"But I got tired of that lifestyle, always trying to keep up with who died, who got shot," he says, disgusted. "You needed a scorecard to keep track. I warned one guy, 'Get out of there, man, before you get wasted.' I heard a couple of weeks ago some guys mugged him down on Avenue D. Stomped on his face and broke all these bones in his cheek."

He began to think about Mountain Home, where he had enjoyed a summer-long visit with his brother, who was stationed at the Air Force base there. "New York's a rat race," he says, describing his feelings then as well as now. "The neighborhood stinks. You got to breathe everybody's bad breath. You slave at work all day. You get ripped off by everybody—seventy-five cents for the bus, another seventy-five for the train, one dollar for cigarettes. I got my taxes back one year and tore the envelope open. I'd been working like a fiend all year, and my refund was only 200 bucks. I said, 'Things can't be any worse in Idaho.'"

Ruben caught the next Greyhound, and sixty hours later he was in Mountain Home to stay. *I saw reds as red as a book,* his poem contin-ues, *I saw greens as green as the sea on a calm, sunny day.* Within a few months he had met an Air Force dental technician from Little Rock, Arkansas, named Becky. In August 1981, Ruben, who is Argentinian, married her—"How's that for integration?" he cracks—and they bought a house, for which their monthly payment is exactly two hun-dred forty-six dollars.

"Guys on Long Island spend a hundred thousand and they still got to wait twenty years for a tree. I got two of them in my front yard at least fifty, sixty years old," he boasts. *I saw yellows as yellow as a golden date tree in the fall.*

Guns are as common in Mountain Home as loose joints are in Central Park, Ruben says, but he's lost his desire to own one. "I don't know if it's that I'm getting old, but mentally I'm different out here," he says. "Idaho mellows you out. You lose all your violence. In the city you're always looking for something. Wake up at three in the morning, you go for a walk, go down to the all-night newsstand on Eighth Street. I wouldn't have done it if I was a girl but as a guy, well, the young male is the baddest animal in the jungle, right? Out here you can't prowl around. I wake up late at night now, I just go out in the backyard and look up at the stars. It's so clear you get a beautiful light show every night."

So had he wanted to get away from the city as far back as 1968, when he was at P.S. 61? Ruben denies it. "I didn't know there was anywhere to get away to," he laughs. *I saw browns as brown as a little squirrel running up a tree,* his poem ended. Poetry had taken him to Idaho long before that Greyhound did.

★   ★   ★

It might be of only passing interest to Ruben today, but the book that he helped write has had a pervasive and deep influence that extends to Idaho and far beyond. Still in print after all these years, *Wishes, Lies, and Dreams* has sold more than 28,000 copies. It has inspired the writing of poetry in grade schools and high schools across the country. Teachers & Writers Collaborative, which sponsored Koch's early visits to P.S. 61, now places about forty poets in New York City schools every year. Formal poets-in-the-schools programs, of which there were exactly none in 1969, are now funded in all fifty states. Koch has traveled all over the United States, as well as to France, Haiti, Italy, and China, to teach poetry to kids. He wrote a book about the poetry of French kids called *Les couleurs des voyelles.* The French Ministry of Education noticed the book and wrote to Koch asking how they might best inspire poetry in their *étudiants.*

★   ★   ★

I wasn't sure if I was supposed to be a person or a bird or something else in my tree, but on my first day of writing poetry that kind of uncertainty didn't even slow me down. I continued, *It is very crowded*

/ *I am stacked up right against a bird* / *But I won't leave my tree.* I did know that this bird was either a big parrot or a vulture; I knew I wanted to keep the lies coming and I knew I wanted to stay in the tree.

★   ★   ★

In another corner of the world, the Eisenhower Elementary School in Boulder, Colorado, one fourth grade class had its poetry writing class last spring. It was based on the assignments Koch devised for *Wishes, Lies, and Dreams*. Eliza Bailey, the student teacher from the University of Colorado who taught the lesson, recalls the scene:

> When the kids were done, they were all shouting, "Come here, come here," and "Read this," and "Is this good?" Some kids would run up to the desk after every line. Others covered up their papers until they were completely done. Some would hand theirs in all embarrassed saying, "This is no good. Don't read it," and they'd slip it at the bottom of the pile.

Eliza admits she got "all choked up" sitting at the teacher's desk that day. In third and fourth grades she had been in Kenneth Koch's classes at P.S. 61, and now her own students were "doing exactly the same things we did." Back then she had written a poem that began *I have a pocketful of laughs* / *I have a dog of dreams*, but today she believes that the poems her fourth graders wrote were better than anything she did.

Eliza received her education degree last summer. One hundred and fifty résumés later she still hadn't found a grade-school teaching job so she moved back to her parents' home in East Meredith, New York, and took a job teaching kindergarten in nearby Oneonta. Now even her four-year-olds write poetry.

"I sit them in a circle and read them some poems from *Wishes, Lies, and Dreams*," she says. "Then I go around and they each give me a line that I write down. Sometimes they get completely off the track. But four-year-olds are so lyrical. One of them said to me, 'I finally figured out how the moon moves without feet. It just blows along in the wind.'"

Teaching, Eliza says, is what she's wanted to do all her life, at P.S. 61 and later, after her family moved from East Seventh Street to East Meredith in 1971. In college she felt certain that Koch had been right, "that there had to be a better way to teach." She remembers P.S. 61 as "a prison and when Mr. Koch came it was like getting out" into a world where she could say *I have a hat made of checkers* / *I have a schoolbag made of crayons*. But Eliza found out things weren't as simple as they had looked in 1968.

"I always thought I was going to be a really 'groovy' teacher," she says. "You know, relate to my kids. I learned it just doesn't work that way." She points out how easy Koch had it. "He could just come in, and the atmosphere of the room would change in one second. But when you're teaching the same class all the time, it's harder than that. You want all that craziness and excitement and energy but you can't have it all the time. You have to say, 'When we write poetry you're allowed to do that; when we're not writing poetry you have to stop and salute.' When I first wrote poetry with my kids in Boulder like that, I realized how much I had changed." *I was given a dress of shoes / I have a sailboat of sinking water*.

Even so, teaching poetry still matters to Eliza because it is her link to poetry now. The faith that Koch instilled—that even as a kid she could write poetry—has been replaced by a resigned suspicion that she could write poetry *only* as a kid. The carefree voice that finished the poem declaring, *I have a house of candy / I was given a piece of paper made of roses / I have a red, blue, and white striped rose* is gone. Eliza says she still writes poetry, "mostly when I'm depressed."

"As you get older you lose spontaneity, freedom," she laments. "At P.S. 61 I felt confident that anything I was doing was going to be good. Now I worry more about what someone will say when they read it than about what I am writing."

She singles out the line *a sailboat of sinking water*, and tries to explain why that line has always stuck with her. "It's a feeling in the pit of my stomach. It's a pulling feeling, going in a lot of different directions. It's turbulent but it's peaceful at the same time. I wrote that in third grade. I don't think I've written a line like that since."

*   *   *

Going back to the old neighborhood, it isn't hard to see why Ruben and Eliza and so many other P.S. 61 kids can no longer be found there. In 1970 the area between Avenues A and D and Ninth and Fourteenth Streets was mostly working-class Puerto Rican, and P.S. 61's enrollment reflected it. Mixed in were Jewish and Irish kids from solidly middle-class Stuyvesant Town, a few blacks, a handful of children of second-generation Italians and Ukrainians who never followed their relatives to Jersey or Long Island, and a few whites with parents like mine who were foolish or idealistic enough to believe that living in a "bad" neighborhood didn't have to be a bad thing.

In the 1970s the middle-class and working-class people began moving out, and the neighborhood was torn apart by the invisible hand of the economy and the desperate hands of the people left behind. The Charles movie theater on Avenue B closed; the lumberyard at Twelfth and C was torched—for the insurance, everyone said. The Avenue B bus line was discontinued. Enrollment at P.S. 61 dropped forty-five percent. Each year from 1970 to 1980 an average of 290 people left the ten-block census tract around P.S. 61; each year an average of 109 housing units were abandoned. Of every 100 area residents in 1970, thirty-six were gone by 1980.

★　　★　　★

I closed my eyes to concentrate. I thought of being blind, which certainly wasn't true, so I wrote *Everything is dark / No light! / I hear the bird sing / I wish I could sing.* I never wanted to sing as a kid, but since I was living in the tree I figured I probably would've wanted to. Thinking about it now, I wonder why it didn't occur to me that parrots and vultures can't sing, and I realize that it was questions like that that ended my poetry career.

★　　★　　★

Fontessa Moore is rocking her two-month-old son in her spacious, dark apartment on the twenty-second floor of an East New York co-op. The curtains are drawn on a gray afternoon; her husband, a systems analyst at Shearson American Express, is at work. Her voice is soft, matter-of-fact, rising and falling on little swells of amused observation of the world. On the dinner table in front of her sits a thick stack of crumpled, torn, or folded sheets of paper, testimony that she has been writing poetry all her life. It is, she says, her peace of mind.

As a kid she was a joyful, crazy poet, reveling in the sheer life of words. *I have a hat / Full of laughs / A book of kisses / A coke came out / like Mr. Coke* began the poem that she read to David Frost and millions of TV viewers.

"If you put restrictions on a person, you cut out part of their feelings, they hold back something, and you won't get the true meaning on paper," she says. "If you leave well enough alone you can really do something to a piece of paper. You really can. When Mr. Koch showed the class an apple and said, 'Make a poem about it,' we made it come to life. We made that apple jump on top of the table."

And jump her poems did: *A monkey jumped out/As a hatful of money came out / Somebody gave me a red / White and blue flag/ As it hit the tank / A pig jumped out.* But as Fontessa grew older her poems lost some of their brightness. A sheet from the pile rages at an unfaithful boyfriend; another tells of loneliness, lying on the beach: *No one to hold me / but the wind / and the air to ask for help.* The time after her graduation from Washington Irving High School was especially difficult. Fontessa majored in chemistry at New York University and worked as a clerk-typist and secretary. But the jobs and the classes weren't the problem. "It just wasn't enough for me," she says. While working as a deposit cashier at a brokerage house, she met her future husband; they were married within two months.

"I thought marriage was for me," she says. "But then again I wanted more. Then the children came and all, but it's still not enough for me. It's like I got married for someone. I had my children for my husband but it wasn't for me. Maybe that is enough for some people but it wasn't enough for me. I need more than a marriage, the kids, the motherhood, because I know there's more to me than just this stage of what I am. There is just much more for me to do. Writing is more for me to do because that's a lifetime thing. When I sign my name to the end of the paper, I know it's mine. I'm still Fontessa Moore."

She makes time to write "even when I don't have time," she says. She wrote a poem, for example, when she was in labor with her son. The nurses thought she was crazy, but Fontessa took time out from her pain to tell God sardonically that she danced the African, Latin, meringue, hustle, bus stop, salsa, two-step, rumba, even the blues *but dear GOD / I never / dance / to you.* She even extended her poetic license to inventing the names of her children: Jacquai for her daughter, Wesley Jhontaine (pronounced Zhawn-taw-nay) for her son. The sassiness that had said *A camel jumped out / As he was a scout / A horse jumped out / An old lady jumped out / With a seesaw hat* has not withered but ripened.

Still on maternity leave from her office, she is contemplating opening a boutique in Brooklyn Heights or downtown Brooklyn featuring African, Asian, and European clothes. Her husband opposes the idea, but she is determined, saying, "I'm the kind of person who takes chances." Store rents are high, though, and she hasn't found the right partners, so she waits. Poetry balances the risks of striking out on her own and the security of her family. When the hatful of laughs was almost empty Fontessa herself popped out: *Out comes a rat / Out comes a sack / Out comes me / Out comes you.* She puts the poems away and bundles up Wesley Jhontaine. It is time to go over to her parents', but before she leaves she says again of poetry, "It's my peace of mind."

*   *   *

I opened my eyes and dropped the idea of being blind, because a scene was now vivid in my mind: an island the size of a pitcher's mound (I was a baseball fanatic back then) supporting my lone tree. This I had to describe: *My eyes they open / and all around my house / The Sea.* I decided this qualified as a lie because I had never been to such a sunny, breezy, tropical place. I thought of otters sliding down bluffs.

*   *   *

"This is me, this is my world," twenty-three-year-old Marion Mackles explains, referring not to the jammed Seventeenth Street coffee shop where she's eating lunch but to the book on the table and the poem she wrote when she was ten. It begins *I saw a fancy dancy dress / hanging on a fancy dancy window / of red roses you could call it a red /rose window I put it on. . . .*

Marion is an actress/ice cream scooper/carpenter, sharing a West Side apartment with a girlfriend and hoping to land a role that will pay the rent. She's short and energetic, with green eyes as shrewd as they are friendly. You get the feeling that if she cross-dressed she could pull off a young Dustin Hoffman.

"I really believed that the world was flowery then, that it was a fancy dancy dress, that I could dance in the streets. I was writing out of total ignorance and naïveté," she says. But that same naïveté led her to believe that the real world around her did not have to be so cruel.

As a kid she gave money to beggars on the streets. She laid a bag of cookies at the feet of a sleeping bum. She made sandwiches for a couple of homeless people who lived in her neighborhood. "I knew they wouldn't take food if I just gave it to them so I'd put the sandwiches in Glad bags and bury them in the garbage nearby where I knew they would find them," she says.

After attending the High School of Performing Arts and graduating "totally neurotic," she went to Ohio University "to be with normal people again." *I fell asleep and I had a dream / of a blue sky of roses / and a house of daisies.* She majored in drama (starring, coincidentally, in a production of a Kenneth Koch play) and earned her degree in three years.

Back in New York in 1981, Marion accepted a friend's invitation to see a sign-language performance of the play *Evangelist* at Circle Rep. Her fascination with the separate world of deaf people reached back to her childhood, when she had watched the kids outside the School of the Deaf at Twenty-third Street and First Avenue near her home.

Even though she had seen the show before, the signed interpretation was a thrill, a revelation, a poem. *And I awoke and it was true / I saw everything I saw / sky of roses house of daisies a tree / of orange a book of apple.*

She immediately enrolled in a sign language course, and says her deaf friends can now understand her sign language fairly well. She aims to do interpretive performances herself someday.

"We can talk around things," she says of people who can hear. "We're spoiled by words. But the deaf, they can't lie, at least not very often or very well. They have their depression and their lovers' quarrels and their killers like everyone else. But they're not too interested in lying because it takes all they've got just to communicate. They don't have our luxury of dancing around words. They can't talk at all without looking the other person in the eye."

Marion recognizes that in the world of the deaf that she wants to reach, there is something very much like the world of her girlhood, a place where the truth is practical and people work to understand and help one another. That, she says, is her confirmation that her poem wasn't just a hopeless dream: *I loved it all and lived with it for / the rest of my life.*

"That was the root," she says of the fancy dancy dress spirit. "It's still there. It's just that different branches have also grown up. A branch that's bitter that the world isn't like that, a branch that believes it was a mistake to ever think it was, a branch that is content."

★   ★   ★

Other poets who paraded around the classrooms of P.S. 61 have spun off in myriad directions. Ana Gomes is an astrophysicist living in the Midwest. Eddy Diaz is a naval airman stationed on the U.S.S. *Coral Sea,* currently docked in Alameda, California. Michael Carlton I could not locate; the Newark nightclub his mother used to operate is now closed.

Tommie Torres (*Everything flows away ready for a new day*), who sat next to me, now works for Texaco in Bayamon, Puerto Rico. Ruben Luyando (*A noisy owl goes woo-woo with its small hair tail on its head*) supervises the night shift of telephone operators at the Waldorf-Astoria. Mercedes Mesen (*Being in school at midnight I can see the wind*) is visiting her grandmother in San José, Costa Rica, and looking for a job there. Chuck Conroy (*Oh green, yellow, orange, pink, red, black, brown / What shall I chartreuse today?*) is an energy conservation engineer for Con Edison. Mayra Morales (*the saddest color I know is orange because it is so / bright that it makes you cry*) works at a telex company on Thirty-sixth

Street. Vivian Tuft (*But best of all Spring is a part of nature like the baby next door / She's grown so big*) works in the finance department of a big Park Avenue advertising agency.

Kenneth Koch is still professor of English and Comparative Literature at Columbia University. He continues to write and publish poetry. He says the point of his poetry classes was never to train future poets any more than the point of gym class is to produce future Reggie Jacksons. "Most people would think it criminal not to let kids run and play or draw and paint," he says. "I think poetry's just as natural in kids—it's a talent they have. If a kid has a good teacher maybe he'll continue writing. More likely, he'll be able to go on reading and enjoying poetry. But so much teaching of poetry just encourages the idea that a poem is a lot of onomatopoeia with a symbol hidden in it, that it's no wonder people feel estranged from poetry. At P.S. 61 I just wanted to say, 'This is something in your life that you can enjoy.'"

One P.S. 61 poet (*I wish I could leap high in the air and land softly on my toes*) can't muster much interest in her former classmates or what they wrote long ago. She tells me, "I think if you took a group of kids from a private school who had something behind them—something like money—then I think you'd see some good stories. But I can't see it from P.S. 61. They weren't too interesting a bunch when I went to school with them. I don't think they'd be too interesting now."

★   ★   ★

I looked around the classroom and shielded my paper from would-be peekers. I knew these really weren't lies I was telling, and I wondered if I had messed up the assignment. But Mr. Koch had said write anything you want. And I wanted to get out of the cramped treehouse. So I went on: *Slowly I get down in the water / The cool blue water / Oh and the space*. No hesitation now. I was writing faster, and in the excitement, getting a little grand.

★   ★   ★

On December 16, 1980, just before noon, twenty-three-year-old Candy Dipini left her two children with a babysitter in her second-floor apartment at 190 Avenue B. She bought a sandwich on Fourteenth Street and went to her clinic on Twenty-fourth Street for her dose of methadone. *When he was down in the yard / and I was in the window/with my father and mother and / him with his mother and father too. . . .* At 12:15 a fire broke out in the living room of Candy's apartment and the artificial Christmas tree went up in flames. The babysitter ran out the back door with five-year-old Marcie. When the firemen arrived the flames were raging out both front windows, and the building was filled with thick black smoke; it took them twenty-two minutes to get the blaze under control. On the living room couch the firemen found the charred bodies of two little boys: four-year-old Tony Dipini and his best friend, three-year-old Junior Santiago. They had been hugging each other when they died.

"I've been through hell," Candy says simply when we first meet, and you can see in her face that the death of her son was the worst, but not the only, part of the passage. Her brown face is a frozen shallow pond: smooth, still, hurt. Her smile is a crack in the ice, full of life but receding even as it appears. She recounts her life since the day of the fire in a hurried, disbelieving voice.

At the coroner's office she saw the little pile of Tony's clothes on a stretcher and "went crazy because I thought that was all that was left of him." Relocated to a welfare hotel, she promptly moved out after an elderly woman living there was stabbed thirty-seven times. No public housing project would accept her because the fire labeled her a risky tenant. In despair she abandoned the methadone treatment and went back to heroin. To support an eighty-dollar-a-day habit, she squandered her welfare check, sold off her household items, borrowed from everyone in the neighborhood, begged for money in the street, shoplifted.

"I was crazy. I was angry at myself because if I had been there Tony wouldn't have died. It's bad to wake up in the morning when you have two children and only find one. Every day I used to cry, and if somebody looked at me funny I would want to hit them," she says.

Finally her brother, on leave from the army in Germany, came back to New York and told her the family was going to take Marcie away from her if she didn't straighten out *and my mother was staring at / me and my father said, "You ugly and little thing what are you / looking at?"*

"My daughter is everything to me. I'd do anything for her," Candy says. So in April 1982 she went back to the methadone treatment. And after sending a four-page letter to Mayor Koch "cursing him out," she obtained an apartment in the new housing project at Thirteenth and C. From the front door of the building you can see the grated windows of P.S. 61, where Marcie attends second grade.

Like most P.S. 61 poets, Candy looks sheepish but proud at the mention of one of her old poems. *And I said, "At / my only lover boy" / and father said, "What is / his name?" I said "His name is Bobby Perez and I love him / a lot. . . ."*

"I always used to like it when I was a little girl and we used to write poetry. It pushed you to say your true feelings, your inside feelings. It might make you sad inside, but even that, once you feel it, feels good. It's sad but you feel calm," she says. She and her boyfriend used to write poems, handing a piece of paper back and forth, each adding a line as they went. Those poems burned in the fire. She had also once taken *Wishes, Lies, and Dreams* out of the library to show to a friend but she left it in a cab and lost it. She asks if she can borrow my copy of the book for the afternoon; she wants to show it to Marcie. She just won't give up on poetry.

I suggest instead that we go buy a copy for her and Marcie. As we walk back toward Avenue B from the bookstore, Candy keeps flipping through the book. Compared with the loss of her little Tony I can't imagine that any poem anywhere can amount to much, but I catch myself. Fencing off tragedy from poetry, like patronizing "slum children" or succumbing to self-consciousness, is one of those restrictions that stifles poetry, that keeps Fontessa's apple from jumping on the table. Tony's death doesn't mean Candy's wishes, lies, and dreams are dead. It doesn't mean Marcie can't find a box holding all the colors of the rainbow or have a sailboat of sinking water or a hat full of laughs or a fancy dancy dress or, like Candy when she was eleven, a secret lover boy. *And I was twenty-three years old / when I got married with my only lover boy / and he was twenty-four, just a / year more than me.* You can go through hell and still not lose any of those things.

*   *   *

A conventional little boy, I had my doubts about getting too carried away. But it was only a poem. And who was going to read it besides Mr. Koch? I decided to finish it exactly the way I wanted to: *I laugh swim and cry for joy / This is my home / For Ever.* I liked it. Poetry wasn't so tough, I thought for the first and last time. I chose to title the poem "The Dawn of Me." That was a little fancy too but . . . I just handed it in. Sure enough, I was embarrassed when it appeared in *Wishes, Lies, and Dreams.* It no longer seemed so great, and I didn't go out of my way to point it out to anyone. But as I looked up my old classmates, I started liking "The Dawn of Me" as much as I had the day I wrote it, maybe even more. Writing poetry was the dawn of all of us; I like to think we're still living in its light.

Notes on Contributors

PRISCILLA ALFANDRE has taught third and fourth grades for many years at Sidwell Friends School in Washington, D.C.

JANE AUGUSTINE is the author of two collections of poems, *Lit by the Earth's Dark Blood* and *Journeys*. Her poems have appeared in many magazines. She teaches at Pratt Institute in Brooklyn.

BILL BERNHARDT teaches writing and reading at The College of Staten Island. He has also taught in China and Brazil. He is the author of *Just Writing* and *Becoming a Writer: A Basic Text* (with Peter Miller).

JOE BRAINARD (1942–1994) was an artist and writer. His books include *Selected Writings, 26 Mini-Essays*, and *I Remember*, which is the original source for the writing assignment of the same name that is now used in schools across the country.

WESLEY BROWN is a playwright and fiction writer. Among his plays are *Love during Wartime* and *Boogie-Woogie and Booker T*. His novels include *Tragic Magic* and *Darktown Strutters*. He teaches at Rutgers University.

FRANCELIA BUTLER is the editor of *Children's Literature* magazine. A leading authority on children's literature, she is the author of an adult novel, *The Lucky Piece*, and *Skipping around the World: The Ritual Nature of Folk Rhymes*.

ROBERT COLES is the author of more than fifty books, among them *The Call of Stories* and *The Spiritual Life of Children*. A recipient of the Pulitzer Prize, he is professor of psychiatry and medical humanities at Harvard University.

JACK COLLOM is a poet and teacher. His books include *Moving Windows: Evaluating the Poetry Children Write, Poetry Everywhere* (with Sheryl Noethe), and *The Fox*. He has received a Poetry Fellowship from the National Endowment for the Arts.

DALE DAVIS is a writer and co-founder of the New York State Literary Center. She conducts interdisciplinary residencies that integrate literature, history, music, translation, theater, media and video productions for students at all levels.

PHILLIP DEPOY is a poet, fiction writer, and playwright currently serving as Artistic Director of Theatrical Outfit in Atlanta. For ten years he was artist-in-residence for the Georgia Council for the Arts. His most recent play is *Angels*.

LARRY FAGIN is a poet and teacher. His books include *Rhymes of a Jerk, I'll Be Seeing You,* and *The List Poem: A Guide to Teaching and Writing Catalog Verse.* For many years he edited and published *Adventures in Poetry* magazine and books. He has worked as a poet-in-residence since 1970.

MARIA IRENE FORNES has won seven OBIEs for her plays, which include *Fefu and Her Friends* and *The Conduct of Life.* She has received a National Endowment for the Arts Distinguished Artist Award, Rockefeller Foundation fellowships, and a Guggenheim fellowship.

ALLEN GINSBERG is the author of *Howl, Collected Poems,* and *Cosmopolitan Greetings,* among many other books. He is co-director of the Jack Kerouac School of Disembodied Poetics at Naropa Institute in Boulder, Colorado. He is also Distinguished Professor at Brooklyn College.

GRADY HILLMAN is a poet who has conducted writing workshops in Texas schools and prisons for many years. His books include *Forces* (poems) and *The Return of the Inca* (translations from the Quechua).

LEWIS HYDE is the author of *This Error Is the Sign of Love* and *The Gift: Imagination and the Erotic Life of Property.* A recipient of a MacArthur fellowship, he is Henry Luce Professor of Art and Politics at Kenyon College.

KENNETH KOCH has written many books of poetry, plays, and fiction. His books on teaching poetry writing are *Wishes, Lies, and Dreams*; *Rose, Where Did You Get That Red?*; and *Sleeping on the Wing* (with Kate Farrell). With Farrell he also edited *Talking to the Sun.*

WILLIAM BRYANT LOGAN is writer-in-residence at New York's Cathedral of Saint John the Divine. He is the co-author of *A Literary Guide to the United States* and the co-translator of *Once Five Years Pass* by Federico García Lorca.

ELLEN LUPTON is a curator, writer, and graphic designer. Among her many books and exhibitions are *Mechanical Brides: Women and Machines from Home to Office* and *Global Signage: Semiotics and the Language of International Pictures.* She is Curator of Contemporary Design at the Cooper-Hewitt, National Museum of Design in New York City.

SHELLEY MESSING, C.S.W., is a psychotherapist in private practice. Her writing has appeared in *Jewish Currents, Women: A Journal of Liberation,* and *Home Planet News.* For years she co-produced "Writer's Block," a monthly poetry magazine for WBAI radio in New York City.

JEFF MORLEY was one of Kenneth Koch's original students featured in *Wishes, Lies, and Dreams.* Morley's articles and essays have appeared in *The Village Voice, The Nation,* and other magazines. Currently he works as editor for the "Outlook" section of the *Washington Post.*

WALTER DEAN MYERS is the author of many books for young adults. His *Young Landlords, Hoops, The Legend of Tarik,* and *Motown and Didi* won ALA Best Book of Year Awards and Coretta Scott King Awards. T&W published his *Sweet Illusions.*

RON PADGETT is a poet and the publications director of T&W. His books of poetry include *Great Balls of Fire, Triangles in the Afternoon,* and *The Big Something.* His translations include *The Complete Poems of Blaise Cendrars* and *The Poet Assassinated* by Guillaume Apollinaire.

JULIE PATTON's poems have appeared in *Transfer.* She is also a visual artist, with exhibitions in Cleveland, New York, and elsewhere. Since 1984 she has taught imaginative writing in the T&W program and written for *Teachers & Writers* magazine.

PETER SCHJELDAHL is a poet and art critic. His many books and monographs include *The 7 Days Art Columns; The Brute;* and *Since 1964: New and Selected Poems.*

JEFFREY SCHWARTZ writes poems and essays on teaching. His first book of poems was *Contending with the Dark.* Recently he co-edited *Students Teaching, Teachers Learning,* a collection of essays. He teaches at Greenwich Academy in Fairfield, Connecticut.

PETER SEARS is a poet and teacher who serves as Community Services Coordinator at the Oregon Arts Commission. He is the author of *Secret Writing* and *Gonna Bake Me a Rainbow Poem,* among other books.

JOHN OLIVER SIMON is a poet who teaches at La Escuelita, an elementary school in Oakland, California. A former director of California Poets in the Schools, he is the editor of *Un techo del tamaño del mundo (A Roof the Size of the World: Poetry across Frontiers).*

LORNA SMEDMAN is a poet currently doing doctoral work in English at the City University of New York. She teaches literature at Hunter College and has worked as a poet-in-the-schools. Her collection of poems and prose poems is called *The Dangers of Reading.*

MARY SWANDER has taught poetry for the Iowa Artists in the Schools program and at the University of Iowa. She is the author of *Succession, Lost Lake,* and *Driving the Body Back.*

MADELINE TIGER is a poet who teaches in the New Jersey Writers in the Schools program. Her books include *Water Has No Color* (poems) and *Creative Writing: A Manual for Teachers* (with Toi Derricote).

STEPHEN VINCENT's most recent book of poems is *Walking*. He was director of Momo's Press, which published the early work of Jessica Hagedorn, Hilton Obenzinger, and Victor Hernandez Cruz. He is the director of Book Studio, a book and CD-ROM packaging house.

MEREDITH SUE WILLIS's novels include *Higher Ground* and *A Space Apart*. For T&W she has written *Personal Fiction Writing, Blazing Pencils,* and *Deep Revision*. The National Endowment for the Arts awarded her a Creative Writing Fellowship. Willis teaches writing at all levels.

BILL ZAVATSKY is a poet, translator, and teacher. His books include *Theories of Rain* and *For Steve Royal*, and his translation of André Breton's *Earthlight* won the PEN/Book of the Month Club Translation Prize. He teaches high school English at Trinity School in New York City.

SUZANNE ZAVRIAN is a poet, editor, and bookseller. For many years she coordinated the New York Book Fair. Her theater piece, *The Autobiography of New York*, was performed at Medicine Show.

ALAN ZIEGLER is a poet, fiction writer, and teacher. His books include *So Much to Do*, a collection of poems, and *The Writing Workshop*. He is director of the Writing Program at Columbia University's School of General Studies.

LARRY ZIRLIN's books of poems include *Awake for No Reason* and *Under the Tongue*. He is also a graphic designer and printer.

DID YOU KNOW

that every piece in this book
appeared originally
in *Teachers & Writers* magazine?

You don't have to wait for years for another collection such as
this. You can be in touch with the newest inspiring and useful
ideas for teaching writing—as they happen, in each new issue
of *Teachers & Writers*.
To subscribe, just send in the card that was inserted in this
book. Or, if the card has gone astray, contact
Teachers & Writers Collaborative,
5 Union Square West,
New York, NY 10003-3306
(212) 691-6590
for current subscription information.
Thank you.

OTHER T&W PUBLICATIONS YOU MIGHT ENJOY

The Teachers & Writers Handbook of Poetic Forms, edited by Ron Padgett. This T&W bestseller includes 74 entries on traditional and modern poetic forms by 19 poet-teachers. "A treasure"—*Kliatt*. "The definitions not only inform, they often provoke and inspire. A small wonder!"—*Poetry Project Newsletter*. "An entertaining reference work"—*Teaching English in the Two-Year College*. "A solid beginning reference source"—*Choice*.

Personal Fiction Writing by Meredith Sue Willis. A complete and practical guide for teachers of writing from elementary through college level. Contains more than 340 writing ideas. "A terrific resource for the classroom teacher as well as the novice writer"—*Harvard Educational Review*.

Playmaking: Children Writing and Performing Their Own Plays by Daniel Judah Sklar. A step-by-step account of teaching children to write, direct, and perform their own plays. Winner of the American Alliance for Theatre & Education's Distinguished Book Award. "Fascinating"—*Kliatt*.

The Story in History: Writing Your Way into the American Experience by Margot Fortunato Galt. Combines imaginative writing and American history. "One of the best idea books for teachers I have ever read"—*Kliatt*.

The List Poem: A Guide to Teaching & Writing Catalog Verse by Larry Fagin defines list poetry, traces its history, gives advice on teaching it, offers specific writing ideas, and presents more than 200 examples by children and adults. An *Instructor* Poetry Pick. "Outstanding"—*Kliatt*.

Poetry Everywhere: Teaching Poetry Writing in School and in the Community by Jack Collom & Sheryl Noethe. This big and "tremendously valuable resource work for teachers" (*Kliatt*) at all levels contains 60 writing exercises, extensive commentary, and 450 example poems.

The Writing Workshop, Vols. 1 & 2 by Alan Ziegler. A perfect combination of theory, practice, and specific assignments. "Invaluable to the writing teacher"—*Contemporary Education*. "Indispensable"—Herbert R. Kohl.

The Whole Word Catalogue, Vols. 1 & 2. T&W's bestselling guides to teaching imaginative writing. "*WWC 1* is probably the best practical guide for teachers who really want to stimulate their students to write"—*Learning*. "*WWC 2* is excellent. . . . It makes available approaches to the teaching of writing not found in other programs"—*Language Arts*.

For a complete free catalogue of T&W books, magazines, audiotapes, videotapes, and computer writing games, contact
Teachers & Writers Collaborative,
5 Union Square West, New York, NY 10003–3306, (212) 691-6590.